PFLR ... HIMVR SIES ...
HOFFNUNG AM! ... IN
HAM EINE PVLSE SCHLAGEN. ... AVF
SEINE DAS HERZ WALLT ... WELCH
SCHÖNE VM SVSS ENTZVCKT ... DOCH WIE? TAVSCH ... FROMME
WEIGEN IHM! WIE NAHTE ... NICHT MEIN OHR? ... AVF ZVM
MIR DER SCHLVMMER ... WIE SCHRITTE! DOCH
STERNE ... VERSCHALLE!
BEVOR ICH IHN GESEH ... INNEN MITTHALLE! ... GELIEBT'S! ER
FEIER ICH IHN GESEH ... HERVOR ER IST'ZVR
A. LIEBE PFLEGT MIT KVMMER ... O WIE DIE LIEBE MAG V
HIMMEL ... DIE FLAGGE DER LIEBE DIE
TETS HAND IN HAND ZV GEH'N ... DEIN MÄDCHEN WACHT NO
GOLDN ... EINEM
OB MOND AVF SEINEM PFA ... DER NACHT! ER SCHEINT
GLANZ ... IN DER
WOHL LACHT? WEICH SCHÖNE ... NOCH NICHT ZV SEH'N! — EIN VITTER
NACHT! LEISE, LEISE, FROMME ... TAVSCT DAS LICHT DES MO
WEISE! SCHWING DICH ... MICH NICHT SO SCHMVCK

MEIN

ZVM STERNENKREISE. ... BLVMENSTRAVSS DEN
DEV, ERSCHALLE FEIERND ... GEWSS, ER HAT DEN BESTEN
ICH ALLE MEIN GEBET ZVR ... GETAN DAS KVNDET NVG ... OHN ANFANG
HIMMELSHALLE! O WIE ... MORGEN AN! O SVSSE HOFF
VND OHN ENDE! VOR ... GEFAHREN VND
JELL DIE GOLDENEN STERNE. ... NEV BELEBTER MVT! ALL
ZV WAHREN SENDE ... DEINE ENGEL-
MIT WIE REINEM GLANZ ... PVLSE SCHLAGEN. VND DAS
SCHAREN ALLES IN ... WALLT VNGESTVM, SVSS ENT ... SCHON
IE GLVHN! NVR DORT ... ENTGEGEN FREVND,
LÄNGST DER ... ZV HOFFEN IHR AVCH
DER BERGE FERNE SCHEINT EIN ... KONNT' IC
WAS WEITZVZIEH'N. DORT ... WAGEN?
VETTER AVFZVZIEH'N ... WANDTE SICH AN INNEN
EIFRIG AVCH SCHWEBT EIN ... NVR
AM WALD ... SCHT. ... DAS
WIR NKLER
BIR SCH ... IM ... WERT

JO-ANNE BIRNIE DANZKER

ROBERT WILSON
STEEL VELVET

PRESTEL

Published on the occasion of the centennial of the Villa Stuck and the exhibition *Robert Wilson/Villa Stuck* at the Museum Villa Stuck, Munich, from November 25, 1997 through February 8, 1998.

Dieses Buch erschien anläßlich des 100jährigen Jubiläums der Villa Stuck und der Ausstellung *Robert Wilson/Villa Stuck* im Museum Villa Stuck, München, vom 25. November 1997 bis 8. Februar 1998.

Robert Wilson/Villa Stuck

Concept/Konzept: Robert Wilson

Artistic Collaboration/Künstlerische Mitarbeit: Stefan Hageneier and/und Hans Thiemann, Design; Heinrich Brunke, Light/Licht; Peter Cerone, Sound/Ton

Exhibition/Ausstellung

Project Curator/Projektleitung: Jo-Anne Birnie Danzker

Project Coordination/Projektkoordination: Michael Buhrs

Exhibition Coordination/Ausstellungskoordination: Susanne Baumann, Sabine Schorer

Exhibition Preparation/Ausstellungstechnik: Robert Matthews

Sculptures/Plastiken: Hans Thiemann (Franz von Stuck, Roman Couple/Römerpaar, Mary as/als Torero, Cupid/Amor, Dogs/Hunde); Theaterplastische Werkstatt Kirsten Prößdorf, Barbara Spaett (Centaur/Flötenspielender Pan, Drunken Centaur/Trunkene Kentaurin, Fantastic Hunt/Phantastische Jagd); Manufaktur (hair and pelt/Fell und Haare der Figuren)

Painting/Malerei: Alfons Ostermeier, Werner Schmidbauer

Objects/Objekte: Birgit Bollweg (vessels/Gefäße), Peter Pfitzner (columns/Säulen), Kirsten Prößdorf, Marion Mayer (birch/Birke), Berthold Reiß (painting of vessels/Bemalung), Michael Ratajcik (arrows/Pfeile), Ingrid Weindl (painting of arrows/Bemalung der Pfeile)

Carpentry/Schreinerarbeiten: Werkhalle: Christian Reinhardt, Peter Junghans, Arthur Bürgel

Snake/Schlange: Thomas Lücke, Reptilienhaus Oberammergau; Dieter Fuchs, Department of Hespitology, State Zoological Collection, Munich/Abt. Hespitologie, Zoologische Staatssammlung, München

Light Design/Licht Design: Heinrich Brunke

Sound Design/Ton Design: Peter Cerone

Sound Recordings/Tonaufnahme (Münchner Kammerspiele): Richard Beek, Bettina Hauenschild, Thomas Holtzmann

Conservators/Restauratorische Betreuung: Elena Agnini, Susanne Eid, Hans Jörg Ranz, Stephan Rudolph

Research/Wissenschaftliche Mitarbeit: Christian Burchard, Sabine Schorer, Franz von Stuck Estate/Nachlaß Franz von Stuck (on/zu Franz von Stuck); Geoffrey Wexler, Archivist/Archivar, Byrd Hoffman Foundation, Steven Bradley Beer, RW Work Ltd., New York (on/zu Robert Wilson)

Administration/Verwaltung: Helene Vetter

Press Office and Public Relations/Presse- und Öffentlichkeitsarbeit: Birgit Harlander

Exhibition Staff/Ausstellungsmitarbeit: Daniel Becker, Miriam Burgauner, Britta Hölzer, Gerhard Lehenberger, Maria Pilzecker, Udayvir Singh, Valentine Weimert, Stefan Zeiler

Technical Services/Technischer Dienst: Wolfgang Leipold, Heinz Kieschke

Book/Buch

Author/Autorin: Jo-Anne Birnie Danzker

Coordination/Koordination: Sabine Schorer

Publications Staff/Mitarbeit: Susanne Baumann, Michael Buhrs

Photographer/Photographin: Brigitte Maria Mayer

Translation English-German/Übersetzung Englisch-Deutsch: Bram Opstelten

Translation German-English/Übersetzung Deutsch-Englisch: John Ormrod

Editors/Lektorat: Gabriele Ebbecke (German/Deutsch), Judith Gilbert (English/Englisch)

Design and Typesetting/Gestaltung und Satz: WIGEL, Munich/München

Lithography/Lithographie; ReproLine, Munich/München

Cover Design/Umschlaggestaltung: Robert Wilson

Printing and Binding/Druck und Bindung: Passavia Druckerei, Passau

Die Deutsche Bibliothek-CIP-Einheitsaufnahme

Robert Wilson, Steel Velvet: [dieses Buch erschien anläßlich des 100 jährigen Jubiläums der Villa Stuck und der Ausstellung Robert Wilson/Villa Stuck im Museum Villa Stuck, München, vom 25. November 1997 bis 8. Februar 1998]/Jo-Anne Birnie Danzker. [Mitarb.: Susanne Baumann ; Sabine Schorer. Übers. engl.-dt.: Bram Opstelten. Übers. dt.-engl.: John Ormrod]. – München ; New York : Prestel, 1997
ISBN 3-7913-1925-6

Cover Image/Auf dem Umschlag: *Drunken Centaur/Trunkene Kentaurin* (see page/siehe Seite 58 ff.)

Endpaper (front)/Vorsatz (vorne): *Fantastic Hunt/Phantastische Jagd* (see page/siehe Seite 42 ff.)

Frontispiece/Frontispiz: Vitrine in the Music Salon/Vitrine im Musiksalon (described on page/beschrieben auf Seite 43)

Endpaper (back)/Vorsatz (hinten): Dining Room/Speisesaal (see page/siehe Seite 46 ff.)

Museum Villa Stuck
   Prinzregentenstr. 60, D-81675 Munich, Germany
   Tel. +49 - 89 - 4 55 55 10, Fax +49 - 89 - 4 55 55 124
Prestel-Verlag
   Mandlstr. 26, D-80802 Munich, Germany
   Tel. +49 - 89 - 38 17 09-0, Fax +49 - 89 - 38 17 09-35

Printed in Germany on acid-free paper

ISBN 3-7913-1925-6

Contents/Inhalt

Acknowledgements

This book has its origins in an event which took place on November 24, 1997 — the premiere of a sculpture, sound, and light installation, an "environment" consisting of twelve tableaux, by the internationally renowned artist and theater director, Robert Wilson, in the historic rooms of a nineteenth-century artist's villa in Munich, Germany. This project, conceived as a centennial celebration for the Villa Stuck, was more than four years in the planning and involved an international team of artists and mastercraftsmen as well as the services of numerous museum personnel and conservators.

It is a privilege to have been able to work with Robert Wilson. I would like to take this opportunity to express my deep appreciation to him — for agreeing to create an installation for the Villa Stuck, for committing himself so whole-heartedly to the project, and for providing us with startlingly new ways to see this extraordinary building. I am also indebted to the Franz von Stuck Estate for agreeing to lend us objects from their collection for the installation and for allowing us to create three-dimensional simulacrums of artworks for which they hold the copyright. They have also generously agreed to the publication of these works in this volume.

An undertaking of this scale and complexity requires an extraordinary concentration of effort and will. Robert Wilson and his colleagues — Stefan Hageneier and Hans Thiemann, design; Heinrich Brunke, light; and Peter Cerone, sound — have remained remarkably generous with their patience, flexibility and good humor despite the numerous, inevitable complications which have arisen. Special mention should be made here of Stefan Hageneier, Robert Wilson's artistic assistant on this project, who was the key liaison between the Museum Villa Stuck and Robert Wilson over the past four years. I would also like to especially acknowledge the contribution of Michael Buhrs, who was project coordinator for the Museum Villa Stuck.

I mentioned earlier that the *Villa Stuck* project involved the services of numerous mastercraftsmen and artists. The various sculptures, objects, and constructions produced for this installation are of extraordinarily fine quality. I would like to acknowledge the contribution of Hans Thiemann, Theaterplastische Werkstatt; Kirsten Prößdorf, Barbara Spaett, Manufaktur; Birgit Bollweg, Peter Pfitzner, Marion Mayer, Berthold Reiß, Michael Ratajczak, and Ingrid Weindl (figures and objects); Alfons Ostermeier and Werner Schmidbauer (painting); and the Werkhalle — Christian Reinhardt, Peter Junghans, Arthur Bürgel (carpentry). The marvelous lighting which transformed each tableau was designed by Robert Wilson's long term collaborator, Heinrich Brunke; the sound scores which brought a new dimension to each work were designed by Peter Cerone. We are indebted to the artistic director of the Munich Kammerspiele, Michael Wachsmann, and the actors Richard Beek, Bettina Hauenschild, and Thomas Holtzmann for their contribution to these sound environments. Thomas Lücke of the Reptilienhaus Oberammergau and Dieter Fuchs of the State Zoological Collection were enormously helpful in obtaining and caring for the tiger python for one of our tableaux.

Special mention should also be made of the Museum Villa Stuck's exhibition technician Robert Matthews and his team, especially Stefan Zeiler and Gerhard Lehenberger, and our exhibition coordinators, Sabine Schorer and Susanne Baumann, for their tireless efforts. Conservators Elena Agnini, Susanne Eid, Hans Jörg Ranz, and Stephan Rudolph assisted us in various

Dank

Dieses Buch geht zurück auf ein Ereignis, das am 24. November 1997 in den historischen Räumen einer Münchner Künstlervilla des 19. Jahrhunderts stattfand: die Premiere einer Skulpturen-, Klang- und Lichtinstallation, eines aus zwölf Tableaus bestehenden Environments des international renommierten Künstlers und Theaterregisseurs Robert Wilson. Die Planungen für das Projekt, das als Veranstaltung zum hundertjährigen Bestehen der Villa Stuck vorgesehen war, erstreckten sich über insgesamt vier Jahre; die Realisierung erforderte die Mitwirkung eines internationalen Teams von Künstlern und Kunsthandwerkern.

Es war eine besondere Ehre, mit Robert Wilson zusammenarbeiten zu dürfen. Ich möchte ihm bei dieser Gelegenheit meinen aufrichtigen Dank aussprechen – für seine Bereitschaft, eine Installation für die Villa Stuck zu schaffen, für das Engagement, mit dem er das Projekt vorangetrieben hat, und dafür, daß er uns die Möglichkeit geboten hat, das bemerkenswerte Gebäude auf ganz und gar neue Art und Weise zu erleben. Ebenso möchte ich den Verwaltern des Nachlasses Franz von Stuck für die Bereitschaft danken, Objekte aus der Sammlung für die Installation als Leihgabe zur Verfügung zu stellen, und für die Erlaubnis, Kunstwerke, für die das Urheberrecht bei ihnen liegt, in dreidimensionaler Form nachzubilden. Sie haben großzügigerweise auch der Abbildung dieser Werke im vorliegenden Band zugestimmt.

Ein Unterfangen dieser Größenordnung und Komplexität erfordert eine besondere Bündelung der Kräfte. Robert Wilson und seine Mitarbeiter – Stefan Hageneier und Hans Thiemann, Design, Heinrich Brunke, Licht, und Peter Cerone, Klang – haben trotz der zahlreichen Komplikationen, die sich zwangsläufig ergaben, stets erstaunliche Geduld und Engagement bewahrt. Hervorgehoben werden sollte an dieser Stelle Stefan Hageneier, Robert Wilsons künstlerischer Assistent bei diesem Projekt, der in den vergangenen vier Jahren als entscheidender Verbindungsmann zwischen dem Museum Villa Stuck und Robert Wilson fungierte. Besondere Anerkennung verdient auch Michael Buhrs für seine engagierte Arbeit als Projektkoordinator für das Museum Villa Stuck.

Das Projekt *Villa Stuck* erforderte, wie gesagt, die Mitwirkung zahlreicher versierter Künstler. Die verschiedenen Skulpturen, Objekte und Konstruktionen, die für diese Installation geschaffen wurden, zeichnen sich durch besonders hochwertige Arbeit aus. Für ihren Beitrag zum Projekt möchte ich folgenden Personen danken: Hans Thiemann, Theaterplastische Werkstatt Kirsten Prößdorf, Barbara Spaett, Manufaktur; Birgit Bollweg, Peter Pfitzner, Marion Mayer, Berthold Reiß, Michael Ratajczak und Ingrid Weindl (Figuren und Objekte); Alfons Ostermeier und Werner Schmidbauer (Malerei) und die Werkhalle: Christian Reinhardt, Peter Junghans, Arthur Bürgel (Schreinerarbeiten). Für die außergewöhnliche Beleuchtung, die den Tableaus eine neue Gestalt verleiht, zeichnete Robert Wilsons langjähriger Mitstreiter Heinrich Brunke verantwortlich; die Klangenvironments wiederum, die jedes Werk um eine zusätzliche Dimension bereichern, wurden von Peter Cerone geschaffen. Unser Dank gilt dem künstlerischen Leiter der Münchner Kammerspiele, Michael Wachsmann, sowie den Schauspielern Richard Beek, Bettina Hauenschild und Thomas Holtzmann für ihren Beitrag zu diesen Klangenvironments. Thomas Lücke vom Reptilienhaus Oberammergau und Dieter Fuchs von der Staatlichen Zoologischen Sammlung waren uns eine enorme Hilfe bei der Beschaffung und Pflege des Tigerpythons für das Tableau in ›Marys Zimmer‹.

aspects of the preparation and presentation of the exhibition. Indeed all members of the staff of the Museum Villa Stuck contributed to the success of both the installation and this publication.

The present volume was originally planned to include only visual documentation of the *Villa Stuck* environment. In an attempt to understand and to describe what was taking place at the Villa Stuck, it became necessary to place this project in the context of other visual art projects undertaken by Robert Wilson in the past thirty years. This was only possible with the assistance of the Byrd Hoffman Foundation and especially its archivist, Geoffrey Wexler, who was generous in providing access to Robert Wilson's archives and in answering our many questions. Geoffrey Wexler also compiled the comprehensive list of solo and group exhibitions and environments published in this volume and assisted us with the location of photographic documentation of these events. I would also like to acknowledge the constant and ongoing support of Steven Bradley Beer from R.W. Work.

Because this project has been so long in the making, numerous persons have assisted us who may no longer be directly involved in the final installation but who nevertheless provided us with support at an early and critical stage. I would like to mention Lucien Terras, formerly of the Paula Cooper Gallery; Ulrich Hauschild, former assistant to Robert Wilson; and especially Piet de Jonge from the Museum Boijmans Van Beuningen, who not only facilitated our first contact with Robert Wilson but also provided us with additional information for the present publication. Paula Cooper and her staff have supported our endeavor in numerous ways over the years. I would also like to express my appreciation to my many colleagues in museums in Europe and in North America who assisted us with the photographic documentation of Robert Wilson's earlier projects.

Last but not least I wish to thank our publisher, Jürgen Tesch, from Prestel; his editors Gabriele Ebbecke and Judith Gilbert; our coordinator Sabine Schorer and our designer, Rainer Lienemann, from WIGEL. Our translators Bram Opstelten and John Ormrod, displayed extraordinary flexibility, patience, and commitment to this book despite constant changes due to last minute alterations in the various tableaux in the Villa Stuck. We are also indebted to Brigitte Maria Mayer for providing us with the marvelous photographs of the Munich installation, again under enormous time constraints.

Robert Wilson took us on a journey into time with this project — time past and time present — which, to paraphrase T. S. Eliot, contains time future. We are grateful to him for this journey.

Jo-Anne Birnie Danzker
Director, Museum Villa Stuck

Besondere Erwähnung verdienen auch der Ausstellungstechniker des Museums Villa Stuck, Robert Matthews, und sein Team, besonders Stefan Zeiler und Gerhard Lehenberger, sowie unsere Ausstellungskoordinatorinnen Sabine Schorer und Susanne Baumann für ihren unermüdlichen Einsatz. Die Konservatoren Elena Agnini, Susanne Eid, Hans Jörg Ranz und Stephan Rudolph waren uns bei der Vorbereitung und Einrichtung der Ausstellung in verschiedenerlei Hinsicht behilflich. Ohne die Hilfe sämtlicher Mitarbeiter des Museums Villa Stuck hätten die Installation sowie der vorliegende Band nicht realisiert werden können.

Dieses Buch sollte ursprünglich lediglich eine Bilddokumentation des Environments *RobertWilson/Villa Stuck* enthalten. Um dieses verstehen und beschreiben zu können, erwies es sich jedoch als notwendig, dieses Projekt in den Kontext anderer bildkünstlerischer Projekte zu stellen, die Robert Wilson im Laufe der vergangenen dreißig Jahre realisiert hat. Dies war nur möglich mit Unterstützung der Byrd Hoffman Foundation und insbesondere des Archivars dieser Stiftung, Geoffrey Wexler, der uns in großzügiger Weise Einsicht in Robert Wilsons Archiv gewährt und unsere zahlreichen Fragen mit viel Geduld beantwortet hat. Geoffrey Wexler hat außerdem das im vorliegenden Band enthaltene umfassende Verzeichnis der Einzel- und Gruppenausstellungen und Environments zusammengestellt und war uns behilflich bei der Suche nach Photodokumenten dieser Veranstaltungen. Ebenfalls danken möchte ich Steven Bradley Beer von R.W. Work, der uns stets hilfreich zur Seite stand.

Weil die Arbeit an diesem Projekt einen derart langen Zeitraum in Anspruch genommen hat, gibt es zahlreiche Personen, die uns in einem frühen und entscheidenden Stadium der Entwicklung behilflich, jedoch nicht mehr unmittelbar an der endgültigen Realisierung beteiligt waren. Hervorheben möchte ich Lucien Terras, ehemals Paula Cooper Gallery, Ulrich Hauschild, ehemaliger Assistent Robert Wilsons, und insbesondere Piet de Jonge vom Museum Boijmans Van Beuningen, der nicht nur die Verbindung zu Robert Wilson hergestellt, sondern uns auch mit ergänzender Information für die vorliegende Publikation versorgt hat. Paula Cooper und ihre MitarbeiterInnen haben unserem Projekt im Laufe der Jahre immer wieder ihre Unterstützung angedeihen lassen. Mein Dank gilt außerdem zahlreichen Kollegen von Museen in Europa und Nordamerika, die uns bei der Photodokumentation zu Robert Wilsons früheren Projekten behilflich gewesen sind.

Nicht zuletzt möchte ich unserem Verleger Jürgen Tesch vom Prestel Verlag danken, seinen Lektorinnen Gabriele Ebbecke und Judith Gilbert, unserer Publikationskoordinatorin Sabine Schorer sowie dem Gestalter des Buchs, Rainer Lienemann, WIGEL. Ebenso den beiden Übersetzern Bram Opstelten und John Ormrod, die, trotz Änderungen in letzter Minute, Flexibilität und Engagement bewiesen haben. Unser Dank gilt außerdem Brigitte Maria Mayer, die, ebenfalls in denkbar knapp bemessener Zeit, die faszinierenden Aufnahmen der Münchner Installation für uns gemacht hat.

Robert Wilson hat uns mit diesem Projekt auf eine Zeitreise in Vergangenheit und Gegenwart mitgenommen, das, um T.S. Eliot zu paraphrasieren, Zukunft in sich birgt. Für diese Reise gebührt ihm unser Dank.

Jo-Anne Birnie Danzker
Direktorin, Museum Villa Stuck

Robert Wilson's Freedom Machines

This strange spectacle, "neither ballet, nor mime, nor opera … calls forth new ways with light and shadow…. [It] is an extraordinary freedom machine."[1] Louis Aragon's oft cited open letter to André Breton on the occasion of the European premiere of Robert Wilson's stage work *Deafman Glance*[2] in 1971 echoes the astonishment and excitement which had greeted Wilson's performance works in America a year earlier. John Perreault, in a review of Wilson's *The Life and Times of Sigmund Freud* exclaimed, "I no longer know the difference between theatre and dance and art…. It was one of the strangest things I have ever seen in my life."[3] Richard Foreman, also writing in the *Village Voice* in 1970, suggested that "Wilson is one of a small number of artists who seem to have applied a very different aesthetic to theatre — one current among advanced painters, musicians, dancers and filmmakers."[4] Wilson's spectacle, he added, "is one of the masterpieces of the 'artist's theatre' which exists almost in secret in this country … that whole *spectrum* of feeling awakened in us is the freedom-bestowing aim of art on the highest level."

Robert Wilson's artist's theater, his freedom machines, were perceived at the beginning of his career in the early 1970s as interdisciplinary performance art. Wilson himself, a painter with a Bachelor of Fine Arts who had studied with Sybil Moholy-Nagy and the visionary architect Paolo Soleri, described his activities in painting, design, dance, music in 1965 as "happenings."[5] In 1968 he created his first sculptural work — a "theater sculpture play environment" — in the fields of Grailville, a Catholic retreat in Loveland, Ohio. 676 telegraph poles, arranged as an amphitheater in a twenty-six-foot square with three oversized gates or passageways, functioned as sculpture, as a play area for children, and as a set for theater works or happenings. The sculpture, now largely overgrown by brush and trees, is still to be seen in Grailville. Nearly

Poles, Grailville, Loveland, Ohio 1968

Robert Wilsons ›Freedom Machines‹

Dieses seltsame Spektakel, »weder Ballett noch Schauspiel noch Oper, … setzt in neuartiger Weise Licht und Schatten ein … [Es] ist eine ungewöhnliche ›Freedom Machine‹«[1] In Louis Aragons vielzitiertem offenen Brief an André Breton anläßlich der europäischen Uraufführung von Robert Wilsons Bühnenwerk *Deafman Glance*[2] im Jahr 1971 klingt die gleiche Verwunderung und Erregung an, auf die Wilsons Bühnenwerke ein Jahr zuvor in Amerika gestoßen waren. In einer Besprechung von Wilsons *The Life and Times of Sigmund Freud* verkündete John Perreault: »Die Grenze zwischen Theater, Tanz und Kunst hat sich für mich verwischt … Es war mit das Seltsamste, was ich jemals in meinem Leben gesehen habe.«[3] Richard Foreman vertrat, ebenfalls 1970 in der *Village Voice*, die Auffassung, daß »Wilson zu der kleinen Gruppe von Künstlern [gehört], die an das Theater mit einer von Grund auf andersartigen Ästhetik herangegangen sind, einer Ästhetik, die unter avantgardistischen Malern, Musikern, Tänzern und Filmemachern gängig ist.«[4] Wilsons Spektakel, so fügte er hinzu, »ist eines der Meisterwerke des ›Künstlertheaters‹, das in diesem Land nahezu im Verborgenen existiert … eben jenes gesamte Spektrum der in uns wachgerufenen Gefühle ist das befreiende Ziel von Kunst auf höchstem Niveau.«

Robert Wilsons Künstlertheater — seine ›Freedom Machines‹ — wurde zu Beginn seiner Laufbahn in den frühen siebziger Jahren als eine gattungsübergreifende Bühnenkunst aufgefaßt. Wilson selbst, ein Maler mit dem akademischen Grad eines Bachelor of Fine Arts, der bei Sybil Moholy-Nagy und dem visionären Architekten Paolo Soleri studiert hat, bezeichnete seine Malerei, Design, Tanz und Musik verbindenden Aktivitäten 1965 als »Happenings«.[5] 1968 schuf er seine erste Skulptur — ein sogenanntes »theater sculpture play environment« — auf dem Gut eines katholischen Refugiums namens Grailville in Loveland, Ohio. 676 Telegraphenmasten, auf einer 63 Quadratmeter großen Fläche angeordnet in Form eines Amphitheaters mit drei überdimensionalen Eingangstoren oder Durchgängen, fungierten zugleich als Skulptur, als Kinderspielplatz und als Kulisse für Bühnenwerke oder Happenings. Die inzwischen von Gestrüpp und Bäumen überwachsene Skulptur in Grailville ist nach wie vor zu besichtigen. Beinahe fünfundzwanzig Jahre sollten vergehen, ehe Wilson wieder eine Skulptur im Freien realisierte, und wiederum war es ein torähnliches Objekt: die *Binnenalster-Tür*, anläßlich der *Mediale '93* in Hamburg aufgestellt. In dem dazwischenliegenden Vierteljahrhundert bestand Robert Wilsons bildhauerische Tätigkeit in erster Linie in der Schaffung von »undurchdringlichen« Objekten, die als Figuren oder Requisiten in seinen »kompositorischen«[6] Theater- und Operninszenierungen Verwendung fanden. Obgleich die meisten dieser Objekte aufgrund ihrer Größe bzw. ihres ätherischen Charakters nicht als rein funktional bezeichnet werden konnten, wiesen sie formale Anklänge an Möbel auf und trugen Titel wie *Rudolf Hess Beach Chairs* (Rudolf-Heß-Strandstühle), *Salome Throne* (Salome-Thron) oder *Saint Sebastien Stools* (St.-Sebastians-Hocker).

Musée Galliera, Paris 1974, Queen Victoria Chairs

twenty-five years were to pass before Wilson created another outdoor sculptural work — this time also in the form of a portal — the *Binnenalster Door* situated in the Alster River in Hamburg on the occasion of *Mediale '93*. In that quarter century Robert Wilson's sculptural activity had consisted primarily of the creation of "impenetrable" objects which had been employed as characters or stage props in his "compositional"[6] theater and opera productions. Although most of these objects, by virtue of their dimension and/or attentuation, could not be described as strictly functional, they echoed the forms of furniture and bore titles such as *Rudolf Hess Beach Chairs*, *Salomé Throne*, or *Saint Sebastien Stools*.

As the interdisciplinary experimentation of the 1960s and '70s gave way to the revival of more traditional art forms, including figurative painting in the 1980s, Robert Wilson's sculptural objects were received by the art press, especially in the United States, with some skepticism. Were these objects sculpture or only stage props? Were they art? Is Robert Wilson even an artist? It is telling that as of September 1997 Robert Wilson is not included in ULAN, the Getty Information Institute's comprehensive list of artists available over the Internet,[7] even though other contemporaries who have continued to be active in the area of performance such as Laurie Anderson are listed. If Robert Wilson's position within the American art community is not yet clearly defined — despite a number of extraordinarily fine museum exhibitions of his work in the United States — his interdisciplinary contribution to the visual arts is virtually unquestioned by European critics. Indeed his first museum exhibition took place in Europe in 1974, at the Musée Galliera in Paris. Marie-Claude Dane, curator of the exhibition, wrote in her introduction that "the

Als die gattungsübergreifende experimentelle Kunst der sechziger und siebziger Jahre in den Achtzigern einer Wiederbelebung traditioneller Kunstformen einschließlich figurativer Malerei wich, stießen Robert Wilsons Skulpturen in der Kunstpresse, insbesondere in den Vereinigten Staaten, auf eine gewisse Skepsis. Handelte es sich bei diesen Objekten um Skulpturen oder lediglich um Requisiten? Handelte es sich um Kunst? War Robert Wilson ein Künstler? Interessanterweise fand sich sein Name im September 1997 nicht in dem umfassenden Künstlerverzeichnis, das unter dem Kürzel ULAN vom Getty Information Institute zusammengestellt wird und über das Internet zugänglich ist;[7] andere zeitgenössische Künstlerinnen und Künstler, die weiterhin im Bereich Performance tätig sind – wie etwa Laurie Anderson – sind dagegen durchaus aufgelistet. Während also Robert Wilsons Stellung innerhalb des amerikanischen Kunstbetriebs – trotz einer Reihe gelungener Museumsausstellungen seines Werkes in den Vereinigten Staaten nach wie vor nicht eindeutig definiert ist, ist die Bedeutung seines die Gattungsgrenzen sprengenden Beitrags zur bildenden Kunst bei der europäischen Kritik im Grunde unbestritten. Seine erste Museumsausstellung hatte Robert Wilson tatsächlich in Europa, und zwar 1974 im Musée Galliera in Paris. Diese Ausstellung sollte, wie die Kuratorin, Marie-Claude Dane, in ihrer Katalogeinführung schrieb, »vor Augen führen, daß dieser junge Schriftsteller, Schauspieler, Filmemacher, Theaterregisseur, Präsident der Byrd Hoffman Foundation usw. usw. genauso gut zeichnet und malt, wie er schreibt, und daß er sich selbst als Bildhauer betrachtet«.[8] In den zwei darauffolgenden Jahrzehnten haben führende europäische Museen und Ausstellungsinstitute wie das Lenbachhaus in München (1982), das Museum Boijmans Van Beuningen in Rotterdam (1983 und 1993), der Kölner Kunstverein und das Centre d'Art Contemporain, Marseille (1984), die Galerie der Stadt, Stuttgart (1987), das Museum Morsbroich, Leverkusen (1989), das Stedelijk Museum, Amsterdam, und die Schirn Kunsthalle in Frankfurt (1990), das Centre Georges Pompidou, Paris, die Städtische Galerie Erlangen, die Kestner-Gesellschaft, Hannover, und die Bayerische Akademie der Schönen Künste, München (1991), das IVAM in Valencia (1992), die Deichtorhallen in Hamburg und die Biennale von Venedig (1993) sowie das Museum Villa Stuck in München (1997) entweder Robert Wilsons Zeichnungen und plastische Arbeiten ausgestellt oder, seit 1991, eine Bühne für seine zunehmend ehrgeizigen und komplexen Installationen geboten. Während dieser Zeit machte sich außerdem seine New Yorker Galeristin Paula Cooper nachdrücklich für ihn stark sowie auch zahlreiche führende Galerien in Europa.[9]

exhibition was to demonstrate that this young author, actor, filmmaker, stage director, president of the Byrd Hoffman Foundation, etc. etc., can draw and paint as well as he writes and that he considers himself a sculptor."[8] In the subsequent two decades, leading European institutions have either exhibited Robert Wilson's drawings and sculptural objects or, since 1991, hosted his increasingly ambitious and complex installations. These include the Lenbachhaus in Munich (1982); the Museum Boijmans Van Beuningen in Rotterdam (1983 and 1993); the Cologne Kunstverein and the Centre d'Art Contemporain, Marseille (1984); the Municipal Gallery in Stuttgart (1987); Museum Morsbroich, Leverkusen (1989); the Stedelijk Museum, Amsterdam, and Schirn Kunsthalle, Frankfurt (1990); Centre Georges Pompidou, Paris; Municipal Gallery Erlangen; Kestner Gesellschaft, Hannover and the Bavarian Academy of Fine Arts, Munich (1991); IVAM, Valencia (1992); Deichtorhallen, Hamburg and the Venice Biennale (1993) and the Museum Villa Stuck, Munich (1997). During the same period, Wilson has not only been strongly supported by his New York gallery owner Paula Cooper but also by numerous leading galleries in Europe.[9]

Robert Wilson's Drawings

It has been noted on various occasions that Robert Wilson's projects all begin with drawings — his installations, sculptural works as well as his theater and opera projects. What is less well known, however, is that Wilson continues to produce drawings not only during the development of a project but also at its conclusion. In other words, a project often begins and ends with drawings. Initial drawings, such as those reproduced in this book, function as a means to develop, to express and to structure his vision.[10] Perhaps produced during a meeting, over dinner or on a plane, they often include handwritten comments and are to be found on scrap paper, in notebooks, or, as in the case of the Villa Stuck project, on the pages of illustrated books or other research material. As ideas are refined, other drawings are produced — "working" drawings which further elucidate a concept, or even change it. When preparation for the project nears its end, sometimes in the last hours before a performance is to be staged, or an exhibition is opened, it is not uncommon for Robert Wilson, in an act of closure, as an epilogue to the project, to work late into the night producing drawings. These have a completely different character than the concept or the working drawings: charcoal, ink or graphite images on fine paper — monumental, transcendental, sometimes claustrophobic — they encapsulate emotional states.

As early as 1965 Robert Wilson acknowledged in an interview that "when painting I let the paint take over…. The response is emotional instead of rational."[11] In Wilson's final drawings for a project the rational is excised. In an emotional and spiritual catharsis, he returns to the source of his work, and its strength, a brooding, non-verbal intuition which expresses itself in images of extinction and apotheosis: "Images of death are a common thread in all my stagings."[12] If in Wilson's theatrical works and sculptural installations one is most aware of the transcendental, redemptive quality of his light, in his drawings as epilogue one is astounded by its absence. There *is* a régie of light and dark, volume and void, as commentators have noted, visual libretti[13] which recall the staged work. If, however, as Wilson once noted, the "stage picture is like a mask,"[14] in his final drawings for a project the brilliant guise has been removed, the masquerade is set aside.

Robert Wilsons Zeichnungen

Es ist schon verschiedentlich festgestellt worden, daß am Anfang von Robert Wilsons Projekten – seinen Installationen, Skulpturen sowie Bühnen- und Operninszenierungen – stets Zeichnungen stehen. Weniger bekannt freilich ist die Tatsache, daß Wilson seine Projekte über das Entwicklungsstadium hinaus und bis in die Abschlußphase hinein zeichnerisch begleitet. Die am Projektanfang entstehenden ›Konzeptzeichnungen‹, wie die im vorliegenden Band abgebildeten, dienen ihm dazu, seine Vorstellungen auszuarbeiten, auszudrücken und zu strukturieren.[10] Häufig unter Einschluß von handschriftlichen Anmerkungen sind sie etwa während einer Konferenz, beim Abendessen oder im Flugzeug auf Papierfetzen, in Notizbüchern oder, wie im Fall des Projekts für die Villa Stuck, auf den Seiten eines bebilderten Buches oder auf anderen Projektunterlagen entstanden. Haben die Vorstellungen einmal eine einigermaßen konkrete Gestalt angenommen, entstehen andere Zeichnungen, ›Arbeitszeichnungen‹, die eine Idee zusätzlich beleuchten oder auch eine Neukonzeption beinhalten. Wenn sich das Projekt dem Ende nähert, kommt es nicht selten vor, daß Robert Wilson in einer Art abschließenden Geste, gleichsam als Epilog zum Projekt, bis spät in die Nacht hinein, ja manchmal sogar noch in den letzten Stunden vor der Aufführung oder Ausstellungseröffnung, Zeichnungen produziert, die sich in ihrem Charakter wiederum grundlegend von den Konzept- und Arbeitszeichnungen unterscheiden: Mit Kohle, Tusche oder Bleistift auf feines Papier gezeichnet, fangen sie in monumentalen, transzendentalen, mitunter auch klaustrophobischen Bildern Stimmungen oder Gemütszustände ein.

Bereits 1965 bekannte Robert Wilson in einem Interview: »Beim Malen überlasse ich der Farbe selbst die Regie … Was sich dabei ergibt, ist nicht rational, sondern emotional.«[11] In Wilsons abschließenden Zeichnungen zu einem Projekt wird das Rationale ausgeklammert. In einer emotionalen und geistigen Katharsis kehrt er zurück zur Quelle seines Werks und zu dessen Kraft, einer grüblerischen, nichtverbalen Intuition, die sich in Bildern der Auslöschung und Verklärung ausdrückt: »Todesbilder ziehen sich wie ein roter Faden durch all meine Inszenierungen.«[12] Drängt sich bei Wilsons Bühnenwerken und skulpturalen Installationen der transzendentale, erlösende Charakter des eingesetzten Lichts geradezu auf, so verblüffen die als Epilog angelegten Zeichnungen durch dessen Fehlen. Es existiert, wie verschiedentlich beobachtet, eine Regie von Licht und Dunkel, von Masse und Leere – Libretti in Bildform,[13] die an das inszenierte Werk erinnern. Während jedoch, wie Wilson einmal angemerkt hat, »das Bühnenbild einer Maske gleicht«,[14] ist in seinen abschließenden Zeichnungen zu einem Projekt diese Maske entfernt, die Maskerade beiseite geschoben worden.

Die Skulpturen

Auch Robert Wilsons Skulpturen funktionieren als eine Art Maske. Stuhl, Sofa oder Thron genannt, kommen sie als Möbel getarnt daher. Tatsächlich handelt es sich bei ihnen um Personifizierungen, Moralitäten, Landschaften und Seinszustände, die die Figuren in Wilsons Opern oder Bühnenwerken begleiten und bestimmen. Ihre Funktionalität im üblichen Sinn ist stark eingeschränkt, sei es durch das Material (Blei) oder durch ihre Plazierung (von der Decke herabhängend). Auf Wilsons erste Möbelskulptur, den 1969 entstandenen *Hängenden Stuhl (Freud)*, folgte bald die fliegende Bank in *Deafman*

The Sculptural Works

Robert Wilson's sculptural objects also function as a mask. Titled chair, or sofa or throne, they are disguised as furniture. In fact they are personifications, cautionary tales, landscapes, and states of being which accompany and situate the characters in Robert Wilson's operas or theater works. Their functionality, in everyday terms, is severely curtailed — through material (lead) or placement (hanging from the ceiling). Wilson's first furniture sculpture, *Hanging Chair (Freud)* produced in 1969, was quickly followed by the flying bench in *Deafman Glance*. As Wilson explained in an interview with Dorine Mignot, they are not conceived as "theatre props, but in terms of space, texture, line, as works of art, as sculpture, drawings etc. My background was in the visual arts ... the work I did in the theatre was a continuation of the work I was doing as a visual artist."[15]

If the hanging chair and flying bench magically defied gravity, other sculptural works such as the *Stalin Chairs* (1973) and the *Queen Victoria Chairs* (1974) are distinguished by their mass and monumentality. It is interesting to note that the latter set was produced in two versions — one in black vinyl, lighter and easier to move for the theater production, and a second version, a third larger in size and made out of lead, for exhibition purposes. The 1974 exhibition at the Musée Galliera in Paris included all of Wilson's furniture works to that date as well as drawings — some as large in scale as the sculptural objects themselves. Four years later, in conjunction with the Berlin Festspiele, Robert Wilson exhibited his sculptural works at the

From a Theater of Images, The Contemporary Arts Center, Cincinnati 1980

Glance. Wie Wilson in einem Interview mit Dorine Mignot erklärte, werden diese Objekte »nicht als Theaterrequisiten konzipiert, sondern unter dem Gesichtspunkt von Raum, Oberflächenbeschaffenheit und Umriß als Kunstwerk, als Skulptur, als Zeichnungen usw. Ich komme von der bildenden Kunst ... das, was ich auf der Bühne machte, war eine Fortsetzung dessen, was ich als bildender Künstler machte.«[15]

Setzten sich der hängende Stuhl und die fliegende Bank auf magische Weise über die Schwerkraft hinweg, so zeichnen sich andere Skulpturen wie die *Stalin Chairs* von 1973 und die *Queen Victoria Chairs* von 1974 wiederum durch ihre Masse und Monumentalität aus. Interessanterweise wurde letztere ›Garnitur‹ in zwei verschiedenen Fassungen produziert – eine leichtere, einfacher zu verschiebende aus schwarzem Vinyl für die Bühneninszenierung und eine um ein Drittel größere aus Blei für Ausstellungszwecke. Die Ausstellung 1974 im Musée Galliera in Paris umfaßte sämtliche bis dahin entstandenen Möbelobjekte Wilsons sowie Zeichnungen, deren Format in manchen Fällen dem der Objekte selbst entsprach. Vier Jahre später zeigte Robert Wilson seine plastischen Arbeiten anläßlich der Berliner Festspiele in der Galerie Folker Skulima. In seinem Beitrag zum begleitenden Katalog schrieb Roland H. Wiegenstein:

»... als Möblierung zu dienen, menschliche Haltungen zu akzentuieren ... erinnern die Objekte: Stuhl, Sessel, Tisch, Bank nur noch für den, der Wilsons Inszenierungen gesehen hat, an diese, sonst lösen sie andere Assoziationen aus, Vergleiche etwa mit Richard Serras riskanten Metallscheiben aus Corten-Stahl oder Blei(!), mit Sol LeWitts minimalistischen Additionen, sogar mit Gerrit Thomas Rietvelds Sitzmöbeln und Häusern. ... Sie sind Prototypen, deren Zweckbestimmung es ist, ihre augenscheinliche Funktion (darauf sitzen, daran sitzen) zugleich – gerade noch – zu ermöglichen und – zu dementieren ... Der erkennbare Zweck transzendiert zur Kunst, zum Kunstwerk.«[16]

In diesen frühen Ausstellungen wurden Wilsons Skulpturen und Zeichnungen, obgleich von den räumlichen Rahmenbedingungen her sorgfältig durchdacht, noch in einer im Grunde traditionellen Art und Weise dargeboten. Gegen 1980 jedoch ging Wilson, angefangen mit seiner zweiten großen Museumsausstellung, die vom Contemporary Arts Center in Cincinnati organisiert wurde, dazu über, nicht mehr nur seine Erfahrung als bildender Künstler für seine Bühnenwerke, sondern auch umgekehrt seine Bühnenerfahrung für seine Ausstellungen fruchtbringend einzusetzen.

Zehn Jahre zuvor hatte Richard Foreman das Prinzip von Wilsons Bühnenwerken als ›Tableau vivant‹ beschrieben.[17]

Galerie Folker Skulima. In his text for the accompanying catalogue Roland H. Wiegenstein noted:

"Objects, such as chairs, tables or benches, may recall … the functions of furnishing a room, or emphasize a physical attitude … but only for those who have seen Wilson's works on the stage; otherwise, they have quite different associations, inviting comparisons with, for example, Richard Serra's menacing discs of steel or lead (!), with Sol LeWitt's minimalist assemblies, or even with the chairs and buildings of Gerrit Rietveld…. They are prototypes, whose purpose is to fulfil, yet simultaneously to disclaim, their function (of providing something to sit on, or at)…. The manifest purpose transcends itself and is transformed into art, into an art work."[16]

In these early exhibitions the presentation of Wilson's sculptural works and drawings, although carefully considered in terms of architectural space, remained essentially traditional. By 1980, however, beginning with Wilson's second major museum exhibition organized by the Contemporary Arts Center, Cincinnati, Wilson began to apply not only his skills as an artist to his theater works but also his theatrical skills to his exhibitions.

From a Theater of Images, Neuberger Museum, State University of New York 1980

Richard Foreman had noted a decade earlier that Wilson's theater works had the character of a series of 'tableaux vivants.'[17] In his review of the Cincinnati exhibition in *Art in America* in 1980, Craig Owens echoed Foreman's comments when he noted that Wilson's exhibition was, "in fact, a series of profoundly arresting tableaux that engaged the viewer directly, without reference to their theatrical origins."[18] Owens argued convincingly that Wilson had identified the tableau as the meeting ground of painting and theater.

In the second venue of the Cincinnati exhibition, in the Neuberger Museum in Purchase, N.Y., Wilson intensified his use of theatrical lighting in the exhibition and — perhaps unintentionally — precipitated an exchange between his own objects and those of other artists.

"Rising from the middle of a reflecting pool, an acetylene-gas torch extending to one side, this ceremonial object [*Overture Chair*] visible upon entering the museum, functioned as both emblem and beacon; approaching it through galleries devoted to a collection of constructivist objects — dwarfed by Wilson's powerful presence — the spectator became a participant in a kind of ritual procession to a consecrated site…. [Wilson] worked to transform the museum into a theater of encounters."[19]

The theater of encounters between objects in a museum's collection and Wilson's own sculptural works which distinguished the Purchase exhibition was not to be repeated again until the 1990s. The creation of a meeting ground between painting and theater in the form of tableau, was, however, to become a hallmark of Wilson's exhibitions during the coming decade.

Craig Owens griff 1980 diese Beobachtung Foremans auf. In seiner Besprechung in der Zeitschrift *Art in America* meinte er, Wilsons Ausstellung in Cincinnati sei »im Grunde eine Folge höchst faszinierender Tableaus, die den Betrachter unmittelbar fesselten, ohne daß ihre Wurzeln im Theater überhaupt eine Rolle spielten«.[18] Owens machte überzeugend geltend, daß Wilson im Tableau eine Form gefunden hatte, die Malerei und Theater in sich vereinte.

Als die Ausstellung anschließend im Neuberger Museum in Purchase im US-Bundesstaat New York gezeigt wurde, griff Wilson bei der Präsentation seiner Werke verstärkt auf Bühnenbeleuchtungstechniken zurück, wodurch er – vielleicht unbeabsichtigt – einer Wechselwirkung zwischen seinen Objekten und denen anderer Künstler Vorschub leistete.

»In der Mitte aus einem reflektierenden Wasserbecken emporragend und mit einem seitlich angebrachten Acetylenbrenner versehen, funktionierte dieser Zeremonialgegenstand [*Overture Chair*], der sich dem Besucher zeigte, sobald er das Museum betrat, zugleich als Symbol und als Leuchtbake: auf seinem Weg dorthin durch Museumsräume, die einer Sammlung konstruktivistischer – durch Wilsons starken Auftritt allerdings in den Schatten gestellter – Objekte vorbehalten war, wurde der Betrachter gleichsam zum Teilnehmer in einer Art ritueller Prozession zu einer Weihestätte … [Wilson] hatte aus dem Museum ein Theater der Begegnungen gemacht.«[19]

Dieses Theater der Begegnungen zwischen Objekten aus einer Museumssammlung und Wilsons eigenen plastischen Arbeiten sollte nach der Ausstellung in Purchase erst wieder in den neunziger Jahren realisiert werden. Das Bemühen, Malerei und Theater in der Form des Tableaus zusammenzubringen, wurde jedoch in den achtziger Jahren zu einem Markenzeichen von Wilsons Ausstellungen.

Environments / Tableaux

The next major exhibition of sculptural work by Robert Wilson took place in 1987 at the municipal gallery in Stuttgart, Germany. Titled *Memory of a Revolution* and described in the catalogue as an environment, the project was developed to coincide with a large scale exhibition titled *Baden and Württemberg in the Age of Napoleon*. A bittersweet "homage" to the French Revolution, Wilson's project took the form of an exhibition/performance which lasted six weeks. In a darkened room, its contours barely visible in a metallic blue light, strains of Callas performing arias from Cherubini's *Medea* in the background, an eighty-two-year-old stand-in actor from the Stuttgart Theater sat motionless, twice a day for two hours, between the toes of a gigantic elephant's foot. Separated from the viewer/voyeur by bars, the actor, dressed in Napoleonic costume, solemnly held a model of an empty stage on his lap.

The environment *Memory of a Revolution* is based on Victor Hugo's 1862 novel *Les Misérables*, in which street urchins seek refuge inside a huge plaster statue of an elephant which is slowly being ravaged by weather and devoured by rats. Hugo's novel is based on historical fact: a twelve-meter-high bronzed plaster statue of an elephant, a model for a fountain commissioned by Napoleon, stood on the Place de la Bastille from 1811 until the 1840s. "After the fall of Napoleon, no one had any further interest in carrying out the project. The rats reclaimed the model of the elephant, and eventually it was demolished." [20] In an exact recreation of the literary and historical facts, Wilson sought permission from the health authorities to allow him to use live rats in his environment, but his efforts were in vain. Instead sculptured rodents scurried motionless in what Johann-Karl Schmidt in his catalogue text "Robert Wilson *still life is real life*" described as "animated stasis, an endless stage scene with no action" — a "continous play in suspended motion." [21]

Room for Salomé, Robert Wilson's next tableau, was presented at Amsterdam's Stedelijk Museum in a 1990 group exhibition titled *Energieën*. [22] For this project Wilson cast his furniture works as protagonists, as actors, [23] as surrogates, in a sound and light environment based on his 1987 staging of Strauss' opera *Salomé* at La Scala in Milan. When asked by the exhibition's curator Dorine Mignot to describe the installation, Wilson replied hesitantly that "in maybe some sense, it has something to do with theatre too." [24] Pressed by Mignot to explain further, Wilson added "there's a sense of poetry about them [the chairs], that they began to tell stories … in the way an artist would tell them…. Even the texture of the floor, the cracked earth, the splitting earth, the light of the room." [25] An abbreviated visual poem, a haiku of colour and physical remains, *Room for Salomé* is, as Wilson expressed it, "a room for experience, which is a way of thinking." [26]

In a major exhibition a year later at the Museum of Fine Arts in Boston, Wilson's furniture works readopted their traditional stance as independent sculptural works. Dramatic lighting, however, and sound environments created by Wilson's long term collaborator Hans Peter Kuhn reinforced their origins in the theater. This retrospective exhibition, which toured to the Contemporary Arts Museum, Houston and the San Francisco Museum of Modern Art, included drawings, paintings, furniture/sculpture and video works from the preceding twenty years. Titled *The Night before The Day*, the exhibition was a metaphysical journey from innocence to experience, a *tour de force* in brilliant white through gray to black, divided into a prologue and three acts.

Environments / Tableaus

Die nächste größere Ausstellung des plastischen Werks von Robert Wilson fand 1987 in der Galerie der Stadt Stuttgart statt. Das im Katalog als ein Environment bezeichnete Projekt mit dem Titel *Erinnerung an eine Revolution* war eigentlich als Begleitveranstaltung zu einer großangelegten Ausstellung über *Baden und Württemberg im Zeitalter Napoleons* geplant. Wilsons Projekt, eine bittersüße ›Hommage‹ an die Französische Revolution, nahm aber die Form einer sechswöchigen Ausstellung beziehungsweise Performance an.

In einem dunklen Raum, dessen Umrisse in schimmerndem metallblauen Licht kaum auszumachen waren und in dem, von der Callas gesungen, Arien aus Cherubinis *Medea* erklangen, saß zweimal am Tag zwei Stunden lang ein 82jähriger Statist des Stuttgarter Theaters zwischen den Zehen eines gigantischen Elefantenfußes. Durch ein Gitter von dem in die Rolle eines Voyeurs versetzten Betrachter getrennt, hielt der in napoleonische Tracht gekleidete Schauspieler feierlich das Modell einer leeren Theaterbühne auf dem Schoß.

Das Environment *Erinnerung an eine Revolution* basiert auf Victor Hugos Roman *Les Misérables* von 1862, in dem Straßenjungen in der riesigen Statue eines Elefanten Zuflucht suchen, die allmählich verwittert und von Ratten zerfressen wird. Hugos Roman liegt eine wahre Begebenheit zugrunde: Von 1811 bis zu den 1840er Jahren stand auf der Place de la Bastille in Paris eine zwölf Meter hohe Gipsstatue eines Elefanten, die das Modell für einen von Napoleon in Auftrag gegebenen Brunnen darstellte. »Nach dem Sturz Napoleons hatte niemand mehr Interesse an der Ausführung des Projekts. Das Tiermodell wurde von den Ratten zurückerobert, schließlich riß man es ab.« [20] Im Bemühen um eine möglichst genaue Rekonstruktion der literarischen und historischen Fakten bat Wilson die zuständigen Behörden um Genehmigung, lebende Ratten in seinem Environment verwenden zu dürfen, jedoch ohne Erfolg. Statt dessen huschten regungslose Rattenskulpturen durch das Environment, das Johann-Karl Schmidt in seinem Katalogbeitrag ›Robert Wilson – *still life is real life*‹ als »bewegte Statik und eine unendliche Bühnenszene ohne Handlung«, als ein »statisches Dauerschauspiel« bezeichnete. [21]

Room for Salomé, Robert Wilsons nächstes Tableau, wurde 1990 im Rahmen einer Gruppenausstellung mit dem Titel *Energieën* im Stedelijk Museum in Amsterdam präsentiert. [22] Für dieses Projekt ließ Wilson seine Möbelobjekte als Protagonisten, als Schauspieler [23] oder Stellvertreter in einem Klang- und Lichtenvironment auftreten, das auf seine Inszenierung der Strauss-Oper *Salome* 1987 in der Mailänder Scala zurückging. Als er von der Ausstellungskuratorin Dorine Mignot gebeten wurde, die Installation zu beschreiben, meinte Wilson zögernd: »In gewisser Weise hat die Sache vielleicht auch mit Theater zu tun.« [24] Auf Mignots Nachhaken hin fügte er hinzu: »Sie [die Stühle] haben etwas Poetisches an sich in dem Sinne, daß sie anfingen, Geschichten zu erzählen … so wie ein Künstler diese erzählen würde … Selbst die Beschaffenheit des Fußbodens, die geborstene, aufgeplatzte Erde, das Licht in dem Raum.« [25] *Room for Salomé* ist ein abgekürztes Gedicht in Bildform, ein Haiku der Farbe und der materiellen Überreste oder, wie Wilson selbst es formuliert hat, »ein Raum für die Erfahrung, die eine Form des Denkens ist«. [26]

In einer größeren Ausstellung ein Jahr später im Museum of Fine Arts in Boston nahmen Wilsons Möbelobjekte wieder ihren traditionellen Status als autonome Skulpturen an. Dramatische Lichteffekte und von Wilsons langjährigem Mitarbeiter Hans Peter Kuhn gestaltete Klangenvironments unterstrichen allerdings

Memory of a Revolution/Erinnerung an eine Revolution, Stuttgart 1987

The prologue or entrance consisted of a narrow passageway through a symbolic forest, the walls covered with Robert Wilson's photographs of tree bark (*Forest Portraits, East Berlin*, 1987). Photographic enlargements of weathered, decaying statues from the castle of Sanssouci in Potsdam[27] hung on the forest wall, framed in mirrored glass which reflected the face of the viewer passing by. Act I consisted of "a big white cube of a room that's almost painfully bright,"[28] in which Wilson's furniture/sculptures either hung from the ceiling or stood in a state of arrested tension in pools of light on the floor. The focus of the room was a golem, a figure made out of clay which, in Jewish mystical literature, is supernaturally brought to life.[29] Wilson's golem's costume, originally worn by actors in *Death Destruction and Detroit II* (1987), consisted of a hat, mask, and a long papier-maché overcoat.[30] The next room, Act II, its gray walls papered with Wilson's drawings, began

ihre Verwurzelung im Theater. Diese Retrospektive, die anschließend in Houston im Contemporary Arts Museum sowie im San Francisco Museum of Modern Art Station machte, umfaßte Zeichnungen, Gemälde, Möbelskulpturen und Video-arbeiten aus den vorausgegangenen zwanzig Jahren. Betitelt *The Night before The Day* (Die Nacht vor dem Tage), war sie eine metaphysische Reise von Unschuld zu Erkenntnis, eine Tour de force in glänzendem Weiß über Grau bis Schwarz, gegliedert in einen Prolog und drei Akte.

Der Prolog oder ›Eingang‹ bestand aus einem schmalen Korridor durch einen symbolischen Wald, angedeutet durch Robert Wilsons Photos von Baumrinde, die die Wände tapezierten (*Forest Portraits, East Berlin*, 1987). Vergrößerte Aufnahmen von verwitterten, verfallenden Statuen des Schlosses Sanssouci in Potsdam[27] hingen hinter verspiegeltem Glas, in dem der Betrachter im Vorbeigehen sein Gesicht an der ›Waldwand‹ widergespiegelt sehen konnte. Der erste Akt bestand aus »dem großen weißen Würfel eines fast schmerzhaft grell ausgeleuchteten Raums«,[28] in dem Wilsons Möbelskulpturen entweder von der Decke herabhingen oder, in erstarrter Spannung, von einem Spot angeleuchtet auf dem Fußboden standen. Den Mittelpunkt des Raumes bildete ein Golem, »eine aus Lehm gefertigte Gestalt, die in der jüdischen Mystik auf übernatürliche Weise zum Leben erweckt wird«.[29] Das – ursprünglich von Schauspielern in *Death Destruction and Detroit II* (1987) getragene – Kostüm von Wilsons Golem bestand aus einem Hut, einer Maske und einem langen Mantel aus Papier-maché.[30] Mit dem nächsten Raum, der den zweiten Akt markiert und dessen graue Wände mit Wilsons Zeichnungen tapeziert waren, begann die Reise hin zur Dunkelheit. Gleichsam eingebettet in diesem Raum befand sich, außen auf einer Seite mit Bühnenbildern verziert, ein zweiter Raum, eine neue Fassung von *Erinnerung an eine Revolution*.

Robert Wilson's Vision (The Night before The Day), Boston 1991, Prologue

the journey towards darkness. In the center of this room was yet another room, one of its outside walls studded with theater sets embedded into it, with a new version of *Memory of a Revolution* inside. If in the original Stuttgart version Wilson had engaged a live actor to "be" the old Bonapartist residing in one of the elephant's legs after Napoleon's demise,[31] in Boston and for the tour the actor was replaced by an animated mannequin. Act III, a completely black room, embodied what the curator of the exhibition, Trevor Fairbrother, termed the "technological aura of urban culture" and its "frightening and dehumanizing guises."[32] Flashing control panels from the spaceship interior of *Einstein on the Beach* (1976) were juxtaposed with casts of cowboy boots and furniture works such as the "aggressively shiny

Während Wilson für die Stuttgarter Urfassung einen lebenden Schauspieler engagiert hatte, um den alten Bonapartisten zu verkörpern, der nach Napoleons Sturz in einem der Elefantenbeine hauste,[31] nahm in der Fassung für Boston und die weiteren Ausstellungsstationen eine bewegliche Puppe dessen Stelle ein. Der dritte Akt, ein ganz in Schwarz gehaltener Raum, verkörperte das, was der Kurator der Ausstellung, Trevor Fairbrother, die »technologische Aura urbaner Kultur« und deren »beängstigender und unmenschlicher Erscheinungsformen« nannte.[32] Neben blinkenden Bedienungsfeldern aus dem Raumschiffinnern von *Einstein on the Beach* (1976) gab es Abgüsse von Cowboy-stiefeln sowie Möbelobjekte wie die »aggressiv glänzenden und kantigen« *Rudolf Hess Beach Chairs* aus *Death Destruction and Detroit* (1979) und ein

Robert Wilson's Vision, Boston 1991, Act I

and angular" *Rudolf Hess Beach Chairs* from *Death Destruction and Detroit* (1979) and a long red lacquer sofa based on the whore's sofa in *Doktor Faustus* (1989).[33] The American journalist April Austin, in a review in the *Christian Science Monitor*, described the final room of the exhibition: "Surrounded by darkness and the sound of an eerie sea whistle, I felt isolated, even though there were reporters all around me. They too had fallen silent."[34]

Robert Wilson's Vision, Boston 1991, Act III

längliches, rot lackiertes Sofa nach dem Bordellsofa in *Doktor Faustus* von 1989 zu sehen.[33] Die amerikanische Journalistin April Austin schrieb in ihrer im *Christian Science Monitor* erschienenen Rezension der Ausstellung über den letzten Raum: »Umgeben von Dunkelheit und dem unheimlichen Klang eines Nebelhorns fühlte ich mich isoliert, obwohl lauter Reporter um mich herum waren. Auch sie waren verstummt.«[34]

Im Verlauf des Jahres 1991 wurde Robert Wilson für seine Arbeit als bildender Künstler in einem bis dahin beispiellosen Umfang gewürdigt. Abgesehen davon, daß seine überaus erfolgreiche Retrospektive immer noch durch die Vereinigten Staaten wanderte, wurde eine größere Ausstellung seiner Möbel unter dem Titel *Monuments* in der Kestner-Gesellschaft in Hannover sowie in der Bayerischen Akademie der Schönen Künste in München gezeigt. Darüber hinaus wurde im November des gleichen Jahres eine der wichtigsten Ausstellungen seines Werkes, *Mr. Bojangles' Memory: og son of fire*, im Centre Georges Pompidou in Paris eröffnet.

Hatte Robert Wilson in seiner Ausstellung im Neuberger Museum in Purchase im US-Bundesstaat New York mehr als ein Jahrzehnt zuvor noch mehr oder weniger unabsichtlich einen Dialog zwischen seinen eigenen Arbeiten und Werken aus dem Bestand des Museums in Gang gesetzt, so waren solche ›Begegnungen‹ in der Ausstellung 1991 im Centre Pompidou ganz und gar gewollt. Wie Wilson selbst in einem im Ausstellungsführer veröffentlichten Interview mit Thierry Grillet aussagte, »unterscheidet sich diese Schau wesentlich von meinen anderen Ausstellungen oder meiner jüngeren Theaterarbeit«. Der Hauptunterschied bestand eben darin, daß Werke anderer Künstler in einen Dialog mit seinen eigenen Arbeiten einbezogen wurden:

Mr. Bojangles' Memory: og son of fire, Paris 1992

In the course of 1991, as at no other time during his career, Robert Wilson was showered with accolades for his work as an artist. Not only was his highly successful American retrospective still touring the United States, but a major exhibition of his furniture works titled *Monuments* was presented at the Kestner-Gesellschaft in Hanover, Germany and at Bavaria's Academy of Fine Arts in Munich. In November of the same year one of the most important exhibitions of his work, titled *Mr. Bojangles' Memory: og son of fire*, opened at the Centre Georges Pompidou in Paris.

If in his exhibition at the Neuberger Museum in Purchase, N.Y. over a decade earlier, Robert Wilson had, somewhat unwittingly, set up a dialogue between his own works and those in the museum's collection, in the Pompidou exhibition in 1991 such "encounters" were fully intentional. In an interview with Thierry Grillet published in the visitors' guide to the exhibition, Wilson noted that "it is very different from my other exhibitions or recent theatre works." The main difference consisted of the inclusion of works of art by other artists in dialogue with his own:

"I chose pieces which would conflict with my work, and others which would complement it.... For example, you see a chair I designed for Einstein, with plumbing pipes. It has tall, vertical lines and it is shown next to a tall figure by Giacometti. There is a relationship between them."[35]

Drawing on nearly twenty years of experience in planning installations of his work, Wilson developed a concept for Pompidou which represented a new direction in his work as well as addressed the problem of presenting his work in the

»Ich suchte Arbeiten aus, die zu meinem Werk im Widerspruch stehen, und andere, die mein Werk ergänzen würden ... Man sieht zum Beispiel einen Stuhl mit Bleirohren, den ich für *Einstein* entworfen hatte. Senkrechten dominieren seine Gestalt, und er wird neben einer hoch aufragenden Giacometti-Figur gezeigt. Es besteht also eine Beziehung zwischen beiden.«[35]

Gestützt auf eine beinahe zwanzigjährige Erfahrung mit der Planung von Installationen seines Werks, entwickelte Wilson ein Konzept für die Schau im Centre Pompidou, das zum einen eine neue Tendenz in seiner Arbeit darstellte und zum anderen den Schwierigkeiten Rechnung trug, welche die eher unbequeme Architektur des Museums einer Präsentation seiner Werke bereitete. Er legte einen Gehweg, einen ›Highway‹, durch eine mehrere Ebenen einnehmende Landschaft mit einem Lava speienden Vulkan an. Im Ausstellungsführer schrieb Wilson: »Der Raum soll die Assoziation mit Ausgrabungen wecken, Ausgrabungen von Zeit und Raum.« Zu den Ausgrabungsfunden zählten seine eigenen Skulpturen sowie Werke von Künstlern des 20. Jahrhunderts aus der Sammlung des Museums: Carl Andre, Giovanni Anselmo, Francis Bacon, Jeanne Bardey, Hans Bellmer, Constantin Brâncuşi, Alfred Coumes, Pablo Gargallo, Alberto Giacometti, Yves Klein, Willem de Kooning, Amedeo Modigliani, Piet Mondrian, Jean Pougny, Germaine Richier und Niki de Saint Phalle.[36]

Die internationale Presse reagierte ein wenig verwundert, insgesamt aber positiv auf Wilsons Konfrontation seines eigenen Werks mit dem anderer Künstler. Der englische Kritiker Robert Hewison schrieb: »Das kühnste Statement, daß es sich <u>nicht</u> um eine konventionelle Kunstausstellung handelt, findet sich gleich im Eingangsbereich, wo der Besucher gezwungen wird, über einen Bronzekopf von Brâncuşi zu gehen, der in einem Plexiglaskasten auf dem Fußboden liegt.«[37] In der *Frankfurter Allgemeinen Zeitung* meinte Joseph Hantmann, die »Bedeutung« der Ausstellung sei nicht in den einzelnen Werken zu suchen, sondern im Neben- und Miteinander von

Mr. Bojangles' Memory: og son of fire, Paris 1992

Monuments, Hannover 1991, Overture Chair

somewhat unforgiving architecture of the museum. He created a walkway, a "highway," through a multi-level landscape with lava flowing from a volcano. Wilson noted in the visitors' guide, "The room is designed to evoke excavations, excavations of time and space." Among the excavation finds were his own sculptural objects as well as works of art by twentieth-century artists from the collection of the museum: Carl Andre, Giovanni Anselmo, Francis Bacon, Jeanne Bardey, Hans Bellmer, Constantin Brâncuși, Afred Courmes, Pablo Gargallo, Alberto Giacometti, Yves Klein, Willem de Kooning, Amedeo Modigliani, Piet Mondrian, Jean Pougny, Germaine Richier, and Niki de Saint Phalle.[36]

The international press was astonished but favorably impressed with Wilson's confrontation of his own work with that of other artists. The British critic Robert Hewison noted: "The boldest statement that this is *not* a conventional art show is made at the entrance, when visitors have to walk over a bronze head by Brâncuși, lying in a perspex box on the floor."[37] In the *Frankfurter Allgemeine Zeitung* Joseph Hantmann suggested that the "meaning" of the exhibition was not to be found in individual works but in the co-existence and juxtaposition of the banal and the meaningful in a series of object and history panoramas:

"Robert Wilson demonstrates in this monographic but by no means monomaniacal staging of the self, that he is a master of precision in ambiguity, a precision which can be located, captured, and represented in an endless flood of images of the urban interior, the source of which can not be identified."[38]

A number of installations which represented unusual and exciting directions in Wilson's work followed the Pompidou exhibition in rapid succession: the temporary floating of the *Binnenalster Door* (1992) in Hamburg's Alster River mentioned earlier (one of his rare outdoor works[39]); the creation of a tableau *Monsters of Grace* (1993) in the Galerie Franck + Schulte, Berlin[40]; the environment *Memory/Loss* which was awarded the Grand Prix de Sculpture, the "Golden Lion," at the Venice Biennale in 1993; and the organization of what was, up to that date, one of the most coherent and successful of his exhibitions, *Portrait, Still Life, Landscape* at the Museum Boijmans Van Beuningen in Rotterdam, also in 1993. Although Wilson continued to exhibit his furniture/sculpture objects and drawings in very fine exhibitions such as that at the prestigious Instituto Valenciano de Arte Moderno (IVAM) in Valencia in 1992,[41] the primary focus of his work as a visual artist was to become tableaux or environments fully independent of his theater work, often in dialogue with the work of other artists both visual and literary.

A letter from the German playwright Heiner Müller written to Wilson in 1987[42] was, for example, a source of inspiration for the stunning installation *Memory/Loss* at the Venice Biennale in 1993:

"… A text by Tshinghis Aitmatov describes a Mongolian torture which served to turn captives into slaves, tools without memory. The technology was simple: the captive, who had been sentenced to survival and not designated for the slave trade but for domestic use by the conquerors, had his head shaved and covered with a helmet made from the skin of a freshly slaughtered camel's neck. Buried to the shoulders, and exposed on the steppe to the sun which dried the helmet and contracted it around the skull, the regrowing hair was forced to grow back into the scalp. The tortured prisoner lost his memory within five days, if he survived, and was, after this operation, a laborer who didn't cause trouble, a 'Mankurt'…. There is no revolution without memory."[43]

Banalem und Bedeutungsvollem in einer Folge von Objekt- und Geschichtspanoramen:

»Robert Wilson … erweist sich auch in dieser monographischen, keineswegs aber monomanischen Selbstinszenierung als ein Meister der Präzision im Ungefähren, die sich im unendlichen Bilderfluß des urbanen Interieurs aufspüren, stellen, darstellen, nie aber herleiten läßt.«[38]

Auf die Ausstellung im Centre Pompidou folgten in rascher Folge mehrere Installationen, die ungewohnte, spannende Tendenzen in Wilsons Werk verkörperten: die *Binnenalster-Tür*, die 1992 für einige Zeit auf der Hamburger Alster trieb (eine der wenigen Arbeiten, die Wilson im Freien realisierte[39]), das Tableau *Monsters of Grace* 1993 in der Galerie Franck + Schulte in Berlin,[40] das Environment *Memory/Loss*, das auf der Biennale von Venedig 1993 mit dem Grand Prix de Sculpture, dem ›Goldenen Löwen‹, ausgezeichnet wurde, sowie ebenfalls 1993 die Schau *Portrait, Still Life, Landscape* im Museum Boijmans Van Beuningen in Rotterdam, eine seiner bis dahin gelungensten, in sich geschlossensten Ausstellungen. Obgleich Wilson weiterhin seine Möbelobjekte beziehungsweise Skulpturen und Zeichnungen in exquisiten Ausstellungen wie etwa 1992 im angesehenen Instituto Valenciano de Arte Moderno (IVAM) in Valencia zeigte,[41] rückten nunmehr in erster Linie von seiner Theaterarbeit völlig unabhängige Tableaus oder Environments, häufig im Dialog mit dem Werk anderer bildender Künstler oder auch von Literaten, in den Mittelpunkt seiner Arbeit als bildender Künstler.

So wurde ein Brief des deutschen Dramatikers Heiner Müller an Robert Wilson aus dem Jahr 1987[42] zur Inspirationsquelle für die hervorragende Installation *Memory/Loss* auf der Biennale von Venedig 1993:

»… Tschingis Aitmatow, der eine mongolische Tortur beschreibt, mit der Gefangene zu Sklaven gemacht wurden, Werkzeugen ohne Gedächtnis. Die Technologie war einfach: Dem Gefangenen, der zum Überleben verurteilt und nicht für den Sklavenexport, sondern für den Eigenbedarf der Eroberer bestimmt war, wurde der Kopf kahlgeschoren und ein Helm aus der Halshaut eines frisch geschlachteten Kamels aufgesetzt. An Armen und Beinen gefesselt, den Hals im Block, damit er den Kopf nicht bewegen konnte, und in der Steppe der Sonne ausgesetzt, die den Helm austrocknete und um seinen Kopf zusammenzog, so daß die nachwachsenden Haare in die Kopfhaut zurückwuchsen, verlor er in fünf Tagen, wenn er sie überlebte, unter Qualen das Gedächtnis und war, nach dieser Operation, eine störfreie Arbeitskraft, ein Mankurt. KEINE REVOLUTION OHNE GEDÄCHTNIS.«[43]

In dem Stuttgarter Environment *Erinnerung an eine Revolution* (1987) hatte Wilson den einstigen, verfallenen Glanz des Bonapartismus in einem anschaulichen Bild festgehalten: der Alte in seinem historischen Kostüm als (einziger) überlebender Zeuge, der, eine leere Bühne auf dem Schoß, alleine mit seinen Erinnerungen und der Gewißheit des Todes zurückgeblieben ist. In *Memory/Loss* sechs Jahre später in Venedig ist aus dem alten Zeugen ein Sklave geworden, ein junger Mann, der seiner Erinnerungen beraubt worden ist, ein zukünftiger Mankurt (eben einer, der keine Schwierigkeiten machen wird), bis zu den Schultern in einen ausgedörrten, aufgeborstenen Lehmboden eingegraben, das Gesicht – dessen Züge an jene von Wilson selbst erinnern – leicht nach unten geneigt zu jener Erde, die seinen Körper verschluckt hat. Man fühlt sich an die verstreuten Trümmer in dem Gedicht von Percy Bysshe Shelley aus dem Jahr 1817 erinnert:

Binnenalster Door/Binnenalster-Tür, Hamburg 1993

Memory/Loss, Venice/Venedig 1993

In Stuttgart's *Memory of a Revolution* (1987) Wilson had vividly recreated the decaying remains of Bonapartist glory and splendor, with its (only) surviving witness, the ancient in his costume, an empty stage in his lap, armed only with his memories and the promise of death. Six years later in Venice, in *Memory/Loss*, the ancient witness has become a slave — a young man stripped of his memories — a Mankurt to be (one who will cause no trouble) — buried to his shoulders in a parched, cracked clay floor, his visage, bearing Wilson's own features, bowed slightly towards the earth which has devoured his body. One is reminded of the shattered remains in Percy Bysshe Shelley's poem of 1817:

" … Two vast and trunkless legs of stone
Stand in the desert … Near them, on the sand,
Half sunk, a shattered visage lies …
And on the pedestal these words appear:
'My name is Ozymandias[44], king of kings:
Look on my works, ye Mighty, and despair!'
Nothing beside remains. Round the decay
Of that colossal wreck, boundless and bare
The lone and level sands stretch far away."[45]

… Zwei Riesenbeine, rumpflos, steingehauen
Stehn in der Wüste. Nahebei im Sand
Zertrümmert, halbversunken, liegt mit rauhen
Lippen voll Hohn ein Antlitz macht-gewöhnt …
Und auf dem Sockel eingemeißelt lies:
»Ich bin Ozymandias,[44] Herr der Herrn.
Schaut, was ich schuf, ihr Mächtigen, und verzagt!«
Nichts bleibt. Um den Verfall her riesengroß
Des mächtigen Steinwracks öd und grenzenlos
Dehnt sich die leere Wüste nah und fern.[45]
                                                (dt. v. Alexander von Bernus)

Eineinhalb Jahrhunderte später ist an die Stelle von Shelleys zum Trümmerhaufen verkommenen, halb im Wüstensand versunkenen Koloß Wilsons und Müllers lebender Sklave getreten.

Die literarischen Bezüge in *Memory/Loss* bechränkten sich nicht auf den Gedankenaustausch zwischen Wilson und Heiner Müller über das Wesen von Revolution und Gedächtnis und einen Anklang an Percy Bysshe Shelley. In einem Interview, das kürzlich in der *Süddeutschen Zeitung* veröffentlicht

A century and a half later Shelley's decaying, colossal wreck half buried in the desert sands has been replaced by Wilson's and Müller's living captive slave.

The literary references in *Memory/Loss* were not limited to the exchange between Wilson and Heiner Müller on the nature of revolution and memory nor even to an unintended reference to Percy Bysshe Shelley. In a recent interview in the *Süddeutsche Zeitung*,[46] Wilson noted that the primary source for *Memory/Loss* was T.S. Eliot's[47] apocalyptic work, *The Waste Land,* written in a sanatorium in Lausanne in 1921. Wilson had sought unsuccessfully to

wurde,[46] wies Wilson darauf hin, daß die Hauptanregung für *Memory/Loss* T.S. Eliots 1921 in einem Sanatorium in Lausanne entstandenes, apokalyptisches Werk *The Waste Land* (Das wüste Land) war.[47] Wilson hatte bereits in den siebziger Jahren in Cambridge und später an der Berliner Schaubühne *The Waste Land* in einer für das Theater bearbeiteten Fassung auf die Bühne zu bringen versucht, allerdings ohne Erfolg.

»Nachdem ich dann mehr als ein Jahrzehnt darüber nachgedacht hatte, beschloß ich, eine Installation dazu zu machen ... *Memory/Loss* ... bestand

Memory/Loss, Venice/Venedig 1993

produce a stage version of *The Waste Land* as early as the 1970s in Cambridge, then again at the Schaubühne in Berlin.

"After thinking about it for more than a decade, I decided to make an installation.... [*Memory/Loss*] consisted of a large space in a granary. There was only one window in the room. Entry was through a narrow door which allowed only one person at a time, and you had to take off your shoes. Only twelve to fifteen people could be in the room at once. So you were alone in this wide space, in another world with light of varying colours. There was also a sound installation, with my voice reading excerpts from *The Waste Land*. And that was continually interrupted by noises, screams. During the twenty minutes or so that it lasted, the text was more or less destroyed."[48]

In *Memory/Loss*, as well as in Boston and at the Centre Pompidou, the sound compositions which played such a central role in Wilson's exhibitions and environments had been produced by his long term collaborator Hans Peter Kuhn.[49] The language/memory/sound score for Venice ("sounds and voices which swayed in the room"[50]) was described by Kuhn:

"The text excerpts are taken from Müller's letter. By cutting up the structure of the sentences and by using only single words one loses the memory of the text and is finally unable to reconstruct the original. The sound-space-structure is an acoustic universe in itself, separated from the outer world and such balance depends on the position of the listener. The composition contains sound effects as dripping water, thunder, a telephone ringing, industrial sounds, a dog barking, text fragments [from *The Waste Land*] spoken by Robert Wilson and a violin solo."[51]

The acoustic universe-in-itself created by Wilson and Kuhn for Venice was not to re-occur on such an ambitious scale until a series of subterranean tableaux two years later in London. In the meantime, indeed concurrently with the Biennale environment, Robert Wilson embarked on a remarkable exhibition project in the Museum Boijmans Van Beuningen in Rotterdam — *Robert Wilson: Portrait, Still Life, Landscape* — in which he engaged in a complex dialogue with the work of other visual artists.

In 1989 Wim Crouwel, then director of the Boijmans Van Beuningen, invited the art historian Harald Szeemann to curate the museum's collection. A second invitation in 1991, this time to the British filmmaker Peter Greenaway, resulted in an "inventorial exhibition," as Crouwel noted later, "driven by the urge we already knew from his films."[52] During the Greenaway exhibition, project curator Piet de Jonge invited Robert Wilson, who was installing his exhibition at the Centre Pompidou in Paris, to "curate" the collection of the Museum Boijmans Van Beuningen two years later, in 1993.

As in the exhibition of his own works in Boston (which was still touring when planning for Rotterdam began), the Boijmans exhibition was to consist of three distinct spaces or states.[53] If in Boston these states represented the metaphorical passage of day through night, in Rotterdam the passage was an art historical one, through the traditional categories of portrait, still life, and landscape. Its structure, Wilson noted, was based on that of a cathedral, on "the idea of a human body."[54]

In the first section of the Rotterdam exhibition, titled *Portrait*, the viewer entered a large, brightly lit space (as in Boston) full of objects, a kind of

aus einem großen Raum in einem Getreidespeicher. In dem Raum war nur ein Fenster. Man betrat ihn durch eine enge Tür, durch die nur eine Person gehen konnte, und man mußte seine Schuhe ausziehen. Nur zwölf bis fünfzehn Leute konnten sich gleichzeitig darin aufhalten. Man war also allein in diesem weiten Raum, in einer anderen Welt, mit verschiedenfarbigem Licht. Dazu kam eine akustische Installation mit meiner Stimme, die Auszüge aus *The Waste Land* las. Und das wurde immer wieder gestört durch Geräusche, Schreie. Während der ungefähr zwanzig Minuten, die das dauerte, wurde der Text mehr oder weniger vernichtet.«[48]

Die Klangkompositionen für *Memory/Loss* ebenso wie für die Ausstellungen in Boston und dem Centre Pompidou waren das Werk von Wilsons langjährigem Partner Hans Peter Kuhn.[49] Ihnen kommt in Wilsons Installationen und Environments eine zentrale Bedeutung zu. Kuhn selbst hat die Sprach-/Erinnerungs-/Klangpartitur für Venedig (»im Raum schwingende Klänge und Stimmen«[50]) wie folgt beschrieben:

»Die Textauszüge sind Heiner Müllers Brief entnommen. Durch das Zerlegen der Struktur der Sätze und die Reduktion auf einzelne Wörter verliert man die Erinnerung an den Text und ist schließlich nicht mehr imstande, das Original zu rekonstruieren. Die Klang-Raum-Struktur ist ein für sich stehendes, von der Außenwelt getrenntes akustisches Universum, und eine solche Ausgewogenheit ist abhängig vom Standpunkt des Zuhörers. Zu der Komposition gehören Klangeffekte wie tropfendes Wasser, Donnergeräusche, ein klingelndes Telephon, Industrielärm, ein bellender Hund, von Robert Wilson gesprochene Textfragmente [aus *The Waste Land*] und ein Geigensolo.«[51]

Das in sich geschlossene akustische Universum, das Wilson und Kuhn für Venedig schufen, sollte in dieser aufwendigen und anspruchsvollen Form erst wieder zwei Jahre später in London bei einer Reihe unterirdischer Tableaus realisiert werden. Unterdessen, genauer gesagt sogar noch während sein Environment auf der Biennale zu sehen war, nahm Wilson ein bemerkenswertes Ausstellungsprojekt, *Robert Wilson: Portrait, Still Life, Landscape*, für das Museum Boijmans Van Beuningen in Rotterdam in Angriff, im Rahmen dessen er sich auf einen vielschichtigen Dialog mit dem Werk anderer bildender Künstler einließ.

Im Jahr 1989 hatte der damalige Direktor des Museums Boijmans Van Beuningen, Wim Crouwel, den Kunsthistoriker Harald Szeemann eingeladen, als Gastkurator eine Ausstellung von Werken aus der Sammlung des Museums zu organisieren. 1991 wurde eine ähnliche Einladung an den englischen Filmregisseur Peter Greenaway ausgesprochen, die, wie Crouwel später schrieb, in eine Ausstellung mündete, die »vom gleichen Impuls zur Inventarisierung getragen wurde, wie wir ihn von seinen Filmen her bereits kannten«.[52] Während der von Greenaway zusammengestellten Schau lud der Kurator des Projektes, Piet de Jonge, Robert Wilson, der gerade seine Ausstellung im Centre Pompidou in Paris aufbaute, ein, 1993 als Gastkurator eine Ausstellung von Werken aus der Sammlung des Museums zu betreuen.

Wie die Ausstellung seiner eigenen Arbeiten in Boston (die ihre Tour noch nicht abgeschlossen hatte, als die Planungen für Rotterdam begannen) sollte die Rotterdamer Ausstellung aus drei verschiedenen Räumen oder Stadien bestehen.[53] Hatten in Boston diese Stadien den metaphorischen Gang des Tages durch die Nacht dargestellt, so handelte es sich in Rotterdam um einen kunsthistorischen Gang durch die traditionellen Malereigattungen Porträt,

Memory/Loss, Venice/Venedig 1993

Portrait, Still Life, Landscape, Rotterdam 1993, Portrait

Stilleben und Landschaft. Seine Gliederung stützte sich, so Wilson, auf die Struktur einer Kathedrale, auf das »Bild eines menschlichen Körpers«.[54]

Im ersten Teil der Rotterdamer Ausstellung mit dem Titel ›Porträt‹ betrat der Betrachter (ähnlich wie in Boston) einen großen, hell ausgeleuchteten Raum voller Gegenstände – eine Art Aladins Höhle, wie der Kurator Piet de Jonge anmerkte. Dieser Teil stellte »die Füße, die Wurzeln, das Archiv« dar. Hier sieht man in einer Art Speicher »die Eingeweide des Museums«.[55] Der zweite Akt der Ausstellung, ›Stilleben‹, bestand aus einem schmalen Korridor, den auf jeder Seite fünf Räume säumten. In jedem der Räume wurden Werke von bildenden Künstlern und Gebrauchskünstlern der Gegenwart und der Vergangenheit in einer Folge von zehn Inszenierungen oder ›Begegnungen‹ zusammengeführt. »Ich sehe in ihnen«, so Wilson, »verschiedene Stadien, verschiedene Wirklichkeiten. Es sind jeweils verschiedene Arten, durch das Leben zu gehen. Verschiedene Konfrontationen, Kontrapunkte. Wie Rippen.« In diesem, wenn man so will, ›Torso‹ der gesamten Installation rückte Wilson bekannte Kunstwerke in neue, überraschende Zusammenhänge. So war etwa Maillols *La Méditerranée* neben einer Pistole aus Glas, ein Film von Marcel Broodthaers sowie ein Objekt von Robert Gober neben einem Stuhl von Alvar Aalto und einem Fernsehgerät Baujahr 1963, eine frühe Dalí-Landschaft neben einem Lautsprecher aus dem Jahr 1927 und Donald Judds *Galvanized Iron* von 1973 hinter dem Schleier eines Chantillyschals aus dem 19. Jahrhundert zu sehen. Im dritten und letzten Teil, gewissermaßen im ›Kopf‹ oder im ›geistigen‹ Teil der Installation stellte Wilson Degas' *Petite danseuse de quatorze ans*, eines der bekanntesten bildhauerischen Werke des 19. Jahrhunderts, in einen langgezogenen, schmalen und leeren Raum, der an einen vulkanischen Strand oder eine Atomwüste erinnerte. Den Rücken den Besuchern und das Gesicht dem Himmel zugewandt, der sich durch-

Aladdin's cave, as curator Piet de Jonge noted. This section represented "the feet, the roots, the archives." Here, in a kind of warehouse,[55] Wilson continued, "you see the bowels of the museum." Act II of the exhibition, *Still Life*, consisted of a narrow passageway with five rooms on each side. In each of the rooms works by contemporary and historical fine and applied artists were brought together in a series of ten stagings or "encounters." Wilson described the rooms: "I think they are different stages, different realities. They are different ways of going through life. Different confrontations, counterpoints. It is like ribs." In this, the "torso" of the installation, Wilson brought well known works of art into new and startling combinations: Maillol's *La Méditerranée* together with a glass pistol, a film by Broodthaers and an object by Robert Gober next to an Aalto chair and a 1963 television set, an early Dalí landscape and a loudspeaker from 1927 and Donald Judd's *Galvanized Iron* from 1973 seen through a nineteenth-century chantilly shawl. In the third and concluding section, in the "head" or "spiritual" part of the installation, Wilson placed one of the nineteenth century's best known sculptural works, Degas' dancer *Petite danseuse de quatorze ans* in an exceptionally long, narrow, and empty space reminescent of a

Portrait, Still Life, Landscape, Rotterdam 1993, Still Life/Stilleben

volcanic beach or a post-nuclear landscape. With her back to the audience, facing the sky which stretched unbroken from the earth to the highest heaven, accompanied by seven bronze lizards (a work by Hans van Houwelingen) and an early sixteenth-century bronze crab, the ballerina waited expectantly, bathed like the reptiles in a pool of light. On stools pressed along the length of the room behind the dancer, the audience also waited expectantly until an extraordinary light-scape by Heinrich Brunke washed the room in varying intensities of cobalt blue, purple, orange, green, yellow, and white, a breathtaking passage of night into day and again into night. As in earlier projects, a sound-scape by Hans Peter Kuhn permeated the room, generating an "experience of something intangible and mysterious."

It is Wilson's capacity to transform the known into the unknown, to take us on a journey into the night which transcends fear, which made the installation in Rotterdam so exceptional. Degas' dancer whom we thought we knew

gehend sichtbar vom Boden in weite Höhen erstreckte, begleitet von sieben Bronzeeidechsen (ein Werk von Hans van Houwelingen) sowie einer bronzenen Krabbe aus dem frühen 16. Jahrhundert verharrte die Ballerina erwartungsvoll. Auf Hockern, die auf der Längsseite des Raums hinter der Tänzerin an die Wand gedrängt waren, harrten auch die Besucher gespannt aus, bis ein außergewöhnliches, von Heinrich Brunke gestaltetes Lichtenvironment den Raum in Kobaltblau-, Purpur-, Orange-, Grün-, Gelb- und Weißtöne verschiedener Intensität tauchte, ein atemberaubendes Schauspiel des Übergangs von Nacht zu Tag und wieder zu Nacht. Wie bei früheren Projekten füllte ein Klangenvironment von Hans Peter Kuhn den Raum und rief »den Eindruck von etwas Ungreifbarem und Geheimnisvollem« hervor.

Es ist Wilsons Fähigkeit, Vertrautes in Fremdes zu verwandeln, uns mitzunehmen auf eine Reise in die Nacht, jenseits der Angst, die die Installation in Rotterdam so außergewöhnlich machte. Degas' Tänzerin, die uns so vertraut

so well is transformed in Wilson's hands into a stranger, a lover, a child, a shaman in the desert accompanied by her beasts. "How can we see this bronze Degas woman?" Wilson asked. "I don't particularly like the figure myself, but how can I see her in a different way.... Suddenly we could see the eyes or the hands, the shape of the dress, the attitude of the head."[56]

In his next environment, *H.G. (Clink Street Installation)*, in a former prison in London in September 1995, Robert Wilson moved in yet another direction with his work. On this occasion the architecture of the exhibition space was to play a central role, as both a motivating and a conceptual force. This is not to suggest that architectural considerations had not been significant in previous installations: on the contrary (one need only recall the importance of the architecture of the former granaries in *Memory/Loss* in Venice in 1993 or in the planning of the Boston exhibition[57]). But it is true that most of the previous installations had located their organizing principles elsewhere — in literary, theatrical, art historical, or even mathematical permutations and combinations. The starting point for *H.G.* (and for the present Villa Stuck project) was the architecture of the space itself.

Portrait, Still Life, Landscape, Rotterdam 1993, Still Life/Stilleben

Portrait, Still Life, Landscape, Rotterdam 1993, Still Life/Stilleben

schien, verwandelt sich unter Wilsons Einwirkung in eine Fremde, eine Liebhaberin, ein Kind, eine Schamanin in der Wüste, begleitet von ihren Tieren. »Wie können wir diese bronzene Degassche Frau sehen?« fragte Wilson. »Mir persönlich gefällt die Figur gar nicht so besonders, aber wie kann ich sie auf eine andere Art und Weise sehen … Plötzlich konnten wir die Augen sehen oder die Hände, die Form des Kleides, die Haltung des Kopfes.«[56]

Mit seinem nächsten Environment, *H.G. (Clink Street Installation)*, das er im September 1995 in einem ehemaligen Gefängnis in London realisierte, ging Robert Wilson wiederum neue Wege. Bei diesem Projekt spielte die Architektur des Ausstellungsraums eine wesentliche Rolle, sowohl als Anregungs- wie auch als konzeptuelles Moment. Das soll nicht etwa heißen, daß architektonische Erwägungen nicht schon bei früheren Installationen eine wichtige Rolle gespielt hatten, im Gegenteil: Man denke nur an die Bedeutung der Architektur der ehemaligen Getreidespeicher in *Memory/Loss* in Venedig oder bei der Planung der Ausstellung in Boston.[57] Es ist aber tatsächlich so, daß bei den meisten früheren Installationen das Leitprinzip anders begründet war, und zwar durch literarische, theatergeschichtliche, kunstgeschichtliche oder gar mathematische Permutationen und Kombinationen. Der Ausgangspunkt für *H.G.* (und für das jetzige Projekt im Museum Villa Stuck) dagegen war die Architektur des Ausstellungsortes selbst.

Die riesigen unterirdischen, labyrinthähnlichen Verliese des ehemaligen, aus elisabethanischer Zeit stammenden Gefängnisses Clink Street Vault in London, das während des Gordon-Aufruhrs von 1780 bis auf die Grundmauern abgebrannt war,[58] dienten nicht nur als Schauplatz, sondern auch als Anregung für *H.G.* »Ich lasse die Räume zu mir sprechen«, erklärte Wilson.[59] In diesen »erstaunlichen, an das Innere einer Kathedrale erinnernden Räumen«[60] schuf er eine Folge von Tableaus, in denen die Besucher in die Vergangenheit reisten, begleitet von ihrem unsichtbaren Gastgeber H.G. Wells, dem Autor des genau hundert Jahre vorher erschienenen Romans *The Time Machine* (Die Zeitmaschine). Überall gab es Spuren von H.G.s Anwesenheit: eine zusammengefaltete Zeitung mit dem Datum 12. September 1895, eine Uhr, ein Likörglas, in das sein Monogramm eingraviert war,[61] und die Überreste eines Mahls »in einem kleinen Eßzimmer, in dem alles zu finden war, was

The vast subterranean, labyrinthine caverns of the former Clink Street Vault, an Elizabethan prison in London which was burned to the ground in the Gordon riots of 1780,[58] were not only the location but also the source of inspiration for *H.G.* "I let the rooms talk to me," Wilson explained.[59] In these "surprising, cathedral-like spaces"[60] Wilson created a series of tableaux in which the public traveled into the past with their invisible host, H.G. Wells, who had authored *The Time Machine* exactly one hundred years earlier.

der kultivierte Luxus des viktorianischen Zeitalters zu bieten hatte. Die Kerzen brennen noch und die Hammelkoteletts und Erbsen auf den Tellern werden allmählich hart.«[62] In einem Tableau »badete in einem Lichtstrahl geschmolzener Lava gleich eine verwesende Mumie, über das traurige, verstaubte Gesicht Blumen gestreut. In einem anderen Bereich gibt es reihenweise grell beleuchtete, metallene Krankenhausbetten. Im Hintergrund erklingt leise eine auf Klavier gespielte Tonleiter. Durch das Eisengitter einer Gefängnistür blickt

Portrait, Still Life, Landscape, Rotterdam 1993, Landscape/Landschaft

Traces of H.G.'s presence were felt throughout the rooms; a folded newspaper dated September 12, 1895, a watch, a liqueur glass engraved with his monogram,[61] and the remnants of a meal "in a small dining room stuffed with the paraphernalia of Victorian gracious living. The candles still burn and mutton chops and peas congeal on the plates."[62] In one tableaux a "decomposing mummy bathed in a shaft of natural light like molten lava, flowers strewn over his sad, dusty face. In another area there is row upon row of harshly lit, metal hospital beds. A piano scale plays softly in the background. Look through iron bars in a prison door and you glimpse a rainforest alive with sound and movement."[63]

In a review for *The Independent* Tom Lubbock observed that the installation "has no scruples at all about being spectacular or voyeuristic. H.G. revels in the many modes of looking, through peep-holes, on to sudden vistas, into hidden cavities, in fleeting glimpses, across unapproachable distances." The "most beautiful and strange creation," he adds, suddenly appears "through a high arch, a seemingly infinite expanse of ultramarine, and floating in the sky a hundred arrows suspended in flight." Especially the first tableaux are "a mouth-opening series of visual and imaginative coups."[64]

Conclusion

Robert Wilson has been active as a visual artist for over thirty years. During this period his "freedom machines," especially his tableaux, have become more and more spectacular. The response to this aspect of his work has not, however, always been unequivocal. Tom Lubbock, for example, in his review of *H.G.*, notes the admirable "promiscuous, prodigal will to beguile and amaze" but he asks whether visitors should lose themselves in the immediacy of its experiences. Does sheer spectacle as such exhaust itself?[65] Lubbock's question on the nature of spectacle, its seductive pleasures and its dangers, is one which has preoccupied other artists and theoreticians in this century.[66] The question is, *has* Robert Wilson engaged in sheer spectacle, is his intent only to beguile and amaze? The answer is, unequivocally no.

"Images of death are a constant thread in all my stagings."[67] Robert Wilson's comment to Rüdiger Schaper in a recent interview identifies a crucial aspect of his work, one which repeatedly expresses itself in images of extinction and apotheosis, as noted earlier in this text. His tableaux, like his drawings as epilogue, are monumental, transcendental, sometimes claustrophobic. They encapsulate emotional *and* intellectual states. Although they are unashamedly spectacular they consistently negate "sheer spectacle" through their cautionary tales of revolution and memory, torture and death, power and its abuse.

The intentional destruction of text (language) in Wilson's installations such as *Memory/Loss* is often interpreted in autobiographical terms (the fact that Wilson had a severe speaking disorder as a child and the fact that he worked with the handicapped). A reliance on the autobiographical and the anecdotal, however, misleads us in our search for a better understanding of Wilson's work. In the second half of the twentieth century Robert Wilson has provided us with increasingly fragmented metaphorical excursions into a night (or day) without language or memory. The stage on our lap, like that held by the ancient in *Memory of a Revolution*, is empty. We are Mankurts,

man in einen von Geräuschen und Bewegung erfüllten Regenwald.«[63]

In einer Besprechung für *The Independent* stellte Tom Lubbock fest, daß die Installation »keinerlei Skrupel hat, spektakulär oder voyeuristisch zu sein. H.G. feiert die verschiedenen Formen des Sehens: der Blick durchs Guckloch, auf ein unerwartetes Panorama, in versteckte Winkel, flüchtige Blicke, der Blick in unerreichbare Fernen«. »Eine unvergleichlich schöne und seltsame Schöpfung« wird plötzlich sichtbar »hinter einem hohen überwölbten Gang, eine schier endlose ultramarinblaue Weite, und am Himmelsgewölbe hängen, angehalten in ihrem Flug, hundert Pfeile.« Insbesondere die ersten Tableaus sind »eine Folge einfallsreicher und optischer Bravourstücke, die einem die Sprache verschlagen«.[64]

Resümee

Robert Wilson ist seit mehr als dreißig Jahren als bildender Künstler tätig. Im Laufe dieser Zeit wurden seine ›Freedom Machines‹, insbesondere seine Tableaus, immer spektakulärer. Die Reaktionen auf diesen Aspekt seines Werkes waren jedoch nicht immer ungeteilt positiv. So registriert Tom Lubbock in seiner Besprechung von *H.G.* zwar den bewundernswerten »totalen, unerschöpflichen Willen zu betören und in Staunen zu versetzen«, wirft aber gleichzeitig die Frage auf, ob sich der Besucher in der Unmittelbarkeit seiner Erlebnisse verlieren sollte? Erschöpft sich reines Spektakel von selbst?[65] Lubbocks kritische Fragen nach dem Wesen des Spektakels, seinen verführerischen Freuden und seinen Gefahren sind solche, die auch andere Künstler und Theoretiker in unserem Jahrhundert beschäftigt haben.[66] Es ist jedoch die Frage, ob Robert Wilson tatsächlich reines Spektakel macht, ob es ihm ausschließlich darum geht, zu betören und in Staunen zu versetzen. Die Anwort darauf ist ein eindeutiges Nein.

»Todesbilder ziehen sich wie ein roter Faden durch all meine Inszenierungen.«[67] Diese Aussage, die Robert Wilson vor nicht allzu langer Zeit in einem Interview mit Rüdiger Schaper machte, bringt einen wesentlichen Aspekt seines Werks auf den Begriff, einen, der, wie bereits erwähnt, wiederholt in Bildern der Auslöschung und Verklärung Ausdruck findet. Seine Tableaus sind ebenso wie seine ein Projekt abschließenden Zeichnungen monumental, transzendental und gelegentlich klaustrophobisch. Sie fangen Gemüts- ebenso wie Geistesverfassungen ein. Obgleich schamlos spektakulär, reduzieren sie sich mit ihren Geschichten über Revolution und Gedächtnis, Folter und Tod, Macht und Machtmißbrauch nie auf »reines Spektakel«.

Die gezielte Zerstörung von Text/Sprache in Wilsons Installationen wie etwa *Memory/Loss* wird häufig unter Hinweis auf biographische Hintergründe erklärt (Wilson hatte als Kind eine schwere Sprachstörung, und er hat mit Behinderten gearbeitet). Im Bemühen um ein besseres Verständnis von seinem Werk führt es jedoch in die Irre, sich auf Biographisches und Anekdotisches zu berufen. In der zweiten Hälfte des zwanzigsten Jahrhunderts hat Robert Wilson uns zunehmend fragmentarische, metaphorische Exkursionen in eine Nacht (beziehungsweise Tag) ohne Sprache oder Erinnerung geboten. Die Bühne auf unserem Schoß, wie die des Alten in *Erinnerung an eine Revolution*, ist leer. Wir sind Mankurts, wir machen keine Schwierigkeiten. Die Environments oder Tableaus, die Robert Wilson für uns kreiert, sind ein mnemotechnisches Training für unseren Körper in seiner kulturellen, sozialen,

we cause no trouble. The environments/tableaux which Robert Wilson creates for us are mnemonics for our bodies — our cultural, social, political and spiritual bodies. He lays this body bare for us — with its short circuits and repetitions, its attenuations and excesses, its decomposition and its smell of fear. It is a body devoured by rats, a mind devoured by itself. Our body, like the acoustic universe in *Memory/Loss*, is increasingly separated from the outside world and unable to reconstruct itself. Robert Wilson seeks to provide us — through his tableaux, his "rooms for experience, which is a way of thinking"[68] — with the means to remember, to recognize and reconstruct ourselves.

politischen und geistigen Dimension. Er führt uns diesen Körper vor Augen – einschließlich aller Kurzschlüsse und Wiederholungen, seiner Ausmergelung und seiner Exzesse, seiner Verwesung und seines Geruchs der Angst. Es ist ein Körper, zerfressen von Ratten, ein Geist, der sich selbst verzehrt hat. Unser Körper ist, wie das akustische Universum in *Memory/Loss*, zunehmend von der Außenwelt getrennt und außerstande, sich selbst zu rekonstruieren. Robert Wilson möchte uns durch seine Tableaus – seine »Räume für die Erfahrung, die eine Form des Denkens ist«[68] – ein Mittel an die Hand geben, uns auf uns selbst zu besinnen, uns selbst zu erkennen und zu rekonstruieren.

H.G., Clink Street Vaults, London 1995

"The Villa Stuck," I wrote to Robert Wilson in August, 1993, "remains, along with Neuschwanstein, one of the great personal stagings in this very baroque set of Bavaria." I was trying to tempt him, to seduce him, into creating an environment for the Villa Stuck, a sumptuous artist's villa, a work of art in itself, designed and decorated by the nineteenth-century Munich painter Franz von Stuck. Mentioning Neuschwanstein and the Villa Stuck in one breath immediately conjured up images of heightened artificiality, utopian longings, and a theatrical aestheticism. An irresistable combination, I hoped.

The castle of Neuschwanstein is situated in a spectacular setting on the edge of the alps south of Munich. King Ludwig II, who had ascended to the throne only four years earlier, decided in 1868 to build a castle on the site, one "more splendid and habitable than the lower castle of Hohenschwangau, which every year is desecrated by the prose of my mother."[1]

Neuschwanstein, which was intended as a temple in honor of Richard Wagner, was more than a refuge and protest against a rapidly industrializing world; it was a place where "dream and reality were blended and history lived again — not merely on a stage."[2] Following the mysterious death of Ludwig II in Lake Starnberg in 1886, construction on the unfinished castle ceased. Three years later the "artist prince" Franz von Stuck took Munich by storm with his painting *Wächter des Paradieses* (Guardian of Paradise). *Die Sünde* (The Sin), exhibited in 1893 in one of the first exhibitions of the Munich Secession, which Stuck co-founded, sealed his reputation as an artist. This painting of a serpent wrapped around the naked body of a decidedly voluptuous Eve generated enormous controversy with its blatant sexuality.[3] The birth of a daughter out of wedlock in 1896 seemed to confirm a bohemian lifestyle. The following year, however, Franz Stuck married the beautiful widow Mary Lindpaintner and embarked on a spectacular climb into the upper echelons of Munich society, eventually being awarded the Order of the Knights of the Cross[4] and the right to name himself Franz von Stuck.

In 1897, eleven years after the death of King Ludwig II and at the height of the rule of Prince Regent Luitpold, Franz Stuck decided to design and build his own refuge from modernity. His luxuriously decorated Villa, situated on a hill overlooking Munich and the Isar River, was one of the first buildings in what was then known as Outer Prinzregent Street, a grand boulevard which Luitpold had constructed to mark his reign. Like Neuschwanstein, Stuck's villa was also a place where dream and reality were blended and history lived again. It was also a stage, a private stage, where Franz Stuck could live out his fantasies of noble life, perhaps at the time of Pompeii, possibly in ancient Greece, surrounded by mythological creatures, rare and luxurious objects, in seclusion from the "prose" of everyday life. While Ludwig II had withdrawn completely from Munich and retreated into the spectacular and isolated landscapes of Neuschwanstein, Linderhof, and Chiemsee, Franz Stuck's withdrawal from society was more symbolic. He remained in Munich as one of its most revered (if sometimes controversial) inhabitants, a highly successful artist and a teacher of renown who attracted artists such as Wassily Kandinsky, Paul Klee, and Josef Albers to his classes. Former students and contemporaries were unified in their description of Stuck as a man of extraordinary personal aura who spoke little and held himself aloof. This distance marked his Villa.

Robert Wilson/Villa Stuck

»Die Villa Stuck«, so schrieb ich Robert Wilson 1993, »ist neben Neuschwanstein eine der großen persönlichen Inszenierungen in dieser barocken Kulisse Bayern.« Ich wollte ihn dazu anregen, ja verführen, ein Environment eigens für die Villa Stuck zu schaffen. Die im 19. Jahrhundert von dem Münchner Künstlerfürsten Franz von Stuck als Gesamtkunstwerk angelegte Villa mußte ihn geradezu reizen. Die Erwähnung von Neuschwanstein und der Villa Stuck in einem Atemzug sollte reflexartig Vorstellungen von gesteigerter Artifizialität, utopischen Sehnsüchten und einem theatralischen Ästhetizismus heraufbeschwören. Eine unwiderstehliche Mischung, hoffte ich.

Schloß Neuschwanstein ist in einer spektakulären landschaftlichen Kulisse am Rande der bayerischen Alpen gelegen. König Ludwig II., der erst vier Jahre zuvor den Thron bestiegen hatte, entschloß sich 1868, ein Schloß an jener Stelle errichten zu lassen: »… in jeder Beziehung schöner und wohnlicher wird diese Burg werden als das untere Hohenschwangau, das jährlich durch die Prosa meiner Mutter entweiht wird«.[1] Neuschwanstein, gedacht als ein Ehrentempel für Richard Wagner, war mehr als ein Refugium und ein Gegenentwurf zur rapiden Industrialisierung, es war ein Ort, wo sich »Traum und Wirklichkeit eins waren und die Geschichte nicht nur auf der Bühne seines Hoftheaters zur Gegenwart wurde«.[2] Nach dem mysteriösen Tod Ludwigs II. im Starnberger See 1886 wurden die Bauarbeiten an dem noch unfertigen Schloß eingestellt. Drei Jahre später eroberte Franz Stuck mit seinem Gemälde *Wächter des Paradieses* München im Sturm. *Die Sünde*, ein Werk, das 1893 in einer der ersten Ausstellungen der von Stuck mitbegründeten Münchner Secession zu sehen war, besiegelte sein künstlerisches Renommee. Diese Darstellung einer Schlange, die den nackten Körper einer entschieden sinnlichen Eva umschlingt, verursachte durch ihre sexuelle Direktheit enorme Aufregung.[3] Die Geburt einer unehelichen Tochter 1896 erschien als weiterer Beweis für einen bohemienhaften Lebensstil. Im Jahr darauf jedoch heiratete Franz Stuck die wunderschöne Witwe Mary Lindpaintner und begann einen spektakulären Aufstieg in die höheren Ränge der Münchner Gesellschaft, die ihm schließlich den Kreuzritterorden[4] und die Nobilitierung einbrachte.

Im Jahr 1897, elf Jahre nach dem Tod König Ludwigs II. und in der Glanzzeit der Regentschaft des Prinzregenten Luitpold, faßte Franz Stuck seinerseits den Entschluß, eine eigene Stätte der Zuflucht vor der modernen Welt zu entwerfen und zu bauen. Seine aufwendig ausgestaltete Villa auf einem Hügel mit Blick über München und die Isar war eines der ersten Gebäude an der, wie sie damals hieß, Äußeren Prinzregentenstraße, einer Prachtstraße, die Luitpold als Denkmal seiner Regierungszeit hatte anlegen lassen. Auch Stucks Villa war ein Ort, wo Traum und Wirklichkeit eins waren und die Geschichte zur Gegenwart wurde. Zugleich war sie eine Bühne, eine private Bühne, auf der Franz Stuck seine Phantasien von einem aristokratischen Leben ausleben konnte, einem aristokratischen Leben etwa in Pompeji oder im Griechenland der Antike, umgeben von mythologischen Geschöpfen, erlesenem Luxus, abgeschieden von der Prosa des täglichen Lebens. Hatte sich Ludwig II. völlig aus München zurückgezogen in die spektakulären, abgelegenen Landschaften von Neuschwanstein, Linderhof und Herrenchiemsee, so war Stucks Rückzug aus der Gesellschaft eher symbolischer Art. Er blieb in München als einer seiner angesehensten (wiewohl gelegentlich umstrittenen) Bürger, ein überaus erfolgreicher Künstler und ein namhafter Lehrer, der wiederum Künstler wie Wassily Kandinsky, Paul Klee und Josef Albers als Schüler anzog. Ehemalige Schüler und Zeitgenossen beschrieben Stuck einmütig als einen ungemein

Unlike other artists' villas in Munich from the period, no splendid garden welcomed guests. The entrance, on a slight rise above street level, consisted of six large steps which climbed steeply to a heavy bronze door with a Medusa head whose open mouth swallowed the daily post and protected its inhabitants against evil and the outside world. The garden, with its columns, mythological figures, and colonnade, remained hidden from view in the private domain. Inside the Villa walls any austerity which may have characterized the exterior facade was quickly shed. Here visitors found a brooding, almost intimidating luxury, walls covered with medieval tapestries, magnificent parquet floors, heavy curtains, Venetian glass windows, and copies of famous sculptures from ancient Greece or Rome. It was these rooms, as well as the former private suites of both Franz and Mary von Stuck, which I offered to Robert Wilson as the site for an environment "Villa Stuck."

At the time I wrote to Wilson, in 1993, he was busy working on his production of *Der Mond im Gras*[5] for the renowned Munich theater, the Kammerspiele.[6] We arranged a meeting at the Villa Stuck to coincide with one of his visits to Munich, and over the next few years discussed the parameters of the project. As other commentators have noted, arranging meetings and developing a project with Robert Wilson can be a complex, lengthy affair. One of our most productive meetings took place at midnight on a warm summer evening in June, 1996, following the preview of *La Maladie de la Mort*.[7] We walked through the still streets of Recklinghausen discussing the complex relationship between Franz von Stuck, his wife Mary, and his daughter Mary, whom the pair adopted in 1904, as well as Stuck's use of photography in the production of his paintings. I believe that it was on this night that the project *Villa Stuck* finally began to take shape.[8] It was now ripe to be taken to Watermill Center on Long Island, New York, a "think tank" where Wilson spends every summer honing his projects into workable shape. Detailed visual documentation on Franz von Stuck, his paintings, drawings, graphic works, sculpture, furniture, and photography as well as a model of the Villa Stuck were given to Robert Wilson's assistant Stefan Hageneier. These he brought to Watermill where, in the summer of 1996, three years after we began discussing the project, precise "Ideas" for the environment *Robert Wilson/Villa Stuck* were developed in dialogue with architects, writers, stage designers, sculptors, actors, assistant directors, and composers who had been invited to Watermill to work with Wilson on his upcoming projects.[9]

The comparatively long period necessary to develop a project with Robert Wilson is only partly due to his extraordinarily hectic work and travel schedule; it is also a consequence of a long process of germination which each project requires.[10] It is therefore not uncommon that planning may span several years or that more than one project may be related to a particular theme, work of art, or piece of literature which has preoccupied Wilson during that period. This was the case with the prize-winning installation *Memory/Loss* for the Venice Biennale in 1993; the play *T.S.E.* in Gibellina, Sicily, in 1994; and the stage work *Persephone* in Delphi, Greece, in 1995 and in Munich in 1997. Each of these projects was linked by Wilson's continued obsession with the person of T.S. Eliot and with Eliot's poetic masterpiece *The Waste Land* (1922). Especially in the case of *Memory/Loss*, 1993 (see page 23), the figure to whom the work is dedicated, T.S. Eliot, is not only invisible but also undetectable. Excerpts from *The Waste Land* read by Wilson in the sound environment *for Memory/Loss* are so disjointed that the text is no longer recognizable. In other words, the personality to whom this environment is dedicated is present only as a fragmented memory which

charismatischen Mann, der wenig sprach und stets Distanz wahrte. Diese Distanz kennzeichnete auch seine Villa.

Anders als bei anderen Künstlervillen in München aus der gleichen Zeit begrüßte kein prächtiger Garten den Besucher. Zu dem von der Straße aus gesehen ein wenig erhöhten Eingang führten sechs steile Treppenstufen. Ein Medusenhaupt mit geöffnetem Mund an der schweren Bronzetür schluckte die tägliche Post und schützte die Bewohner des Hauses vor Unglück und der Außenwelt. Der Garten mit seinen Säulen, mythologischen Figuren und einer Kolonnade war Privatsphäre und blieb fremden Blicken entzogen. Im Innern der Villa fand sich jedwede Strenge oder Nüchternheit, die die äußere Fassade gekennzeichnet hatte, sogleich abgestreift. Den Besucher erwartete im Innern ein üppiger, ja geradezu einschüchternder Luxus: Wände tapeziert mit mittelalterlichen Tapisserien, herrliche Parkettfußböden, schwere Vorhänge, Fenster mit venezianischen Glasscheiben und Kopien berühmter Skulpturen aus der Antike. Ebendiese Räume sowie die ehemaligen Privatgemächer von Franz und Mary von Stuck bot ich Robert Wilson als Schauplatz für ein ›Villa Stuck‹-Environment an.

Als ich Wilson 1993 schrieb, war er gerade mit seiner Inszenierung von *Der Mond im Gras*[5] für die Münchner Kammerspiele[6] beschäftigt. Wir vereinbarten ein Treffen in der Villa Stuck während eines seiner nächsten Aufenthalte in München und erörterten in der Folgezeit die Parameter des Projektes. Die Vereinbarung von Treffen mit Robert Wilson und die Entwicklung eines Projektes mit ihm kann, wie andere bereits verschiedentlich festgestellt haben, eine komplizierte und langwierige Angelegenheit sein. Eine unserer fruchtbarsten Begegnungen fand zu mitternächtlicher Stunde an einem warmen Sommerabend im Juni 1996 im Anschluß an die Probeaufführung von *La Maladie de la Mort* statt.[7] Wir gingen durch die stillen Straßen von Recklinghausen und sprachen über das schwierige Verhältnis zwischen Franz von Stuck, seiner Frau Mary und seiner Tochter Mary, die das Ehepaar 1904 adoptierte, sowie über die Rolle, die die Photographie bei der Entstehung von Stucks Gemälden spielte. Es war, glaube ich, an diesem Abend, daß das Projekt *Villa Stuck* schließlich konkrete Gestalt anzunehmen begann.[8] Es war jetzt reif für das Watermill Center auf Long Island, eine ›Denkfabrik‹, wo Wilson jeden Sommer verbringt, um seine Projekte zu realisierbarer Form auszufeilen. Robert Wilsons Assistenten Stefan Hageneier wurde ausführliches Bildmaterial zu Franz von Stuck, seinen Gemälden, Zeichnungen, druckgraphischen Arbeiten, Skulpturen, Möbeln und Photographien sowie ein Modell der Villa übergeben. Alles wurden nach Watermill verfrachtet. Im Sommer 1996, also drei Jahre nachdem wir erstmals über das Projekt gesprochen hatten, wurden in einem regen Gedankenaustausch mit Architekten, Schriftstellern, Bühnenbildnern, Bildhauern, Schauspielern, Regieassistenten und Komponisten, die nach Watermill eingeladen worden waren, um mit Wilson an seinen bevorstehenden Projekten zusammenzuarbeiten, präzise ›Ideen‹ für das Environment *Robert Wilson/Villa Stuck* entwickelt.[9]

Die Tatsache, daß die Entwicklung eines Projektes mit Robert Wilson einer vergleichsweise langen Zeit bedarf, ist nur zum Teil dem ungemein dichten Terminplan des weltweit operierenden Künstlers zuzuschreiben. Sie ist eben auch ein Ausfluß des langen Gärprozesses, den jedes Projekt erfordert.[10] Es kommt daher nicht selten vor, daß sich die Planungen für eine Projekt über mehrere Jahre erstrecken oder daß mehrere Projekte mit ein und demselben Thema, Kunstwerk oder Werk der Literatur zu tun haben, das während jener Zeit im Mittelpunkt von Wilsons Interesse gestanden hat. So verhielt es sich

is barely able to be reconstructed. In the Stuttgart environment *Memory of a Revolution*, 1987, described on page 14 of this volume, Napoleon is also "off stage," as is the mysterious H.G. Wells, author of the *Time Machine* in London's *H.G. (Clink Street Installation)*, 1995 (see page 28). In the environment *Villa Stuck* Robert Wilson allows the personality to whom the work is dedicated for the first time to appear "on stage." He is present, however, as a ghost.

The Watermill "Ideas"

At Watermill a total of twenty-one "Ideas" for tableaux in the Villa Stuck were developed. In the final environment thirteen were realized. It is interesting to note that the original Ideas were not designed for specific rooms. In other words, although Wilson reacted to the architectural spaces offered to him, and certainly reacted to the feelings the spaces generated, the concept or Idea came first, and then the appropriate space for it was located.

The Villa Stuck complex consists of three buildings: the "historical" Villa built as Stuck's residence and atelier in 1897, the atelier (originally a generous, well lit, two-storey addition) constructed in 1914/15, and the former servants' quarters. The original plans developed by Wilson at Watermill called for tableaux throughout the Villa and in three floors[11] of the atelier. For a number of reasons, however, it became increasingly clear that the environment should be restricted to the so-called historical Villa and timed to coincide exactly with the 100th anniversary of its construction.

It is interesting to observe the original sequence of Ideas — where the first and most intuitive reaction of Robert Wilson to the art, photography, architecture, and furniture of Franz von Stuck is to be located — and also how, if at all, these Ideas have changed once the spaces were allocated. The first five Ideas, indeed more than half of the Ideas developed in Watermill,[12] are based on photographs by Mary and Franz von Stuck. Wilson used these photographs in several ways:
– as information to enable him to construct ghost-like simulacrums of Franz von Stuck and his family (including his dog);
– as the basis for excursions into theoretical discussions on photography and its relationship to painting.

These quite different uses of Stuck's photography resulted in two kinds of tableaux: ones which are an exact, three-dimensional transposition of the original photograph, and others which involve a "translation" of the original photograph into a new and unexpected form.

Wilson created nine ghost-like simulacrums (Franz and Mary von Stuck as a Roman couple, Stuck with his dog, Mary as Torero with Pips, a family dog), and three slightly different versions of Franz von Stuck in an artist's smock). Two photographs were "translated" into a new form: a landscape photograph became a theatrical-style set (see *Smoking Salon* on page 54 ff.) and in *Franz von Stuck's Bedroom* on page 68 ff., Stuck's photograph of the turn-of-the-century actor Ernst von Possart as Napoleon was transposed into two paintings. In other words, both Stuck and Wilson produced a painting based on the same photograph. Wilson's painting, however, was designed to look like a photograph.[13]

One of the most interesting Ideas for the Villa Stuck, not realized in the final version,[14] was planned for the splendidly decorated, historic atelier. A white

zum Beispiel mit der preisgekrönten Installation *Memory/Loss* für die Biennale von Venedig 1993, dem Stück *T.S.E.* 1994 in Gibellina auf Sizilien und dem Bühnenwerk *Persephone* 1995 im griechischen Delphi und 1997 in München. Das verbindende Element dieser Projekte war Wilsons anhaltende Beschäftigung mit der Person T.S. Eliots und dessen dichterischem Hauptwerk *The Waste Land* (Das wüste Land, 1922). Insbesondere im Falle von *Memory/Loss* (siehe Seite 23) ist die Person, der das Werk gewidmet ist, eben T.S. Eliot, nicht nur unsichtbar, sondern geradezu unauffindbar. Von Wilson selbst gesprochene Auszüge aus *The Waste Land*, die einen Teil des Klangenvironments von *Memory/Loss* bilden, werden bis zur Unkenntlichkeit zerstückelt. Die Person, der dieses Environment gewidmet ist, ist also nur als fragmentierte, kaum mehr zu rekonstruierende Erinnerung gegenwärtig. In dem Stuttgarter Environment *Erinnerung an eine Revolution* von 1987 (siehe Seite 14) ist Napoleon ebenfalls ›hinter die Bühne‹ verbannt, desgleichen der mysteriöse H.G. Wells, Autor des Romans *The Time Machine*, in *H.G. (Clink Street Installation)* 1995 in London (siehe Seite 28). In dem Environment *Villa Stuck* läßt Robert Wilson die Person, dem das Werk gewidmet ist, erstmals auf der ›Bühne‹ auftreten. Sie ist anwesend, allerdings als Geistererscheinung.

Die Watermill-›Ideen‹

In Watermill wurden insgesamt 21 ›Ideen‹ zu Tableaus für die Villa Stuck entwickelt. Dreizehn davon sind im endgültigen Environment realisiert worden. Dabei sei angemerkt, daß die ursprünglichen ›Ideen‹ nicht für bestimmte Räume entwickelt wurden. Wilson ließ sich zwar allgemein von der Architektur und zweifellos insbesondere von der Stimmung anregen, die von den ihm zur Verfügung gestellten Räumen ausging, doch die Idee oder das Konzept war zuerst da, danach erst wurde der passende Raum dafür ausgesucht.

Die heutige Villa Stuck besteht aus drei Gebäuden: der ›historischen‹ Villa, 1897 als Stucks privates Wohnhaus mit Atelier errichtet, dem Atelier, einem 1914/15 errichteten, ursprünglich geräumigen und hellen zweistöckigen Anbau, sowie den ehemaligen Unterkünften der Hausangestellten. Die ursprünglichen Pläne, die Wilson in Watermill entwickelt hatte, sahen Tableaus verteilt über die gesamte Villa sowie über drei Stockwerke[11] des Ateliers vor. Aus einer Reihe von Gründen wurde jedoch immer deutlicher, daß eine Beschränkung des Environments auf die Räume der sogenannten historischen Villa geboten war; zudem wurde nunmehr vorgesehen, das Environment pünktlich zum 100jährigen Bestehen der Villa Stuck zu realisieren.

Interessant ist, wie die ursprüngliche Reihenfolge der Watermill-›Ideen‹ aussah – in die ja Robert Wilsons erste, intuitive Reaktion auf die Kunst, die Photographien, die Architektur und die Möbel Franz von Stucks eingeflossen ist – und welche Abwandlungen diese auf die Zuordnung der jeweiligen Räume hin erfahren haben. Den ersten fünf, ja insgesamt mehr als der Hälfte aller in Watermill entwickelten ›Ideen‹,[12] liegen Photographien von Mary und Franz von Stuck zugrunde. Wilson bediente sich dieser Photographien auf folgende Art und Weise: um nach ihrer Vorlage wie Geistererscheinungen wirkende Figuren von Franz von Stuck und seiner Familie (einschließlich des Hundes) gestalten zu können und als Ansatzpunkt für theoretische Exkurse über die Photographie und deren Verhältnis zur Malerei. Diese durchaus unterschiedlichen Ansätze ergaben zweierlei Arten von Tableaus: solche, die eine originalgetreue dreidimensionale Umsetzung des Photos darstellen, und solche, die eine ›Umsetzung‹ des Originalphotos in eine neue, unerwartete Form beinhalten.

swan with a pearl necklace (evoking associations of King Ludwig II) was to have been placed in the center of the room. Three large, minimalist "gray walls — drawings" of the reverse side of a photograph of Stuck's favorite model, Lydia Feez — were to have been installed along two walls and in front of the entranceway (so that visitors to the museum would have to walk *through* the image). The sound score for this tableau was to have been that of a lake, of Lake Starnberg, where Ludwig II mysteriously drowned.

It should be mentioned that most of the photographs used by Franz von Stuck in the production of his paintings were portraits or studies, probably taken by his wife, Mary, who then enlarged them before they were drawn on and traced by Stuck. On both the front and the reverse of the original photographs one can see masterly, expressive strokes as Stuck gouged new details into the photograph, added a feature, narrowed the neck, or elongated the face. It was the visible remains of this process which particularly fascinated Robert Wilson.[15]

Eight Ideas from Watermill were based on paintings, drawings, and sculpture by Stuck. Again Wilson used the original works of art in different ways:
– as information to enable him to construct life-like simulacrums of the fabulous creatures which populated Stuck's paintings;
– as the basis for excursions into theoretical discussions on painting/drawing/ sculpture and their relationship to theater and architecture.

It is interesting to note that the simulacrums which Wilson transposed from photographs are "ghost-like," while those transposed from paintings (no matter how fantastic) create the illusion of being "real."

Wilson's selection of paintings for tableaux in the Villa is unexpected in that it excludes Franz von Stuck's most famous works. Three paintings were transposed in the final version: *Amor* (Cupid), *Trunkene Kentaurin* (Drunken Centaur), and *Frühling* (Spring). Only one painting, *Der Nibelungen Not* (The Distress of the Nibelungen), was to have been translated into a new — and, given its subject matter, perhaps expected form — a theater set. This Idea was not carried out. In addition to paintings Wilson also included preliminary drawings for the relief *Tänzerinnen* (Dancers) in the music salon. These were translated into wall paper in one room in the atelier (see page 62/63). The most spectacular "translation", however, occured in the *Dressing Room* where a tableau consisting of a live tiger python and a sculpture by Stuck, *Monna Vanna*, became a provocative substitute for, and re-interpretation of, Franz von Stuck's most famous painting, *Die Sünde*.

Given Robert Wilson's fascination with furniture, it was to be expected that at least some of the marvelous chairs designed by Franz von Stuck would be included in the final installation. Indeed in the *Boudoir* we see a simulacrum of Stuck seated in the artist's "Red Chair;" in Mary's room his daughter is seated on a Spanish chair (not designed by Stuck but in his possession). In addition, the *Phantastische Jagd* takes place in the reception room and music salon among the furniture which Stuck designed for his Villa and for which he won the Golden Medallion at the Paris World's Fair in 1900. One Idea which was not realized was described as follows: "one leg of Stuck's chair [Bergère] stands on a lightbulb on the floor."

Earlier the question was posed — how, if at all, did Robert Wilson's Ideas change once the spaces in the Villa were allocated? Surprisingly little. In

Wilson schuf neun Geistern ähnliche Figuren: Mary und Franz von Stuck in römischem Kostüm, Stuck mit seinem Hund, die Tochter Mary als Torero mit Pips, einem Hund des Hauses, und drei geringfügig voneinander abweichende Figuren von Franz von Stuck im Malerkittel. Zwei Photographien wurden in eine neue Form übertragen: eine als eine Art Bühnenbild nach einer Landschaftsaufnahme (siehe *Rauchsalon*, Seite 54 ff.) und die zweite (ein Photo eines Schauspielers in der Rolle Napoleons) wurde zweifach als Gemälde umgesetzt (siehe *Franz von Stucks Schlafzimmer*, Seite 68 ff.). Sowohl Stuck als auch Wilson fertigten also ein Gemälde nach derselben Photographie an, mit dem Unterschied, daß das von Wilson wie eine Photographie aussehen sollte.[13]

Eine der interessantesten, letzten Endes aber nicht realisierten Ideen für das Projekt *Villa Stuck* war für das herrlich ausgeschmückte, historische Atelier vorgesehen.[14] Ein weißer Schwan mit einer Perlenkette (der automatisch Assoziationen mit König Ludwig II. erwecken würde) sollte in der Mitte des Raums plaziert werden. Drei große, minimalistische »graue Wände – Zeichnungen« von der Rückseite eines Photos, das Stucks Lieblingsmodell Lydia Feez zeigt – hätten an zwei Wänden entlang und vor dem Eingang aufgestellt werden sollen (so daß der Besucher des Museums das Bild hätte ›durchschreiten‹ müssen). Untermalt werden sollte dieses Tableau vom Geräusch der Wellenbewegung eines Sees, genauer des Starnberger Sees, in dem Ludwig II. auf mysteriöse Weise ertrank.

Es sollte erwähnt werden, daß die überwiegende Mehrzahl der Photos, derer sich Franz von Stuck bei der Arbeit an seinen Gemälden bediente, Porträts oder Studien waren, die vermutlich von seiner Frau Mary aufgenommen und vergrößert wurden, ehe Stuck auf sie zeichnete und sie abpauste. Sowohl auf der Vorder- wie auf der Rückseite der Originalphotographien finden sich meisterhafte, ausdrucksstarke Bleistiftstriche Stucks, mit denen er das Photo ausfeilte und ihm neue Details hinzufügte, indem er etwa einen Hals ein wenig schlanker oder ein Gesicht etwas länger machte. Die sichtbaren Spuren dieser Bearbeitung übten auf Robert Wilson eine besondere Faszination aus.[15]

Für acht der in Watermill entwickelten Ideen dienten Gemälde, Zeichnungen und Skulpturen Franz von Stucks als Ausgangspunkt. Sie fanden wieder in verschiedener Art und Weise Verwendung: um nach ihrer Vorlage lebensechte Nachbildungen der Fabelwesen machen zu können, die Franz von Stucks Gemälde bevölkern oder als Ansatzpunkt für theoretische Exkurse über Malerei, Zeichenkunst und Plastik und deren Verhältnis zu Theater und Architektur. Interessanterweise haben die Nachbildungen, die Wilson nach Photographien machte, stets etwas Geisterhaftes, während diejenigen, für die – wenn auch noch so phantastische – Gemälde als Ausgangspunkt dienten, viel ›lebensechter‹ wirken.

Die Auswahl der Gemälde für Wilsons Tableaus überrascht insofern, als Franz von Stucks berühmteste Werke keine Berücksichtigung fanden. Drei Tableaus der endgültigen Fassung des Environments sind nachgestellte Gemälde: *Amor*, *Trunkene Kentaurin* und *Frühling*. Nur ein Gemälde, *Der Nibelungen Not*, hätte in eine neue – und angesichts seiner Thematik vielleicht nicht überraschende – Form übertragen werden sollen, nämlich in ein Bühnenbild. Diese Idee wurde nicht realisiert. Neben Gemälden bezog Wilson auch Vorzeichnungen für Stucks Relief *Tänzerinnen* ein, das den Musiksalon schmückt. Sie fanden im Tableau im Atelier Verwendung (siehe Seite 62/63). Die spektakulärste ›Umsetzung‹ jedoch vollzog sich im Ankleidezimmer, wo ein

some cases changes were necessary for either technical, conservation, or financial reasons; occasionally a sound-scape would be modified, or a detail would be added. The majority of ideas, however, remained as originally planned. This reflects not only the length of time (four years) Wilson worked on this project but also the extraordinary intuition he brought to it. Even though virtually all the research material he was provided with for this project was written in a language he does not understand, Wilson repeatedly made decisions, based on a purely intuitive response, which were astonishingly razor-sharp and unerring.

What exactly is the Villa Stuck project? How does it relate to Wilson's other exhibitions and environments? To answer the latter first: *Robert Wilson/Villa Stuck* is not an exhibition in the classic sense of the word. It bears little resemblance to Wilson's many exhibitions in which he presented his own drawings or sculptural objects. The present project is, however, related to earlier environments such as *Memory of a Revolution*, 1987, in Stuttgart; *Memory/Loss*, 1993, in Venice; and *H.G.*, 1995, in London. As if to stress this, Wilson cites some of these works in the *Villa Stuck*. The "presence" of Napoleon in *Franz von Stuck's Bedroom* reminds us of Wilson's first environment, *Memory of a Revolution*, 1987; in the *Dining Room* we see Mary and Franz von Stuck dressed as Romans under a heaven filled with frozen golden arrows reminiscent of the tableau in *H.G.* reproduced on page 31. Nevertheless there are significant differences between the *Villa Stuck* and earlier environments. The grand themes of revolution, slavery, and military might are missing. Instead one finds aging, jealousy, domestic conflict, vanity, and loss of prowess, both artistic and sexual. The battleground has become personal, the confrontation between Wilson's own work and that of another visual artist one-to-one.

Robert Wilson has often engaged in intense dialogue with the work of living, and deceased, literary artists. One needs only recall his many collaborations with Heiner Müller and Wilson's repeated projects based on the writings of T.S. Eliot. His still lifes created with the objects of other visual artists have been astonishing and revelatory. Nevertheless, in comparison with those tableaux based on literary themes, Wilson's art-based projects have remained somewhat distanced, cooler. With the present project Robert Wilson has abandoned this distance and engaged in a complex, comprehensive dialogue with the work and fantasy life of another visual artist. For the first time Wilson not only re-interprets or re-contextualizes art objects but also re-creates them in two- and three-dimensional form. Indeed the entire production of a single artist — his paintings, drawings, sculptures, architecture, and furniture — is placed under a microscope, as is his person. Franz von Stuck's personal and mythological universe becomes Robert Wilson's playing field.

Throughout the *Villa Stuck* the visitor is constantly surprised by the presence of fabulous creatures in unlikely places and positions and by rapid shifts in the sequencing of time. In the vestibule Franz von Stuck greets us, already an apparition, shortly before his death. A few steps further, in the *Dining Room*, he is a young man at the height of his success. Still a few steps further, in the *Boudoir*, Stuck is a fifty-year-old increasingly under attack for the irrelevance of his work. This fragmented, non-sequential narrative, and the unexpected juxtapositions one finds in each tableau, are strategies which Wilson learnt from Sybil Moholy-Nagy at the Pratt Institute in Brooklyn in 1963 when he was still a student:

Tableau, das einen lebenden Tigerpython und eine Skulptur Stucks mit dem Titel *Monna Vanna* vereinte, zu einem provozierenden, eine Neudeutung enthaltenden Ersatz für Franz von Stucks berühmtestes Gemälde, *Die Sünde*, wurde.

In Anbetracht der Faszination, die Möbel auf Robert Wilson ausüben, konnte man erwarten, daß zumindest einige der wunderbaren Sessel, die Franz von Stuck selbst entworfen hat, in die endgültige Installation einbezogen werden würden. Tatsächlich begegnen wir im Tableau im Boudoir der nachgebildeten Figur Stucks sitzend auf seinem sogenannten Roten Sessel. In Marys Zimmer wiederum schwebt seine Tochter sitzend über einem (nicht von Stuck entworfenen) spanischen Stuhl aus dem Besitz des Künstlers. Außerdem spielt sich die *Phantastische Jagd* in Empfangsraum und Musiksalon inmitten der Möbel ab, die Stuck eigens für die Villa entworfen hat und für die er auf der Pariser Weltausstellung 1900 mit der Goldmedaille ausgezeichnet worden war. In der Beschreibung einer Idee, die nicht realisiert wurde, hieß es: »Ein Bein von Stucks Sessel [Bergère] steht auf einer auf dem Boden liegenden Glühbirne.«

Weiter oben wurde die Frage aufgeworfen, inwiefern, wenn überhaupt, Robert Wilsons Ideen sich gewandelt haben, nachdem die Zuordnung der jeweiligen Räume der Villa Stuck erfolgt war. Überraschend wenig, lautet die Antwort. In manchen Fällen mußten aus technischen, konservatorischen oder finanziellen Gründen Änderungen vorgenommen werden; gelegentlich wurde ein Klangenvironment abgewandelt oder ein neues Detail hinzugefügt. Die Mehrzahl der Ideen jedoch blieb grundsätzlich unverändert. Dies ist nicht nur ein Ergebnis der langen Zeit (vier Jahre), die Wilson auf dieses Projekt verwendete, sondern auch der erstaunlichen Intuition, mit der er an die Sache herangegangen ist. Obgleich nahezu sämtliche Unterlagen, mit denen er für dieses Projekt versorgt wurde, in einer ihm fremden Sprache geschrieben sind und seine Ideen vielfach aus einer rein intuitiven Verarbeitung dieses Materials heraus entwickelt wurden, brachte Wilson mit seinen Entscheidungen immer wieder erstaunlich sicher Wesentliches auf den Punkt.

Worum genau handelt es sich beim Projekt *Villa Stuck*? Wie verhält sich das Projekt zu Wilsons übrigen Ausstellungen und Environments? Um letzteres zuerst zu beantworten: *Robert Wilson/Villa Stuck* ist keine Ausstellung im herkömmlichen Sinn des Wortes. Sie hat wenig Ähnlichkeit mit Wilsons zahlreichen Ausstellungen, in denen er seine eigenen Zeichnungen oder Skulpturen gezeigt hat. Das jetzige Projekt ist vielmehr verwandt mit früheren Environments wie *Erinnerung an eine Revolution* 1987 in Stuttgart, *Memory/Loss* 1993 in Venedig und *H.G.* 1995 in London. Als wollte er dies noch unterstreichen, zitiert Wilson einige dieser Werke im Environment *Villa Stuck*. Die Gestalt Napoleons im Tableau in Franz von Stucks Schlafzimmer erinnert uns an Wilsons erstes Environment *Erinnerung an eine Revolution* von 1987; das Tableau im Speisesaal zeigt uns Mary und Franz von Stuck in römischem Kostüm unter einem Himmelsgewölbe voller im Flug angehaltener goldener Pfeile, das wiederum an das auf Seite 31 des vorliegenden Bandes abgebildete Tableau in *H.G.* erinnert. Gleichwohl bestehen zwischen *Villa Stuck* und früheren Environments wesentliche Unterschiede. Die großen Themen Revolution, Sklaverei und militärische Macht fehlen. Statt dessen geht es um das Altern, um Eifersucht, Familienkonflikte, Eitelkeit und das Schwinden der – künstlerischen wie sexuellen – Potenz. Das Schlachtfeld ist nunmehr ein privates.

Robert Wilson hat sich oft auf einen intensiven Dialog mit dem Werk von Dichtern der Gegenwart oder der Vergangenheit eingelassen. Man denke nur an seine zahlreichen Gemeinschaftsarbeiten mit Heiner Müller und die ver-

"She'd turn out the lights — you couldn't take notes — and show slides of all sorts of things, rapid-fire. A Ming vase, the Acropolis, a city street, a forest, a train station. She'd talk about anything that came to mind, drawing amazing parallels. You came out of class in a daze."[16]

The impact of Robert Wilson's tableaux in the Villa Stuck on us is not that dissimilar; we come out in a daze. Like Sybil Moholy-Nagy he insists that we don't take notes, he refuses to provide interpretations.

In an interview with Robert Enright in 1994 Wilson noted that, "regardless of what the work is, we have to approach it with an idea of saying what is it, instead of saying what it is."[17] Nearly a decade earlier, in an interview with Jacqueline Brody,[18] he declared that we are all "the innocent fool.... And as soon as we say what it is, it's finished, fascistic, everything that's messed up, once it's tied up in a box, it's finished." Wilson's passionate resistance to providing interpretions of his work, and his plea that we approach it as "innocent fools" must be respected. What exactly is the Villa Stuck project? In one of the few public statements prior to the opening of the exhibition Robert Wilson tells us:

"This is an installation of sculptures, sound, and light in the historic rooms of the Villa; a very personal project about Franz von Stuck. The man fascinates me, he had strange visions."[19]

schiedenen Projekte, für die das Werk T.S. Eliots einen Ausgangspunkt bildete. Die Stilleben, die Wilson mit den Objekten anderer bildender Künstler geschaffen hat, waren überraschend und aufschlußreich. Im Vergleich zu den Tableaus, denen literarische Motive zugrunde lagen, wirkten die auf bildende Kunst bezogenen Projekte Wilsons jedoch immer eher ein wenig distanziert, kühler. Mit dem jetzigen Projekt hat Robert Wilson diese Distanz aufgegeben und sich auf einen vielschichtigen, umfassenden Dialog mit dem Werk und der Phantasiewelt eines anderen bildenden Künstlers eingelassen. Erstmals unterzieht Wilson Kunstobjekte nicht nur einer Neudeutung oder rückt sie in einen neuen Zusammenhang, sondern er gestaltet sie tatsächlich in zwei- oder dreidimensionaler Form nach. Das gesamte Schaffen eines einzelnen Künstlers – seine Gemälde, Zeichnungen, Skulpturen, Architektur und Möbel – wird ebenso wie die Person selbst unter die Lupe genommen. Stucks private und mythologische Welt wird zur Spielwiese Robert Wilsons.

Im Environment *Villa Stuck* begegnet der Besucher an den unerwartetsten Stellen immer wieder Fabelwesen oder erlebt jähe Wechsel in der Zeitabfolge. Im Vestibül begrüßen uns zwei bereits geisterhafte Stucks kurz vor dem Tod des Künstlers. Nur wenige Schritte weiter, im Speisesaal, ist Franz von Stuck ein junger Mann auf dem Gipfel seines Erfolgs. Wieder einige Schritte weiter, im Boudoir, ist er ein Fünfzigjähriger, der sich wegen der angeblichen Banalität seines Werks zunehmender Kritik ausgesetzt sieht. Diese bruchstückhafte, nichtlineare Erzählung und die unerwarteten Nebeneinanderstellungen, die sich in jedem Tableau finden, sind Strategien, die Wilson 1963 als Student von seiner Lehrerin Sybil Moholy-Nagy am Pratt Institute in Brooklyn gelernt hat:

»Sie pflegte das Licht auszuschalten (man konnte sich also keine Notizen machen) und daraufhin Schlag auf Schlag Dias von allen möglichen Sachen vorzuführen. Eine Ming-Vase, die Akropolis, eine Großstadtstraße, einen Wald, einen Bahnhof. Sie redete über alles, was ihr in den Sinn kam, und zog verblüffende Parallelen. Man verließ den Unterricht am Ende ganz benommen.«[16]

Die Wirkung, die die Tableaus Robert Wilsons auf uns ausüben, ist nicht ganz unähnlich: wir verlassen die Villa Stuck am Ende ganz benommen. Ebenso wie Sybil Moholy-Nagy möchte er nicht, daß wir uns Notizen machen, er weigert sich, uns Erklärungen oder Interpretationen anzubieten.

In einem Interview mit Robert Enright 1994 meinte Wilson: »Ganz unabhängig von der Art des Werkes sollten wir, wenn wir darauf zugehen, nicht etwa von vornherein sagen, was es ist, sondern vielmehr uns fragen, was ist es?«[17] Beinahe zehn Jahre zuvor hatte er im Gespräch mit Jacqueline Brody ausgesagt, wir alle seien »unschuldige Narren ... Und sobald wir sagen, was es ist, ist es vorbei, ist es faschistisch, alles ist vermasselt, wenn es einmal in eine Schublade gesteckt wurde, ist es vorbei.«[18] Wenn sich Wilson so entschieden dagegen sträubt, Interpretationen seines Werkes anzubieten, und er uns dazu aufruft, als »unschuldige Narren« auf sein Werk zuzugehen, sollten wir dies respektieren. Die Antwort auf die Frage, worum genau es sich beim Projekt *Villa Stuck* handelt, überlassen wir daher ihm. In einem der wenigen öffentlichen Statements erklärt uns Robert Wilson: »Es ist eine Installation aus Skulpturen, Klang und Licht im alten Haus der Villa, ein sehr persönliches Projekt über Franz von Stuck. Der Mann fasziniert mich, er hatte seltsame Visionen.«[19]

Vestibule

Franz von Stuck's vestibule functions as a prologue to the Villa Stuck. With its Medusa head, serpent mosaic floor, theater mask, and copies of Greek and Roman sculptures and reliefs, it tells visitors that they are in another, more perfect world, a world of the gods. Robert Wilson, in his prologue to the Villa Stuck, brings us into a less perfect world, that of an aging and disillusioned Franz von Stuck. It is 1919, more than twenty years after the construction of the Villa. Two slightly different simulacrums of Franz von Stuck stand in the center of a simple, blue-gray room; fluorescent tubes are scattered at their feet

on a white fabric floor. A replica of a 1903 Dutch Rozenburg vase from the museum's collection has been placed on the floor in front of the two figures. Next to the vase is a beetle. Another beetle rests on Stuck's shoulder, a third on the artist's palette. Stuck is reading a letter aloud.[1] Written in July, 1919, it is addressed to Stuck's colleague and friend, the painter Friedrich August von Kaulbach.[2]

Vestibül

Franz von Stucks Vestibül fungiert gewissermaßen als Prolog zur Villa Stuck. Mit seinem Medusenhaupt, dem Schlangenmotiv des Mosaikfußbodens, der Theatermaske und den Kopien griechischer und römischer Skulpturen und Reliefs signalisiert es dem Besucher, daß er nunmehr in eine andere, eine vollkommenere Welt, eben in eine Welt der Götter eingetreten ist. Robert Wilson wiederum führt uns in seinem Prolog zur Villa Stuck in eine weniger vollkommene Welt, in die Welt eines alternden und desillusionierten Franz von Stuck. Wir schreiben das Jahr 1919, mehr als zwanzig Jahre sind seit der Fertigstellung der Villa vergangen. In der Mitte eines schlichten, blaugrauen Raums stehen zwei geringfügig voneinander abweichende Figuren, die Franz von Stuck darstellen. Zu ihren Füßen liegen Leuchtröhren auf dem weißen Stoffboden verstreut; auf der Schulter der einen Figur, auf der Palette der anderen sowie auf dem Boden sitzen drei Käfer. Auf dem Fußboden steht die Replik einer holländischen Porzellanvase aus dem Jahr 1903; sie stammt aus der Jugendstilsammlung des Museums Villa Stuck. ›Stuck‹ liest mit lauter Stimme einen Brief[1] vom Juli 1919, der an seinen Malerkollegen und Freund Friedrich August von Kaulbach gerichtet ist.[2]

In diesem ersten Tableau ist Franz von Stuck 56 Jahre alt und seine sorgfältig aufgebaute, ›vollkommenere‹ Welt bricht um ihn herum zusammen. Wenige Monate vorher, im April 1919, hatte während der sogenannten Vierten Revolution die Rote Garde eine Reihe prominenter Münchner Bürger als Geisel genommen, darunter Stuck. In seinem Brief an Kaulbach spricht er von diesem Ereignis und der Tatsache, daß er nur knapp dem Tod entronnen war, nur noch als »den anderen Aufregungen«[3]. Obgleich erst ein knappes Jahr zuvor eines seiner Hauptwerke, das stark erotisch aufgeladene Gemälde *Die Versuchung*, entstanden war, ist Stucks Stern als Künstler von Rang nunmehr im Sinken. »Wochenlang konnte ich nicht arbeiten, so hat mich der Zusammenbruch unseres armen Vaterlands niedergedrückt«, berichtet er Kaulbach. Tatsächlich haben seine tiefe Niedergeschlagenheit und seine Unfähigkeit zu arbeiten jedoch ihren Grund viel eher darin, daß seine Frau wegen schwerer Strahlenschäden im Krankenhaus liegt; sie wird wegen Krebs behandelt und die Heilungsaussichten sind ungewiß.

»Todesbilder«, so meinte Robert Wilson vor nicht allzu langer Zeit in einem Interview, »ziehen sich wie ein roter Faden durch all meine Inszenierungen.«[4] Sein Eröffnungstableau zum Environment *Villa Stuck* macht uns bekannt mit einem alternden Künstler am Ende seiner Laufbahn und seiner schöpferischen Kräfte, der mit der eigenen Sterblichkeit und der seiner Frau konfrontiert wird. Es führt uns zudem in das Familiendrama ein, das für die Geschichte der Villa Stuck so prägend war: das Dreiecksverhältnis zwischen Franz von Stuck, seiner Frau Mary und seiner unehelichen Tochter Mary, die das Ehepaar 1904 adoptierte. Im Brief an Kaulbach spricht Stuck von der Freude, die ihm die Nähe seiner Tochter bereite.

Die Figuren, die im Mittelpunkt des Tableaus stehen, basieren auf einer 1928 von Friedrich Witzel aufgenommenen Photographie. Diese zeigt den Künstler vor seinem Gemälde *Sisyphos* von 1920 und einer späten Skulptur mit dem Titel *Helena* (um 1925). Ungewöhnlich ist, daß Stuck im Malerkittel zu sehen ist: Normalerweise ließ er sich nur in Gesellschaftskleidung ablichten. Robert Wilson hat also ein ›privates‹ Bild von Stuck ausgewählt, eines, das nur wenige Monate vor seinem Tod aufgenommen wurde. Die einer Geistererscheinung gleichenden Figuren Franz von Stucks, ein Werk Hans Thiemanns, sind

In this first tableau Franz von Stuck is fifty-six years old and his carefully constructed (more perfect) world is collapsing around him. Only months earlier, in April, 1919, during the so-called Fourth Revolution, the Red Guard had taken a number of Munich's leading citizens hostage, Franz von Stuck among them. In his letter to Kaulbach he understatedly refers to this event, and his narrow escape from death, as "the other excitement."[3] Although less than a year earlier he had produced one of his major works, the highly erotic *Versuchung* (The Temptation), Stuck's work as an artist of significance is drawing to a close. "For weeks on end I was unable to work, distressed as I was by the collapse of our poor fatherland," Stuck tells Kaulbach. His deep depression, however, and his inability to work, has much more to do with the fact that his wife is in hospital suffering from severe radiation burns: she is being treated for cancer, the prospects for cure are uncertain.

In a recent interview Robert Wilson commented that "images of death are a common thread in all my stagings."[4] In his opening tableau to the *Villa Stuck* we are introduced to an aging artist at the end of his career and creativity, confronted by his own mortality and that of his wife. We are also introduced to the family drama which dominates the history of the Villa Stuck, the triangle relationship between Franz von Stuck, his wife Mary, and his illegitimate daughter Mary, whom the pair adopted in 1904. In his letter to Kaulbach, Franz von Stuck speaks of his joy at having his daughter nearby.

The simulacrums of Franz von Stuck, which are the focus of this tableau, are based on a photograph taken by Friedrich Witzel in 1928. The artist stands in front of his painting *Sisyphos* (1920) and a late sculpture *Helena* (c. 1925). Unusual is the fact that Stuck is in an artist's smock; normally he allowed himself to be photographed only in formal dress. Robert Wilson has therefore chosen a "private" image of Stuck, one taken only months before his death. Hans Thiemann's apparition-like figures of Franz von Stuck are constructed out of paper whose surface has been treated with fluid in order to create a particularly smooth surface. The facial features have been taken from a mould of Stuck's death mask which is in the possession of the Museum Villa Stuck. In the initial concept drawing for this tableau Robert Wilson noted that he wanted "maybe 3 white figures the same, like ghosts." In the final version of the environment *Villa Stuck*, Franz von Stuck appears five times as a phantasm — twice here, in the vestibule, and in the dining room, the boudoir, and the secret stairwell. The three figures "the same" are now, however, slightly different in glance and position. They also depict Stuck as a young, middle-aged, and elderly man.

In Robert Wilson and Peter Cerone's sound environment two different actors portray Stuck reading the letter. By alternating and interspersing the identical-but-different sound texts, Wilson creates a fracturing and unexpected intensification of the text. These revelatory "moments of discord," as one commentator called them, are to be found in other sound scores for tableaux in the Villa Stuck.

aus Papier hergestellt; dieses wurde mit Flüssigkeit behandelt, um eine besonders glatte Oberfläche zu erzielen. Für die Gesichtszüge verwendete man eine Gußform von Stucks Totenmaske, die sich im Besitz des Museums Villa Stuck befindet. Auf der ursprünglichen Konzeptzeichnung für dieses Tableau vermerkte Wilson, ihm schwebten »vielleicht 3 weiße Gestalten, identisch, geistergleich« vor. In der endgültigen Fassung des Environments *Villa Stuck* ist Franz von Stuck insgesamt fünfmal als ›Geist‹ zu sehen: zweimal hier im Vestibül und des weiteren im Speisesaal, im Boudoir und in dem geheimen Treppenhaus. Die drei ›identischen‹ Figuren weichen jetzt in Blick und Stellung leicht voneinander ab. Sie stellen Stuck als jungen Mann, in mittlerem Alter und als älteren Mann dar.

In Robert Wilsons und Peter Cerones Klangenvironment verkörpern zwei Schauspieler Stuck beim Lesen des Briefes. Durch das Abwechseln der eigentlich gleichen, aber verschieden gesprochenen Texte erzeugt Wilson eine seltsame Fragmentierung und zugleich eine unerwartete Intensivierung des Brieftextes. Diese aufschlußreichen »Momente der Dissonanz«, wie ein Kommentator sie genannt hat, finden sich auch in den Klangenvironments für andere Tableaus des Projektes *Villa Stuck*.

München, Villa Stuck, 20. Juli 1919

Lieber Freund!

Dein lieber Brief hat mich sehr gefreut und die so liebenswürdige Einladung, zu Euch zu kommen, nicht minder. Es ist mir aber ein Bedürfnis geworden, meine Frau täglich zu sehen und zu trösten, sodaß ich mich nicht entschließen kann, von hier weg zu gehen, so gerne ich Dich und Deine liebe Familie nach so langer Zeit wieder sehen und sprechen möchte. Meiner Frau geht es wesentlich besser, das heißt allerdings nur so viel, daß jetzt wenigstens Aussicht auf Heilung besteht, während noch vor vierzehn Tagen Geheimrat Sauerbruch ungewiß war, ob die Wunde überhaupt jemals heilen würde. Das hat er mir erst jetzt eingestanden. Das Schwerste hat meine Frau nun überstanden – hoffentlich hält die Besserung an. Ich selbst bin ganz wohl und da meine Mary seit drei Tagen wieder ganz in München ist, bin ich auch nicht mehr allein. Sie kommt oft zu mir und ich besuche sie auch täglich und freue mich über mein Enkelkind, die kleine Hilde, die ganz sonnengebräunt ist und sich sehr kräftig entwickelt hat. Es würde jetzt niemand auf den Gedanken kommen, daß es ein Siebenmonatskind ist. Wochenlang konnte ich nicht arbeiten, so hat mich der Zusammenbruch unseres armen Vaterlands niedergedrückt. Dazu kamen dann die anderen Aufregungen und nun auch noch die unglückliche Röntgen-Verbrennung meiner Frau. Jetzt fange ich aber allmählich wieder zu arbeiten an, das hilft mir über vieles hinüber.

Und nun danke ich Dir nochmals herzlich für alles Liebe, empfehle mich Deiner Frau und grüße die Kinder! Meine Frau erwidert Eure freundlichen Grüße auf das Herzlichste.

Immer Dein getreuer Stuck

Reception Room and Music Salon

The reception room and music salon of the Villa Stuck are undoubtedly among the most spectacular and important of Franz von Stuck's architectural stagings. During Stuck's lifetime visitors were astonished by the sculptures, paintings, mirrors, and gold mosaic walls which shimmered in the dusk-like glow of the reception room. This special lighting effect was created by a window out of transparent Tiffany glass, which could be shuttered in the evening with panels made out of antique Venetian mirrors. Although Stuck intended that the visitor would enter the reception room and move through the boudoir and dining room before leaving the Villa through the music salon, both rooms were treated as one complex: "Their spatial unity is barely interrupted by a partition, resembling a stage backdrop, which at one time could also be closed off by a heavy curtain."[5]

The music salon is distinguished not only by its wall decorations and reliefs produced by Stuck's own hand but also by its ceiling, the *Sternenhimmel* (Heaven of Stars) which reputedly represents an evening in August, 1895, the month in which his daughter Mary was conceived. The cobalt blue heaven and its stars are viewed through a painted pergola, an illusionist construction reminiscent of Pompeien or Etruscan wall paintings.[6] One of the walls in the music salon is dedicated to Orpheus, the other to the dance — a theme which Robert Wilson later takes up in the tableau *Atelier*, where he incorporates a drawing for the relief *Tänzerinnen* (Dancers) in the music salon. In the decorative pediments on this wall are three theater masks — comic, tragic, and demonic.

Incorporating these rooms into Robert Wilson's environment originally posed considerable difficulties. Not only are both spaces highly decorated and filled with furniture designed by Stuck, but they are also under monument protection and in very fragile condition, making elaborate construction virtually impossible. Wilson's first concept called only for "historical rooms lit decadently." It was not until January, 1997, when he saw a painting by Franz von Stuck, *Phantastische Jagd* (Fantastic Hunt), 1890,[7] which had just been purchased by the museum for its collection, that he decided to create a tableau here of a Centaur[8] pursuing a Deer-Man-Centaur — a three-dimensional transposition of Stuck's painting.

The *Phantastische Jagd* captures the hunt at the exact moment the Deer-Man-Centaur is fatally struck by an arrow in the breast. In the vestibule, at the entrance way to the music salon, a detail from one of the ancient world's most famous images of the hunt, from the palace of Ashurbanipal at Nineveh, also captures the exact moment when the pursued creature is struck by an arrow. By placing a transposition of the *Phantastische Jagd* in the music salon, in the vicinity of Ashurbanipal's *Dying Lioness*,[9] Wilson introduces us to the fabulous creatures and phantasmic world of Franz von Stuck. He also reiterates the theme of death in both his own, and Stuck's, tableau in the vestibule and carries it over into the reception room and the music salon.

Robert Wilson and Peter Cerone's sound score for this tableau, three arias and a modified, attenuated excerpt from the Overture to *Der Freischütz* by Carl Maria von Weber, accentuated the themes of the supernatural and the hunt, while refering to Stuck's dedications to famous composers, including Weber, on the walls of the music salon. It also recalls a 1990 collaboration between Robert Wilson, William Burroughs, and Tom Waits, *The Black Rider:*

Empfangsraum und Musiksalon

Der Empfangsraum und der Musiksalon der Villa Stuck zählen zweifellos zu den spektakulärsten und bedeutendsten Architekturinszenierungen Franz von Stucks. Besucher zu Lebzeiten Stucks staunten angesichts der Skulpturen, Gemälde, Spiegel und goldenen Mosaikwände, die im Dämmerlicht des Empfangsraums schimmerten. Verantwortlich für diesen besonderen Lichteffekt war ein Fenster aus transparentem Tiffanyglas, das abends mit Fensterläden aus antiken venezianischen Spiegeln verschlossen werden konnte. Obgleich nach Stucks Vorstellung der Besucher zunächst in den Empfangsraum eintreten und auf dem Weg über das Boudoir bzw. den Speisesaal die Villa durch den Musiksalon wieder verlassen sollte, wurden Empfangsraum und Musiksalon als Einheit betrachtet: »Die räumliche Einheit beider wird durch eine bühnenprospektartige Zwischenwand, die früher noch durch einen schweren Vorhang geschlossen werden konnte, kaum getrennt.«[5]

Der Musiksalon beeindruckt nicht nur durch seine Wanddekorationen und die Reliefs von der Hand Stucks, sondern auch durch seine Decke, den ›Sternenhimmel‹, der angeblich den Himmel an einem Abend im August 1895 darstellt, dem Monat, in dem seine Tochter Mary gezeugt wurde. Das kobaltblaue Himmelsgewölbe ist durch eine gemalte Pergola hindurch gesehen, eine illusionistische Bildanlage, die an pompejanische oder etruskische Wandmalereien erinnert.[6] Eine der Wände im Musiksalon ist Orpheus gewidmet, die andere dem Tanz – ein Thema, das Robert Wilson in seinem Tableau im Atelier wieder aufgreift: er integriert hier eine Entwurfszeichnung für das Relief *Tänzerinnen* im Musiksalon. Drei Theatermasken, eine komische, eine tragische und eine dämonische, schmücken den Ziergiebel dieser Wand.

Die Einbeziehung dieser Räume in Robert Wilsons Environment bereitete zunächst erhebliche Schwierigkeiten. Nicht nur sind beide Räume reich dekoriert und mit von Stuck entworfenen Möbeln ausgestattet, sie sind auch mit strengen Denkmalschutzauflagen belegt und ihr Zustand ist so empfindlich, daß sie aufwendige Einbauten nicht zulassen. Wilsons ursprüngliches Konzept sah lediglich »dekadent beleuchtete Räume« vor. Erst im Januar 1997 sah er ein Gemälde Stucks, *Phantastische Jagd* von 1890, welches das Museum gerade für seine Sammlung erworben hatte;[7] es inspirierte ihn zur Realisierung eines Tableaus, in dem ein Kentaur einen Hirschmensch-Kentauren[8] verfolgt – eine dreidimensionale Umsetzung von Stucks Gemälde.

Die *Phantastische Jagd* zeigt genau den Moment der Jagd, da der Hirschmensch-Kentaur von einem Pfeil tödlich in der Brust getroffen wird. Im Vestibül, beim Eingang zum Musiksalon, zeigt ein Ausschnitt aus einer der berühmtesten Jagddarstellungen der Antike – aus dem Palast Assurbanipals in Ninive – ebenfalls genau den Augenblick, in dem die verfolgte Kreatur von einem Pfeil getroffen wird. Mit seiner Fassung der *Phantastischen Jagd* im Musiksalon, also in der Nähe von Assurbanipals *Sterbender Löwin*,[9] bringt Robert Wilson uns nicht nur die Fabelwesen und die Phantasiewelt Franz von Stucks nahe, sondern er greift auch das Thema des Todes wieder auf, das sowohl in seinem eigenen wie auch in Stucks Tableau im Vestibül im Mittelpunkt gestanden hatte, und überträgt es in den Empfangsraum und den Musiksalon.

Robert Wilsons und Peter Cerones Klangenvironment für dieses Tableau, drei Arien und ein modifizierter, abgeschwächter Auszug aus der Ouvertüre zu *Der Freischütz* von Carl Maria von Weber, unterstreicht die Thematik des

The Casting of the Magic Bullets, based on Weber's opera. Wilson also placed the text to Agathe's aria from *Der Freischütz* in gold lettering on the glass door and two walls of a vitrine in the corner of the music salon, creating a sculptural, three-dimensional effect. A Tiffany goblet and a mask by Despret of the dancer Cléo de Mérode wearing a floral diadem, from the museum's collection, were also placed in the vitrine.

Übernatürlichen und der Jagd. Es verweist auch auf Stucks Huldigungen an berühmte Komponisten, einschließlich Weber, an den Wänden des Musik-zimmers. Außerdem erinnert es an die 1990 uraufgeführte Gemeinschafts-arbeit von Robert Wilson, William Burroughs und Tom Waits, *The Black Rider: The Casting of the Magic Bullets*, der Webers Oper zugrunde lag. Auf den Wänden und auf der Glastüre der Eckvitrine des Musiksalons hat Wilson in goldener Schrift Teile des Textes von Agathes Arie aus dem *Freischütz* an-gebracht, was einen skulpturalen und dreidimensionalen Effekt hervorruft. In der Vitrine sieht man ein Stengelglas von Louis Comfort Tiffany sowie von Despret eine Maske der Tänzerin Cléo de Mérode, die ein Blütendiadem trägt.

Im Unterschied zur repräsentativen Pracht von Empfangsraum und Musik-salon hatte der Speisesaal eher privaten Charakter. Seine Dekorationen spiegelten den bürgerlichen Geschmack des späten 19. Jahrhunderts wider. Wohn- und Speisezimmermöbel im Stil der Zeit, massive Holztäfelung, chinesische Porzellanbilder, von Franz von Stuck entworfene Lampen und schwere Teppiche sorgten für eine an »flämische oder englische Landhaus-dielen« erinnernde Atmosphäre.[10] Wegen seiner großen Fenster mit Blick auf den Garten wird der Speisesaal heute häufig Gartenzimmer genannt; ledig-lich die Originallampen sowie die Holzdecke und die Türrahmen mit ihren geschnitzten Schlangenornamenten sind erhalten. Diesen Raum hatte Robert Wilson auserkoren, um eines seiner aufwendigsten Tableaus in der Villa Stuck zu realisieren.

In der Mitte des Zimmers, unter einem Himmel aus hundert goldenen, im Flug angehaltenen Pfeilen,[11] befinden sich wie Geistererscheinungen wirkende lebensgroße Figuren von Franz und Mary von Stuck in römischem Kostüm. Hans Thiemann gestaltete sie nach einer Photographie von Adolf Baumann, die anläßlich eines Faschingsballs am 15. Februar 1898 aufgenommen wor-den war.[12] Unter der Leitung eines anderen Münchner ›Künstlerfürsten‹, Franz von Lenbach, sowie der beiden berühmten Archäologen Adolf Furtwängler und Heinrich Bulle hatte man das Münchner Hoftheater in eine einzige Bühnenlandschaft verwandelt, die dem Thema ›In Arkadien‹ gewidmet war. Das alte Athen, die Akropolis und eine überdimensionale Skulptur der Göttin Athene wurden rekonstruiert für ein Bacchanal, zu dem sich Tausende von Nymphen, Kentauren, Satyrn, Faunen, kostümierten Assyrern, Ägyptern, Griechen und Römern, darunter Mary und Franz von Stuck, einfanden.[13]

In Robert Wilsons Tableau sehen wir das kostümierte Ehepaar vor einer großen Tempelfassade mit Säulen (Nachbildungen der Säulen im Eingangs-bereich der Villa Stuck), die »wie das Werk eines Dekorateurs aussieht«.[14] Die Trümmer zerbrochener, in sich zusammengestürzter Säulen liegen ver-streut auf einem falschen Boden aus Dämmplatten. Begleitet wird diese höchst kulissenhafte ›Ruine‹ von den Aufziehgeräuschen eines Glockenspiels.

Obgleich sich in der Villa Stuck zahlreiche kostbare Materialien finden und insgesamt der Eindruck eines unerschöpflichen Luxus vorherrscht, besteht doch ein Großteil der Dekorationen aus bemaltem Gips. Der kulissenhafte Charakter der Stuckschen Villa verstärkt sich noch durch die enorme Kunstfer-tigkeit von Robert Wilsons Mitarbeitern an diesem Projekt und wird gerade-zu augenfällig. Wilsons zerbrochene Styroporsäulen bilden in unmittelbarer Nähe zu Stucks Gipskopie der Pallas Athene eine interessante Paarung; sie rufen die Bemerkung Julius Meier-Graefes in Erinnerung, der im Jahr 1904 Franz von Stuck abschätzig »die größte Leistung der Münchner Faschings-renaissance« bescheinigt hatte. In seinem Tableau für diesen Raum, dem Herz der historischen Villa Stuck, macht Robert Wilson das Theatralische, die Maskerade und Selbstinszenierung anschaulich, die im ausgehenden 19. Jahrhundert weite Teile des Münchner Kulturlebens prägte und die ihre extremste Ausformung in der Architektur – und dem Lebensstil – des Künstler-fürsten Franz von Stuck fand.

Dining Room

Unlike the splendid reception room and music salon, the dining room was a domestic space, decorated to reflect late nineteenth century, bourgeois taste. Living and dining room furniture of the period, heavy wooden paneling, Chinese porcelain paintings, lamps designed by Franz von Stuck, and rich carpets provided the atmosphere of a "Flemish or English countryhouse."[10] The dining room, now often referred to as the garden room because of its large windows and the view onto the garden, has retained only its original lamps and the wooden ceiling and doorways with their carved, ornamental serpents. It is in this space that Robert Wilson decided to create one of the most ambitious tableaux in the Villa Stuck.

In the center of the room, under a heaven of one hundred golden arrows frozen in flight,[11] are ghostly, life-size figures of Mary and Franz von Stuck dressed as a "Roman couple." Constructed and costumed by Hans Thiemann, they are based on a photograph taken by Adolf Baumann on the occasion of a Fasching Ball on February 15, 1898.[12] Under the direction of another Munich "artist prince," Franz von Lenbach, and the renowned archaeologists Adolf Furtwängler and Heinrich Bulle, Munich's Royal Theater was transformed into enormous theater sets dedicated to the theme, "In Arcadia." Ancient Athens, the Acropolis and an oversized sculpture of the goddess Athena were recon-structed for a bacchanalia attended by thousands of nymphs, centaurs, satyrs, fauns, costumed Assyrians, Egyptians, Greeks, and Romans, among them Mary and Franz von Stuck.[13]

In Robert Wilson's tableau we see the costumed couple in front of a large temple facade with columns (imitating those at the entrance to the Villa Stuck) constructed and painted "as if there was a decorator who did something."[14] Broken and fallen columns lie scattered on a false floor constructed out of insulating material. This highly theatrical "ruin" is accompanied by the sounds of a carillon being wound.

Although the Villa Stuck contains many precious materials and the overwhelming impression is one of unboundless luxury, much of its decoration consists of painted plaster. The superb workmanship of Robert Wilson's collaborators on this project intensifies and makes visible the theatricality of Stuck's villa. Wilson's broken, styrofoam columns in the vicinity of Stuck's plaster copy of Pallas Athene create an extraordinary dialogue and recall the comment of Julius Meier-Graefe in 1904, in which he somewhat dismissively described Franz von Stuck as the greatest achievement of Munich's "Fasching Renaissance." In his tableau for this room, the physical heart of the historic Villa Stuck, Robert Wilson makes manifest the theatricality, costume, and self-staging which characterized much of Munich's cultural life in the late nineteenth century and which found its most extreme form in the architecture — and the lifestyle — of the "artist prince" Franz von Stuck.

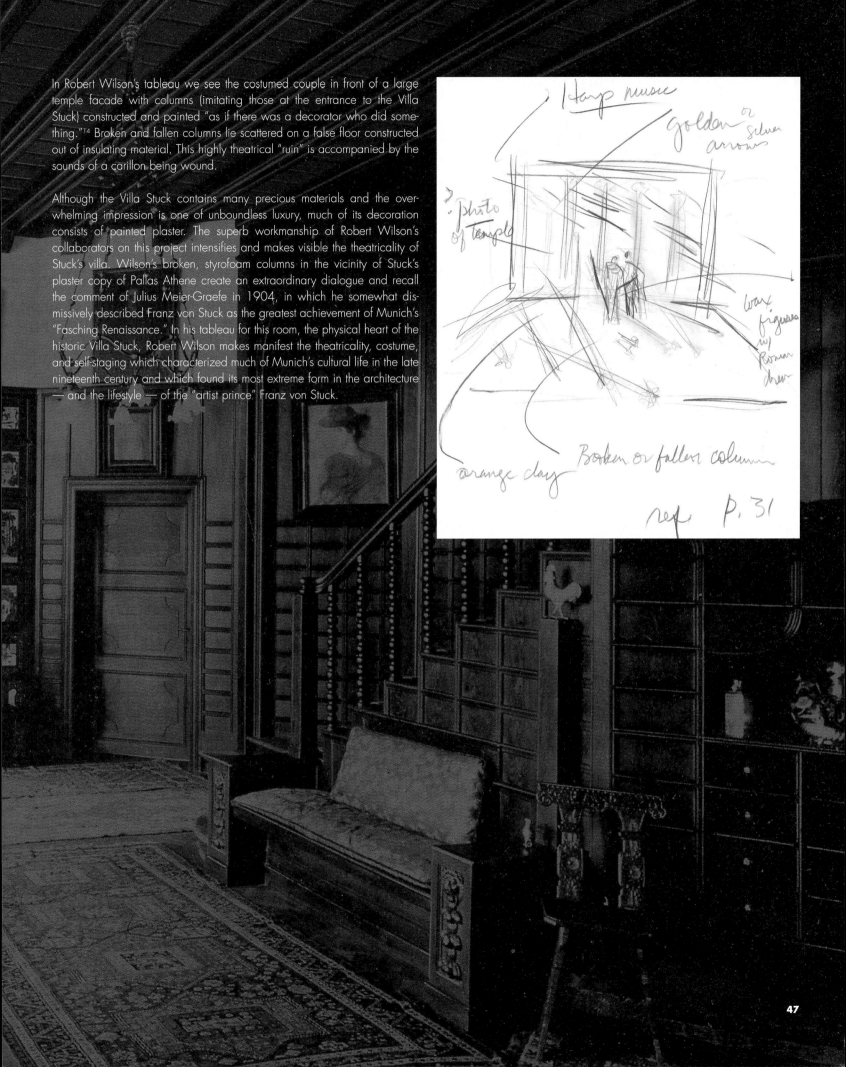

The boudoir or women's salon may be entered either from the reception room, through a narrow passageway which serves as a library, or directly from the dining room. Today the boudoir is distinguished by its ceiling reliefs based on Greek mythology; in Stuck's time also by magnificent medieval tapestries which decorated its walls.

The photograph of Franz von Stuck on which this tableau is based was taken by Theodor Hilsdorf in 1914. The artist, seated in a chair of his own design, the so-called Red Chair, plays with a family dog. Even though this scene is supposedly a domestic one, in both the original photograph and in Robert Wilson's tableau, Franz von Stuck appears in formal attire more appropriate for a public appearance. The sound environment consists of the whining and barking of a dog.

Family dogs appear twice in Robert Wilson's environment — here and in the last tableau, *Mary's Room*. It has been suggested that a barking or growling dog has a particular, personal significance for Robert Wilson. This observation was made in connection with a scene in Wilson's monumental theater work *the CIVIL warS*, 1984, where Frederick the Great first plays with a dog and then shoots it.

Unlike most other tableaux in *Robert Wilson/Villa Stuck*, those in the dining room, boudoir, and smoking salon are visible in their entirety from one another and should, therefore, be considered to be in dialogue with one another. In the *Dining Room* a youthful, handsome Franz von Stuck is at the height of his success and influence, newly married and in the middle of constructing his Villa; in the *Boudoir* he is fifty years old and increasingly under attack for the anachronism, indeed irrelevance, of his work.[15] A visitor to the *Dining Room* tableau, one of the few celebratory images of Stuck in Wilson's environment, is therefore simultaneously aware of the tableau in the boudoir, and of its cautionary tale of the transience of life and fame. As if to stress this, Wilson placed Franz von Stuck's death mask (and autumn leaves) in the library shelves at the entrance to the tableau.

Boudoir

In das Boudoir, auch Damensalon genannt, gelangt man entweder vom Empfangsraum durch einen schmalen Durchgang, der als Bibliothek dient, oder direkt aus dem Speisesaal. Heute beeindruckt das Boudoir durch seine Deckenreliefs mit Motiven aus der griechischen Mythologie. Zu Stucks Lebzeiten schmückten zudem großartige mittelalterliche Tapisserien die Wände.

Das Photo von Franz von Stuck, das diesem Tableau zugrunde liegt, wurde 1914 von Theodor Hilsdorf aufgenommen. Es zeigt den Künstler in dem von ihm selbst entworfenen sogenannten Roten Sessel beim Spiel mit einem Hund des Hauses. Obgleich es sich anscheinend um eine häusliche Szene handelt, ist Stuck sowohl auf dem ursprünglichen Photo wie auch in Wilsons Tableau eher wie für einen Auftritt in der Öffentlichkeit gekleidet. Das Klangenvironment besteht aus dem Gewinsel und Gebell eines Hundes.

Hunde treten in Robert Wilsons Environment zweimal in Erscheinung, hier und im letzten Tableau in Marys Zimmer. Im Zusammenhang mit einer Szene in Wilsons monumentalem Bühnenwerk *the CIVIL warS* von 1984, in der Friedrich der Große zunächst mit einem Hund spielt und diesen anschließend erschießt, wurde behauptet, ein bellender oder knurrender Hund hätte für Robert Wilson eine bestimmte persönliche Bedeutung.

Im Unterschied zu den übrigen Tableaus des Environments *Robert Wilson/ Villa Stuck* sind diejenigen in Speisesaal, Boudoir und Rauchsalon von jedem dieser Räume aus zur Gänze sichtbar, weshalb sie im Zusammenspiel betrachtet werden sollten. Im Speisesaal steht der jugendliche, gutaussehende, frisch verheiratete Franz von Stuck im Zenit seines künstlerischen Ruhms und Wirkens, die Bauarbeiten an seiner Villa sind zu dieser Zeit in vollem Gang; im Boudoir ist er fünfzig Jahre alt und sieht sich immer häufiger der Kritik ausgesetzt, sein Werk sei unzeitgemäß, ja unerheblich.[15] Dem Betrachter des Speisesaal-Tableaus, einer der wenigen verherrlichenden Darstellungen Stucks in Wilsons Environment, ist also gleichzeitig das Tableau im Boudoir vor Augen, eine Gegenüberstellung, die von der Vergänglichkeit des Lebens (und des Ruhms) erzählt. Als wollte er dies noch stärker betonen, hat Wilson Franz von Stucks Totenmaske (und Herbstblätter) auf den Regalen der Bibliothek am Eingang zu diesem Tableau plaziert.

Atelier Friedrich Müller/Theodor Hilsdorf, *Franz von Stuck mit seinem Hund*, 1914 (Kat. 37)

gen, gelegentlich ins Grobe abgleitenden »Bauernjungen« mit »langen Gliedern und breitem schwarzhaarigen Bauernschädel« beschreibt,[42] stammte aus einem Bergdorf (Oberammergau) und hatte es über die Schnitzschule, Kunstgewerbeschule und Kunstakademie »zu etwas gebracht«. Nach Jahren des bohemehaften Herumtrödelns hatte Gwinner – bereits sein Name verpflichtete zum Erfolg – einen überraschenden künstlerischen Durchbruch auf einer Secession-Ausstellung dank der Beteiligung von fünf in prächtige Goldrahmen gefaßte Gemälden erlebt, einem *Raub der Proserpina* und »vier bescheidene(n) Genossen in dem handlichen Sofaformat, alle aber mythologischen Charakters.«[43] Wie Stuck mit Bruno Piglhein über einen frühen Förderer verfügte, besaß auch Gwinner einen Akademieprofessor als Protektor. Mehr aus wirtschaftlichem Kalkül hatte Gwinner sich auf mythologische Themen spezialisiert, was sich als erfolgversprechende Methode erwies: »Man malte etwas Lustiges, wie's einem gerade einfiel, und erfand sich nachher einen recht blöd' wirkenden Titel mit alten Göttern. Nichts

einfacher als das! Und man hatte so gleich die im Handel geschätzte persönliche Note, die einem nicht auswendig genug an seinen Werken kleben kann, weil sie ihren praktischen Zweck verfehlt, wenn nicht auch der Begriffsstutzigste sie sofort bemerkt und davon spricht.«[44] Besondere Aufmerksamkeit sollte Gwinner mit dem Gemälde *Der Friede vertreibt die Kriegsdämonen von der Erde* erregen – eine Parodie auf Stucks Gemälde *Der Krieg* –, das den Maler zu weiteren Versuchen reizte und ihm den Titel eines ›Friedens-Gwinner‹ einbrachte.

Der gesellschaftliche und künstlerische Erfolg des jungen Gwinner verlief in ähnlichen Bahnen wie Stucks Aufstieg. Zu Wohlstand gekommen, erbaute Gwinner sich zunächst nach eigenen Entwürfen eine Villa mit Atelier in einem Münchner Vorort, sodann eine palastartige Luxusvilla im Herzogpark, die »über die Grenzen Deutschlands hinaus den Ruf einer Sehenswürdigkeit« besaß.[45] Nach der Ernennung zum Professor folgte die Berufung in den persönlichen Adel, und fortan latinisierte der Maler seinen Vornamen, um seine Werke als Antonius von

Smoking Salon

Visible from both the dining room and the boudoir is a small salon to which gentlemen would retire following the evening meal to smoke.[16] The heavy wooden doorway which separates the smoking salon from the dining room, its lintel bearing a carved serpent, functions in Robert Wilson's tableau as a frame for a three-dimensional, painted landscape based on a photograph taken by Franz von Stuck.

The extreme theatricality, indeed artificiality, which one finds in the Villa Stuck — and in the adjacent tableau, *Dining Room* — is intensified by Robert Wilson in the smoking salon. A study photograph of a carriageway lined with birch trees, attributed to Stuck and presumably taken in 1890 during a sojourn at the Osternberg artists' colony,[17] is transposed by Wilson into a multi-layered theater set. A live tree trunk over three-and-a-half meters high, stripped of its natural leaves and then decorated with meticulously handmade, artificial leaves, stands erect in a foreshortened, sloping, painterly foreground designed to create the illusion of distance. Although Franz von Stuck did not produce a painting of this image, Wilson commissioned Alfons Ostermeier to create an exact facsimile of the photographic landscape as if Franz von Stuck had painted it.

In a previous exhibition, *The Night Before The Day*, organized by the Museum of Fine Arts in Boston in 1991 (see page 14 ff.), Robert Wilson created a prologue which incorporated his own photographic studies of trees, taken as part of his research for his 1988 production *The Forest* in Berlin, a collaboration with Heiner Müller and David Byrne. In the same year he created a landscape of "excavations of time and space" for his exhibition at the Centre Pompidou in Paris (see page 20). Two years later, at the Museum Boijmans Van Beuningen in Rotterdam, his exhibition *Portrait, Still Life, Landscape* concluded with a (post-nuclear) landscape which he described as the "spiritual" part of the installation (see page 27). This fascination with issues of landscape takes an interesting turn in the present tableau. Various levels of displacement occur: a photograph becomes a "painting," a two-dimensional construction becomes three-dimensional, a "real" tree becomes artificial, reality becomes illusion becomes real.

Rauchsalon

Vom Speisesaal wie auch vom Boudoir aus ist ein kleiner Salon sichtbar, in den sich die Herren nach dem Abendessen zum Rauchen zurückzuziehen pflegten.[16] Der massiv hölzerne, von einer in den Türsturz geschnitzten Schlange gekrönte Türrahmen, der den Rauchsalon vom Speisesaal trennt, dient in Robert Wilsons Tableau als Rahmen für eine dreidimensionale gemalte Landschaft nach einer von Franz von Stuck aufgenommenen Photographie.

Die ausgeprägte Kulissenhaftigkeit, ja Künstlichkeit, die die Villa – und die Installation im angrenzenden Speisesaal – kennzeichnet, ist im Tableau im Rauchsalon noch einmal gesteigert. Wilson hat hierzu eine photographische Studie von einem von Birken gesäumten Karrenweg, die Stuck zugeschrieben wird und vermutlich 1890 während eines Aufenthalts in der Künstlerkolonie Osternberg entstanden ist,[17] in eine vielschichtige Bühnenkulisse umgesetzt. Ein echter, mehr als dreieinhalb Meter hoher Baumstamm, entblättert und anschließend mit überaus detailgenau von Hand nachgebildeten Blättern verziert, steht in einem verkürzten, ansteigenden gemalten Vordergrund, der die Illusion von Ferne erzeugen soll. Obgleich Franz von Stuck niemals ein Gemälde nach diesem Photo schuf, beauftragte Wilson Alfons Ostermeier mit der Schaffung einer genauen, wie von Stuck gemalten Nachbildung der photographischen Landschaft.

In einer früheren Ausstellung, *The Night Before The Day*, die 1991 vom Museum of Fine Arts in Boston organisiert wurde und auf die im vorliegenden Band, Seite 16, näher eingegangen wird, gestaltete Robert Wilson einen Prolog, der eigene photographische Studien von Bäumen einschloß; er hatte sie im Rahmen seiner Vorarbeiten für die Inszenierung von *The Forest*, einer 1988 in Berlin uraufgeführten Gemeinschaftsarbeit mit Heiner Müller und David Byrne, aufgenommen. Im selben Jahr schuf er für seine Ausstellung im Pariser Centre Georges Pompidou (siehe Seite 18) eine Landschaft, die Assoziationen mit »Ausgrabungen von Zeit und Raum« hervorrufen sollte. Zwei Jahre später schloß die Ausstellung *Portrait, Still Life, Landscape* im Museum Boijmans Van Beuningen in Rotterdam mit einer (an eine Atomwüste erinnernden) Landschaft, die Wilson als den »geistigen« Teil der Installation bezeichnete (siehe Seite 26). Dieses Fasziniertsein von Landschaft erfährt eine interessante Wendung im Rauchsalon-Tableau. Es gibt ›Verschiebungen‹ auf mehreren Ebenen: Aus einem Photo wird ein ›Gemälde‹, aus einem zweidimensionalen Gebilde ein dreidimensionales, aus einem echten Baum ein künstlicher. Wirklichkeit wird Illusion, die wiederum real ist.

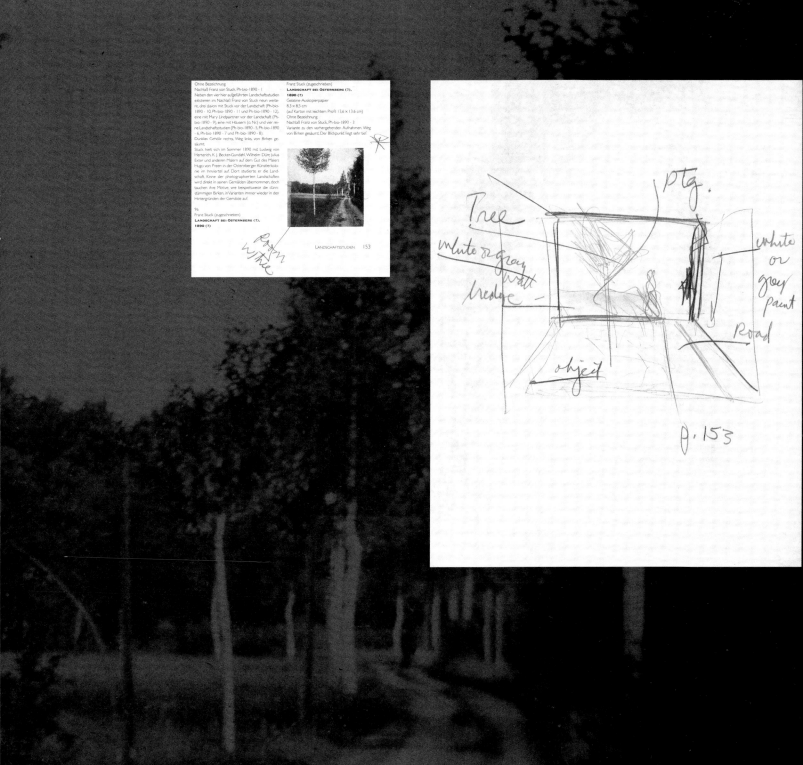

"Here, painting takes on a cultic significance; the production of art becomes a sacred act. Here, a painter does not 'work,' a genius blessed by the gods 'creates.'"[18] Franz von Stuck's magnificently decorated atelier with its medieval tapestries, decorated ceiling, marble columns, and altar dedicated to his own paintings, was the stage on which he proclaimed his genius, marketed his paintings, and hosted special feasts, such as that for his fiftieth birthday. It is in this temple consecrated to art that one finds Robert Wilson's most extravagant tableau in the Villa Stuck.

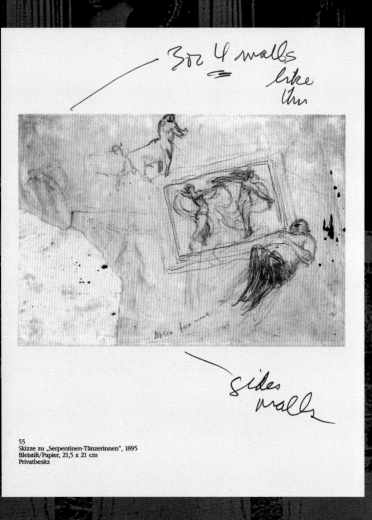

55
Skizze zu „Serpentinen-Tänzerinnen", 1895
Bleistift/Papier, 21,5 x 21 cm
Privatbesitz

A large dark brown wooden square, 4.75 meters long and 2.75 meters high, is divided into two rooms. The first is closed, its interior only visible through two circular windows, one set lower for children. The walls are decorated with pencil drawings of centaurs and swirling dancers, Serpentine dancers, on what appears to be aged, slightly discolored paper. A hare sits on the floor. This room is dedicated not to Franz von Stuck but to the American turn-of-the-century dancer Loïe Fuller, whose Serpentine Dance took Europe by storm in the early 1890s. Her spectacular use of movement, light, and voluminous fabric brought ecstatic reviews of her first appearance in Germany on December 10, 1892:

»Hier wird das Malen zum Kultakt, das künstlerische Schaffen zur sakralen Handlung. Hier ›arbeitet‹ kein Maler, sondern hier ›erschafft‹ das von den Göttern begnadete Genie.«[18] Franz von Stucks herrlich ausgestaltetes Atelier mit seinen mittelalterlichen Tapisserien, der verzierten Decke, den Marmorsäulen und dem seinen eigenen Gemälden geweihten Altar war die Bühne, auf der er seine Genialität proklamierte, seine Gemälde vermarktete und besondere Feste wie das zu seinem 50. Geburtstag ausrichtete. In diesem Kunsttempel hat Robert Wilson sein extravagantestes Tableau innerhalb des Environments *Villa Stuck* realisiert.

Ein 4,75 m langes und 2,75 m hohes blockartiges Gebilde aus dunkelbraunem Holz ist in zwei Räume aufgeteilt. Der erste Raum ist geschlossen, einsehbar nur durch zwei runde Fenster, von denen eines für Kinder etwas niedriger angebracht wurde. Die Wände sind geschmückt mit Bleistiftzeichnungen von Kentauren und wirbelnden Tänzerinnen – sogenannten Serpentintänzerinnen – auf einem Untergrund, der wie gealtertes, leicht verfärbtes Papier wirkt. Auf dem Boden sitzt ein Hase. Dieser Raum ist weniger Franz von Stuck als vielmehr der amerikanischen Tänzerin Loïe Fuller gewidmet, die Anfang der neunziger Jahre des vorigen Jahrhunderts mit ihrem Serpentintanz Europa im Sturm eroberte. Bei ihrem ersten Auftritt in Deutschland am 10. Dezember 1892 erhielt sie für ihre spektakuläre Darbietung, eine Mischung aus Tanz und Lichtshow unter Verwendung von riesigen, sich bauschenden Stoffbahnen, begeisterte Kritiken:

»Die Bühne stellt eine phantastisch ausgestattete Höhle vor. Durch eine Felsspalte betritt Miß Fuller die Szene. Plötzlich bestrahlt elektrisches Licht ihre schöne Gestalt. Sie beginnt sich wie ein Kreisel zu drehen, die Falten ihres langen, weißen, mit Schlangen und Schmetterlingen bestickten Seidenkleides heben sich und bilden im Wirbel des Tanzes Figuren ... Die stets wechselnden Reflexe und Farben des elektrischen Lichtes tragen wesentlich dazu bei, den Effekt der ganzen Vorführung derartig zu erhöhen, daß die Zuschauer sich in den Glauben versetzt fühlen könnten, Miß Fuller in einer diamantenen Atmosphäre tanzen zu sehen, sodaß auch in dieser Hinsicht die Bezeichnung Serpentintänzerin vollkommen gerechtfertigt erscheint.«[19]

Obgleich es keinen eindeutigen Beleg dafür gibt, daß Franz von Stuck jemals einer Darbietung Loïe Fullers beigewohnt hat, steht außer Zweifel, daß die ›Göttin des Lichts‹ die Inspiration für seine 1895 entstandenen (und hier abgebildeten) Zeichnungen von zwei Serpentintänzerinnen und das nahezu identische Relief *Tänzerinnen* im Musiksalon sowie für die Photographien war, die er ab 1907 von seiner Tochter Mary als Serpentintänzerin machte.[20] Daß Wilson ausgerechnet diese Werke in seinem Tableau zitiert, kann angesichts seiner vielfach belegten Passion für den Tanz nicht überraschen. Auf die Geschichte von Miss Bird Hoffman, einer Tanzlehrerin, die Wilson half, eine Sprachstörung zu überwinden, ist ebenso häufig verwiesen worden wie auf den Einfluß, den Tänzerinnen und Tänzer wie Martha Graham, Merce Cunningham und Alwin Nikolais auf sein Werk ausgeübt haben. Wilson selbst hat einmal gesagt: »Aber mein ganzes Werk ist Tanz.«[21]

Das Klangenvironment für diesen Raum – das Geräusch von Wasser – soll an den Ertrinkungstod von König Ludwig II. erinnern. Ursprünglich war es für ein anderes Tableau im Atelier vorgesehen (siehe Seite 35).

"The stage is like a magically decorated cave. Miss Fuller enters the scene through a gap in the rock. Suddenly, her attractive figure is illuminated by electric light. She begins to spin like a top, the folds of her long white silk dress, embroidered with snakes and butterflies, rising to form figures in the whirlwind of her dance.... The ever-changing reflections and colors of the electric light play an important part in enhancing the overall effect of the performance, to such a degree that the spectators may feel they are watching Miss Fuller dance in an atmosphere of diamonds, so that in this respect, too, the appellation 'serpentine dancer' appears entirely warranted."[19]

Although there is no direct evidence that Franz von Stuck saw a performance by Loie Fuller, there is no doubt that the so-called Goddess of Light inspired his 1895 drawings of two Serpentine dancers (copied here), an almost identical hand painted relief in the music salon, *Tänzerinnen*, as well as photographs of his daughter Mary as a Serpentine dancer from 1907.[20] That Robert Wilson chose to cite these works in his tableau is not surprising; his passion for dance has been well documented. The story of Miss Bird Hoffman, a dance instructor who helped cure Wilson of a speech impediment, has been recounted many times, as has the influence of dancers such as Martha Graham, Merce Cunningham, and Alwin Nikolais on his work. Wilson himself has noted, "But all my work is dance."[21]

The sound score for this room, that of water, was designed to evoke associations of the drowning of King Ludwig II. This was originally planned for another tableau in the atelier (see page 35).

The second component of the tableau, a room which opens to the rear of Franz von Stuck's atelier, contains a three-dimensional transposition of a painting by Stuck titled *Trunkene Kentaurin* (Drunken Centaur) from c.1889.[22] Although Wilson's tableau has the characteristic of a still life, such as those he created for the Rotterdam exhibition, *Portrait, Still Life, Landscape* (see pages 24ff.), an important difference between the two environments is that the Villa Stuck tableau is a transposition of the work of art, not the object itself, and one which is able to be physically entered by the viewer. The curator of the Rotterdam exhibition, Piet de Jonge, noted in a recent letter that the traditional art historical categories of portrait, still life, and landscape were applied by Wilson in Rotterdam in a very untraditional way. "They were referring to the distance of the viewer towards the object."[23]

Wilson's choice of *Trunkene Kentaurin*, rather than better known works by Stuck such as *Die Sünde* or *Wächter des Paradieses*, for a three-dimensional tableau, is unexpected but instructive. For Stuck's contemporaries and admirers, such as Otto Julius Bierbaum, who wrote about his work in 1893, *Trunkene Kentaurin* was a particularly artificial work whose subject "would be more at home in the 'Antiquities Room at the Academy' than in the wild."[24] In his commentary on the still life section of the Rotterdam exhibition, however, Robert Wilson noted, "I hate naturalism. I think to be natural is a lie.... If I accept the fact that I am artificial, and my behavior, then I can perhaps be more natural."[25]

Wilson's *Trunkene Kentaurin* not only recalls the *Phantastische Jagd* one floor below in the music salon, it brings us once again into Stuck's universe of fabulous creatures. Ancient vessels on the ground remind us, as Hans Ottomeyer has pointed out, "of an ancient Arcadian dream world, where Stuck makes time stand still in order to capture a fleeting moment."[26]

Der zweite Bestandteil des Tableaus, ein Raum, der in den hinteren Bereich von Franz von Stucks Atelier führt, enthält eine dreidimensionale Umsetzung eines um 1889 entstandenen Stuckschen Gemäldes mit dem Titel *Trunkene Kentaurin*.[22] Wilsons Tableau hat zwar den Charakter eines Stillebens, ähnlich denen, die er für die Rotterdamer Ausstellung *Portrait, Still Life, Landscape* schuf (siehe Seite 26ff.), doch besteht ein wesentlicher Unterschied zwischen beiden Environments darin, daß es sich beim Tableau in der Villa Stuck nicht um das Kunstobjekt selbst, sondern eben um eine Umsetzung desselben handelt, die für den Betrachter begehbar ist. Piet de Jonge, schrieb jüngst in einem Brief, Wilson habe in Rotterdam die traditionellen kunsthistorischen

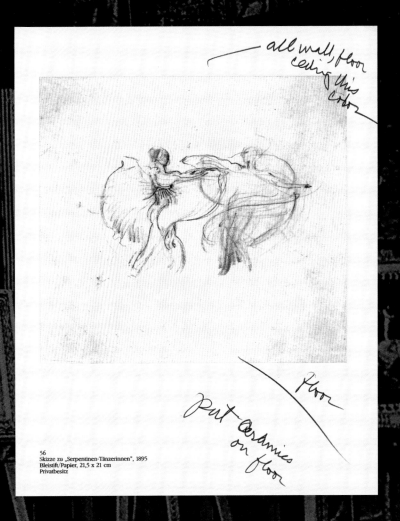

56
Skizze zu „Serpentinen-Tänzerinnen", 1895
Bleistift/Papier, 21,5 x 21 cm
Privatbesitz

Gattungen Porträt, Stilleben und Landschaft in einem höchst untraditionellen Sinn angewandt: »Sie bezogen sich auf die jeweilige Entfernung des Betrachters vom Gegenstand.«[23]

Daß Wilson die *Trunkene Kentaurin* und nicht bekanntere Werke Stucks wie *Die Sünde* oder *Wächter des Paradieses* als Vorlage für ein dreidimensionales Tableau auswählte, ist zugleich überraschend und aufschlußreich. Für Stucks Zeitgenossen und Bewunderer war die *Trunkene Kentaurin* ein besonders artifizielles Werk. So schrieb Otto Julius Bierbaum 1893, die dargestellte Kreatur würde sich »eher im ›Antikensaal der Akademie‹ zu Hause

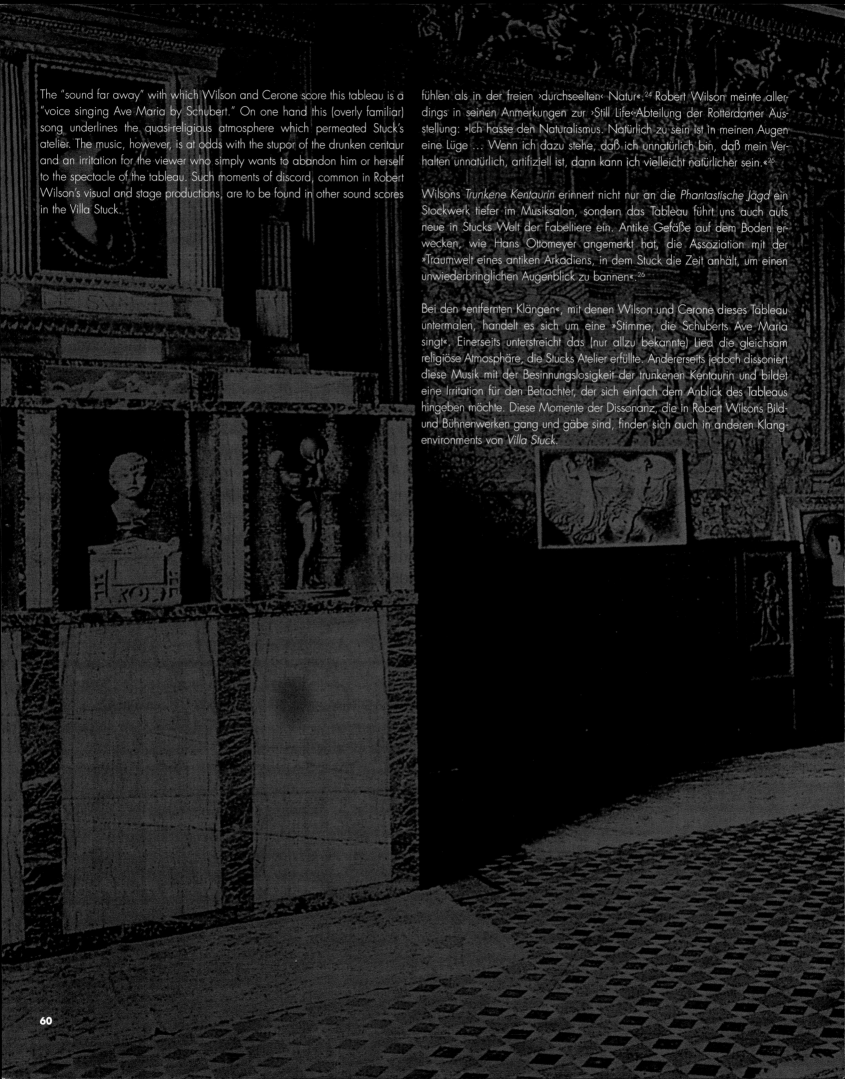

The "sound far away" with which Wilson and Cerone score this tableau is a "voice singing Ave Maria by Schubert." On one hand this (overly familiar) song underlines the quasi-religious atmosphere which permeated Stuck's atelier. The music, however, is at odds with the stupor of the drunken centaur and an irritation for the viewer who simply wants to abandon him or herself to the spectacle of the tableau. Such moments of discord, common in Robert Wilson's visual and stage productions, are to be found in other sound scores in the Villa Stuck.

fühlen als in der freien ›durchseelten‹ Natur«.[24] Robert Wilson meinte allerdings in seinen Anmerkungen zur ›Still Life‹-Abteilung der Rotterdamer Ausstellung: »Ich hasse den Naturalismus. Natürlich zu sein ist in meinen Augen eine Lüge … Wenn ich dazu stehe, daß ich unnatürlich bin, daß mein Verhalten unnatürlich, artifiziell ist, dann kann ich vielleicht natürlicher sein.«[25]

Wilsons Trunkene Kentaurin erinnert nicht nur an die Phantastische Jagd ein Stockwerk tiefer im Musiksalon, sondern das Tableau führt uns auch aufs neue in Stucks Welt der Fabeltiere ein. Antike Gefäße auf dem Boden erwecken, wie Hans Ottomeyer angemerkt hat, die Assoziation mit der »Traumwelt eines antiken Arkadiens, in dem Stuck die Zeit anhält, um einen unwiederbringlichen Augenblick zu bannen«.[26]

Bei den »entfernten Klängen«, mit denen Wilson und Cerone dieses Tableau untermalen, handelt es sich um eine »Stimme, die Schuberts Ave Maria singt«. Einerseits unterstreicht das (nur allzu bekannte) Lied die gleichsam religiöse Atmosphäre, die Stucks Atelier erfüllte. Andererseits jedoch dissoniert diese Musik mit der Besinnungslosigkeit der trunkenen Kentaurin und bildet eine Irritation für den Betrachter, der sich einfach dem Anblick des Tableaus hingeben möchte. Diese Momente der Dissonanz, die in Robert Wilsons Bild- und Bühnenwerken gang und gäbe sind, finden sich auch in anderen Klangenvironments von Villa Stuck.

seen thru a door

3
Betrunkene Kentaurin, 1892
Öl/Holz, 25 x 73 cm

3D here

Room

Letters decorate the walls of this room, letters meticulously copied by Alfons Ostermeier in the Sütterlin script common in Germany at the turn-of-the-century. One is addressed to Martin Gerlach, the publisher of *Karten und Vignetten*, in which Stuck published many drawings and caricatures at the beginning of his career. Stuck's letter to Friedrich August von Kaulbach (read aloud in the sound environment in the *Vestibule*) is also included as well as a private letter to his beloved daughter Mary, written in the last years of his life: "And now, fond embraces and kisses to you all. And especially to you, Mary my dear, from your ever-affectionate Bawali."

Robert Wilson is fascinated with language not only in its spoken but also in its written form. Since the beginning of his career, but especially in recent years, he has incorporated letters and words into drawings and installations (see the exhibition in Cincinnati in 1980 and his installation *Waterjug Boy* at the Cologne Art Fair in 1996, based on an Indian legend). In the present tableau Wilson has incorporated a form of writing which is no longer in use and which cannot be interpreted by many German speaking adults today. By selecting correspondence written over a forty-year period in the original Sütterlin script, Wilson has created a sequential narrative which is able to be deciphered only with difficulty, if at all.

In the center of the room, a masked figure of cupid coyly holds an arrow to his mouth in one hand and a large fan in the other. The image on which the figure is based is a popular and inexpensive reproduction of a painting by Franz Stuck which was distributed in 1889 by the Photographische Union. Stuck was among the first artists in Munich to use photographic reproductions as a medium to promote his work, to gain additional income, and to ensure mass distribution of his images. This particular work, *Amor auf dem Maskenball* (Cupid at a Masked Ball), is one of many which Stuck produced on the theme of Cupid in the late 1880s.[27] This particular image was possibly inspired by an artist's ball in Munich in 1887 which was attended by guests dressed as gods. Among the most popular costumes was that of Cupid.[28] It also recalls the legendary Fasching Ball attended by Franz and Mary von Stuck in Roman costume, which is referred to in Wilson's tableau in the dining room.

The original use of this small room which is adjacent to both the atelier and Franz von Stuck's bedroom has not been determined. In the earliest plans for the Villa Stuck it is simply referred to as "room." Oral tradition suggests two possible uses, one as a dressing room for Franz von Stuck, the other as a room to store his paintbrushes and supplies.

The saccharine sweetness of this tableau, its "am I not adorable" appeal, is rudely disrupted by Robert Wilson's and Peter Cerone's sound environment, the sound of a child learning to play exercises from Béla Bartók's *Mikrokosmos* (1926–1937).

Zimmer

Briefe schmücken die Wände dieses Zimmers, Briefe, die von Alfons Ostermeier akribisch in Sütterlinschrift kopiert wurden. Einer davon ist an Martin Gerlach gerichtet, den Herausgeber und Verleger des Vorlagenwerks *Karten und Vignetten*, in dem Stuck zu Beginn seiner Künstlerlaufbahn zahlreiche Zeichnungen und Karikaturen veröffentlichte. Stucks Schreiben an Friedrich August von Kaulbach, der für das Klangenvironment im Vestibül Verwendung gefunden hat, wurde ebenso einbezogen wie der Brief an die geliebte Tochter Mary, den er in seinen letzten Lebensjahren geschrieben hatte: »Und nun seid innig umarmt und geküßt alle miteinander. Und besonders Du von Deinem Dich immer innig liebenden Bawali.«

Robert Wilson fasziniert Sprache nicht nur in der gesprochenen, sondern auch in ihrer geschriebenen Form. Vor allem in jüngerer Zeit bezieht er Buchstaben und Wörter in Zeichnungen und Installationen ein (vgl. die Ausstellung 1980 in Cincinnati und seine Installation *Waterjug Boy* auf der Kölner Kunstmesse 1996, der eine indianische Legende zugrunde liegt). In unserem Tableau hat er eine Schrift verwendet, die längst nicht mehr im Gebrauch ist und die viele Deutsche heute nicht mehr lesen können. Durch die Auswahl von Briefen aus einem fast vierzig Jahre umspannenden Zeitraum hat Wilson eine Erzählung geschaffen, die sich vom Betrachter nur mühsam, wenn überhaupt, entziffern läßt.

In der Mitte des Zimmers hält Amor schüchtern einen Pfeil an seinem Mund, in der anderen Hand hat er einen großen Fächer. Die Bildvorlage für diese Figur ist eine populäre und billige Reproduktion eines Gemäldes von Franz von Stuck, die 1889 von der Photographischen Union vertrieben wurde. Stuck war einer der ersten Künstler in München, die in photographischen Reproduktionen ein Mittel sahen, um für ihre Werke Reklame zu machen. Er erzielte damit zusätzliche Einkünfte und sorgte für die Massenverbreitung seiner Bilderfindungen. Unser Bild *Amor auf dem Maskenball* ist eines von vielen die Figur Amors thematisierenden Werken, die Stuck in der zweiten Hälfte der 1880er Jahre schuf.[27] Inspiriert wurde es möglicherweise durch einen Künstlerball 1887 in München, zu dem sich die Besucher als Götter verkleidet einfanden. Besonders beliebt war dabei die Verkleidung als Amor.[28] Zugleich erinnert es an den legendären Faschingsball, dem Franz und Mary von Stuck in römischem Kostüm beiwohnten und auf den sich Wilsons Tableau im Speisesaal bezieht.

Wozu dieses kleine Zimmer, das sowohl an das Atelier wie an Franz von Stucks Schlafzimmer angrenzt, ursprünglich genutzt wurde, ist bisher nicht eindeutig geklärt. In den frühesten Plänen für die Villa Stuck wird es schlicht ›Zimmer‹ genannt. Mündlichen Überlieferungen zufolge könnte es entweder als Ankleidezimmer für Franz von Stuck oder aber als ›Pinselraum‹, einem Raum zur Aufbewahrung von Pinseln und anderem Malerbedarf, gedient haben.

Der süßliche ›Ist-er-nicht-niedlich‹-Charakter dieses Tableaus wird rüde durchbrochen durch Robert Wilsons und Peter Cerones Klangenvironment, die Aufnahme eines klavierspielenden Kindes, das die Übungen aus Béla Bartóks *Mikrokosmos* (1926–1937) zu spielen lernt.

Registered — Geschützt.

1880
Franz Stuck
Amor auf dem Maskenball

MODERNE GALLERIE.

PHOTOGRAPHISCHE UNION IN MÜNCHEN

New-York: Geo. Kirchner & Co.

Franz von Stuck's Bedroom

It is in Franz von Stuck's most intimate and private space in the Villa, in his bedroom, that Robert Wilson most clearly articulates the vanity, the ambition, even the self-exaltation, which motivated Franz von Stuck and which, to a large extent, defines the character of the Villa Stuck. Wilson expresses this in his tableau by incorporating a photograph, attributed to Mary and Franz von Stuck, of an eminent turn-of-the-century actor, Ernst von Possart,[29] in the role of Napoleon. In 1905 Possart retired from the position of General Director of Munich's prestigious Royal Theater. On this occasion Franz von Stuck produced a drawing of Possart, based on this photograph, which was distributed the following year as an inexpensive reproduction,[30] on which he inscribed "To the great artist/Ernst von Possart/28th September 1905/with respect and admiration/Franz/Stuck." In the year prior to his retirement, Possart had re-performed his most famous roles, among them, Napoleon.

Robert Wilson's 1987 environment dedicated to Napoleon, *Memory of a Revolution*, is documented on pages 14f. of this volume. Numerous commentators have noted Wilson's predilection for larger-than-life characters in his work. Jill Johnston has written that "in Wilson's oeuvre there are three types of heros: the (male) child, the disabled, and the fabulously great.... They certainly are personas with which Wilson himself closely identifies."[31]

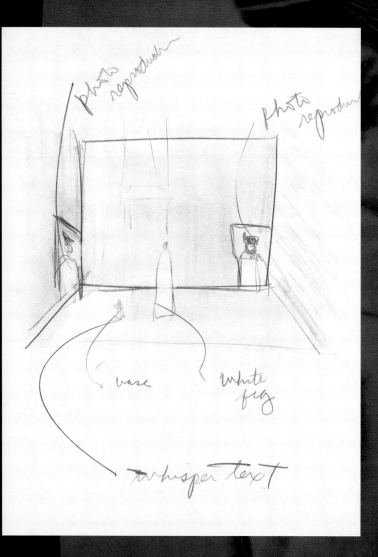

Franz von Stucks Schlafzimmer

In Franz von Stucks intimstem, privatestem Raum innerhalb des Hauses, seinem Schlafzimmer, hat Robert Wilson eindeutig die Eitelkeit, den Ehrgeiz, man möchte sogar sagen: die Selbstverherrlichung unterstrichen, die Stuck befeuerte und die in einem hohem Grade den Charakter seiner Villa prägt. Wilson bringt dies in seinem Tableau zum Ausdruck, indem er eine Mary und Franz von Stuck zugeschriebene Photographie einbezieht, die den berühmten, um die Jahrhundertwende tätigen Schauspieler Ernst von Possart[29] in der Rolle Napoleons zeigt. Im Jahr 1905 nahm Possart seinen Abschied als Generalintendant des renommierten Münchner Hoftheaters. Aus diesem Anlaß porträtierte Stuck ihn in einer Zeichnung, für die diese Photographie als Vorlage diente. Die Zeichnung kam im Jahr darauf als billige Reproduktion[30] auf den Markt, versehen mit der Widmung: »Dem großen Künstler/Ernst von Possart/zum 28. September 1905/Verehrungsvoll/Franz/Stuck«. In seiner letzten Spielzeit hatte Possart noch einmal seine berühmtesten Rollen gespielt, darunter auch die des Napoleon.

Robert Wilsons Environment *Erinnerung an eine Revolution* aus dem Jahr 1987, die Napoleon gewidmet war, ist im vorliegenden Band, Seite 14f., näher beschrieben. Zahlreiche Kommentatoren haben auf Wilsons Vorliebe für überlebensgroße Gestalten in seinem Werk hingewiesen. Nach Auffassung von Jill Johnston gibt es »in Wilsons Œuvre dreierlei Heldentypen: das (männliche) Kind, den Behinderten und den sagenumwobenen Großen ... Sie sind ohne Frage Figuren, mit denen sich Wilson identifiziert«.[31] Nach Aussage von Wilson selbst sieht er in diesen Figuren allerdings eher »mythische Personen. Der Mann auf der Straße hat eine gewisse Ahnung von Einstein, von Freud, von Josef Stalin, es ist also ein wenig wie mit den griechischen Mythen in den Zeiten des griechischen Theaters, wo die Zuschauer, die kamen, um eine Geschichte dargestellt zu sehen, ein bestimmtes Wissen teilten, mit der Geschichte vertraut waren ... Wir haben also bereits gewisse Assoziationen, Bilder, Geschichten im Kopf, wenn wir uns dieses Stück ansehen wollen.«[32] Wenn Wilson ein Bild Napoleons in Franz von Stucks Schlafzimmer anbringt, stützt er sich auf dieses gemeinsame Wissen und erweckt sogleich die Assoziation übersteigerter Ehrgeiz und damit verbundenes Verderben.

In die Mitte von Stucks Schlafzimmer hat Wilson ein kleines Notizbuch mit aufgeschlagenen weißen Seiten gelegt, das von oben angestrahlt wird. Zwei vergrößerte Bilder von Possart als Napoleon hängen nebeneinander an einer der Wände. Obgleich sie aus der Entfernung wie Photos wirken (Wilson hatte in seinem ersten Entwurf für dieses Tableau tatsächlich Photos vorgesehen), wurden sie in Wirklichkeit von Alfons Ostermeier von Hand gezeichnet und in Airbrush-Technik gemalt. Ebenso wie im Tableau für den Rauchsalon wird also ein Originalkunstwerk einem Prozeß der Übertragung und Umsetzung unterzogen: Ein Photo, das von Franz von Stuck vergrößert, abgepaust, zeichnerisch ausgefeilt und daraufhin zum Zwecke der Verbreitung photographisch reproduziert worden war, ist von Robert Wilson aufs neue vergrößert und in Malerei übertragen worden.

Das Löwengebrüll, das dieses Tableau untermalt, beschwört zahlreiche Assoziationen herauf: Kraft, eine gewisse Würde, raubtierhafte und sogar sexuelle Potenz. Dadurch, daß er Napoleon – stellvertretend für Stuck – als älteren Mann darstellt, entzieht Wilson solchen gedanklichen Verbindungen jedoch brüsk den Boden. Das Gebrüll wirkt hier leer, grotesk, ja beinahe schon peinlich.

Wilson himself has argued that the figures are not necessarily ones with which he identifies but "mythic subjects. The man on the street knows something about Einstein, something about Freud, about Joseph Stalin, so it's a little like the Greek myths and the time of the Greek theater where the audience came sharing a certain knowledge, a story already known … so we have already some associations, some images, some stories in mind when we come and see this piece."[32] By placing an image of Napoleon in Franz von Stuck's bedroom, Wilson draws on this shared knowledge and immediately evokes associations of great ambition — and its ruin.

In the center of Franz von Stuck's bedroom Wilson has placed a small notebook with blank pages which is spotlit from above. Two enlargements of Possart as Napoleon hang next to one another on one wall.

Although from a distance they appear to be photographic (which Wilson originally planned in his first concept for this tableau), they are in fact hand drawn and airbrushed by Alfons Ostermeier. As in the tableau in the smoking salon, an original work of art has undergone a process of translation and transformation: a photograph which was enlarged by Franz von Stuck and then traced, drawn, and photographically reproduced for distribution purposes has, in Robert Wilson's hands, been enlarged once again and painted.

The sound of a roaring lion for this tableau evokes numerous associations — power, a certain nobility, the predatory, even sexual prowess. By presenting Napoleon, and by implication, Stuck, as an elderly man, Wilson brutally undercuts such aspirations. The roaring becomes hollow, grotesque, even embarrassing.

Bathroom

Franz von Stuck's bathroom, situated between his bedroom and that of his wife, retains little of its original character; its "Roman" marble bath and the platform on which it rested, as well as the original wall tiles, have long been removed. Nevertheless it remains one of the most interesting spaces in the Villa Stuck, with its vault ceiling, mask above the door, and a frieze of reliefs from the classical world.

It is in this space that Robert Wilson once again brings us into Franz von Stuck's world of fabulous creatures. A centaur over 160 cm long defies gravity by climbing vertically up a wall. The three-dimensional figure is based on a painting by Stuck, *Frühling* (Spring), *c.*1920, in which the centaur plays a flute in a landscape similar to that re-created by Wilson in the smoking salon. In his original concept Robert Wilson considered painting the landscape in *Frühling* on three adjacent walls (see concept drawing right).

The music of a flute in this pure white space, and the presence of an over-sized centaur clambering somewhat awkwardly among the gods in Stuck's frieze, creates a curious mixture of the meditative and the bizarre, which is reinforced by Stefano Scavani's untitled composition, a circular motif composed especially for this installation.

Badezimmer

Franz von Stucks Badezimmer, zwischen seinem Schlafzimmer und dem seiner Frau gelegen, hat nur wenig von seinem ursprünglichen Charakter bewahrt: Das ›römische‹ Marmorbad mitsamt seinem Podest sowie die ursprünglichen Kacheln sind längst entfernt worden. Gleichwohl ist das Badezimmer mit der gewölbten Decke, der Maske über der Tür und dem Fries von antiken Reliefs nach wie vor einer der stimmungsvollsten Räume der Villa Stuck.

In diesem Raum führt uns Robert Wilson erneut in die Stucksche Welt der Fabelwesen. Ein Kentaur von mehr als 160 cm Körperlänge läuft unter Mißachtung der Schwerkraft eine senkrechte Wand hinauf. Die dreidimensionale Gestalt dieses Fabelwesens geht auf ein um 1920 entstandenes Gemälde Stucks mit dem Titel *Frühling* zurück, auf dem der Kentaur Flöte spielt in einer Landschaft ähnlich derjenigen, die Wilson im Rauchsalon nachgebildet hat. Im ursprünglichen Entwurf hatte Robert Wilson erwogen, die Landschaft in *Frühling* auf drei benachbarte Wände zu malen (siehe nebenstehende Konzeptzeichnung).

Die Klänge einer Flöte in diesem rein weißen Raum sowie die Gegenwart eines überdimensionalen Kentauren, der ein wenig unbeholfen inmitten der Götter in Stucks Fries klettert, ergeben eine seltsame Mixtur aus Besinnlichem und Bizarrem, die durch Stefano Scavanis Komposition ohne Titel, ein zyklisch wiederkehrendes Motiv, das speziell für diese Installation entstand, noch verstärkt wird.

34
Frühling, um 1920
Öl/Leinwand, 34,5 x 31,3 cm
Privatbesitz

Mary von Stuck's Bedroom

The American-born widow Mary Lindpaintner née Hoose (1865–1929) was considered at the time of her marriage to Franz von Stuck to be one of Munich's great beauties. Her devotion to Stuck[33] included agreeing to the adoption of Stuck's only daughter, Mary, although her husband had not particularly welcomed her own children into the marriage.[34] Following Stuck's unexpected death in 1928, what had appeared to be an affectionate relationship between the two Marys was permanently shattered in a bitter dispute over the artist's will.[35] The Villa Stuck and most of the family's collection of his paintings were auctioned off. In frenzied bidding Stuck's daughter succeeded in re-purchasing the Villa; Mary von Stuck, seriously ill with cancer, retained the right to live in the Villa but died only a matter of weeks later, on October 27, 1929. At her burial she was described as "a creative woman, an artist and singer whose grasp of technical matters was of great assistance to her husband, and who helped create works of beauty."[36]

Mary von Stuck's bedroom, with its doorway to a terrace overlooking the garden, was certainly one of the most pleasant and inviting rooms in the Villa during Stuck's lifetime. Marcella Wolff, who played regularly with Stuck's daughter, recalls Mary von Stuck as one of the "truly beautiful women I have met in the course of my life … with her blue eyes and regal stature, she looked exactly like the goddess Athena. Her rich Munich dialect provided a certain contrast to her appearance. She showed great kindness and warmth to me, continually showering me with presents. She was the Good Fairy of my childhood."[37]

In his tableau for this room Robert Wilson hung a large photographic reproduction of Mary von Stuck to the left of the terrace door. Transparent, sepia toned, and printed on silk, it is based on a photographic enlargement from around 1900 which was drawn upon and traced by Franz von Stuck in the preparation of a painting of his wife, one of several in which she glances at him (and at us) over her shoulder. A band of light runs the length of the image covering much of Mary's face. The original photograph was probably enlarged by Mary von Stuck herself in the basement of the Villa Stuck, where a photographic laboratory had been installed.

The simple wooden parquet floor in Mary von Stuck's bedroom has been covered with granulate cork. Wilson has placed what appears at first glance to be a pile of sulphur in the middle of the room. A hidden doorway in the bedroom wall has been literally broken open to reveal a secret stairwell from the dining room to the bedroom suites which Stuck would use to escape unwelcome guests. In this space, which Wilson painted yellow, is the third ghost-like figure of Stuck, a pile of sulfur-yellow pigment, and a vacuum cleaner — an unexpected, discordant addition to this space. The sound environment consists of the noise of the vacuum cleaner. In the early hours of the morning of April 25, 1944, the Villa Stuck was struck by fire bombs. The roof and entire second floor of the Villa were severely damaged and fire broke out in the secret stairwell. The broken wall and the unused, empty staircase recall not only the bombing of the Villa Stuck during the Second World War but also the psychological devastation[38] which the artist's death precipitated.

Mary von Stucks Schlafzimmer

Die aus Amerika gebürtige Witwe Mary Lindpaintner geb. Hoose (1865–1929) galt zur Zeit ihrer Eheschließung mit Franz von Stuck als eine der großen Schönheiten Münchens. Sie war Stuck so sehr ergeben,[33] daß sie unter anderem der Adoption von Stucks einziger Tochter, Mary, zustimmte, obgleich umgekehrt ihr Mann ihre eigenen Kinder nicht gerade liebevoll in die Ehe aufgenommen hatte.[34] Nach Stucks überraschendem Tod im Jahr 1928 brach die bis dahin zumindest nach außen hin herzliche Beziehung zwischen beiden Marys wegen erbitterter Erbstreitigkeiten endgültig entzwei.[35] Die Villa Stuck und der Großteil der Gemälde Stucks in Familienbesitz wurden versteigert. In einem wüsten Bietgefecht bekam die Tochter Stucks den Zuschlag für das Anwesen. Der schwer krebskranken Mary von Stuck wiederum wurde das Wohnrecht in der Villa zugesprochen, doch sie starb nur wenige Wochen später, am 27. Oktober 1929. Bei ihrem Begräbnis wurde sie beschrieben als »eine schöpferische Frau, Künstlerin und Sängerin, die mit der Beherrschung technischer Wissenschaften dem Gatten zur Seite war und half, Werke der Schönheit zu schaffen.«[36]

Mary von Stucks Schlafzimmer, von dem eine Tür auf die Terrasse mit Blick über den Garten führte, war zu Lebzeiten Stucks zweifellos einer der angenehmsten Räume der Villa. Marcella Wolff, die regelmäßig mit Stucks Tochter spielte, erinnert sich an Mary von Stuck als eine der »wirklich schönen Frauen, denen ich im Leben begegnet bin … mit ihren blauen Augen und ihrem königlichen Wuchs sah sie wirklich wie Pallas Athene aus, das unverfälschte Münchnerisch, das sie sprach, bildete einen gewissen Kontrast zu ihrer Erscheinung. Sie war von großer Güte und Herzlichkeit zu mir und hat mich dauernd beschenkt als gute Fee meiner Kinderzeit.«[37]

In seinem Tableau für diesen Raum hat Robert Wilson eine großformatige photographische Reproduktion von Mary von Stuck links von der Tür zur Terrasse aufgehängt. Diesem – transparenten – sepiafarbenen Seidendruck liegt eine um 1900 entstandene und vergrößerte Photographie zugrunde, auf die Franz von Stuck im Zuge seiner Vorarbeiten für ein Gemälde seiner Frau gezeichnet und die er abgepaust hat. Es ist eines von mehreren Bildern, auf denen Mary von Stuck ihrem Gatten (und dem Betrachter) über ihre Schulter in die Augen sieht. Ein Lichtstreifen zieht sich der Länge nach über das Bild und verdeckt einen Großteil ihres Gesichts. Das Originalphoto wurde vermutlich von Mary von Stuck im Photolabor im Keller der Villa Stuck vergrößert.

Der einfache Parkettfußboden in diesem Zimmer wurde mit granulierten Korkplatten bedeckt. In die Mitte des Raums plazierte Wilson einen Pulverhaufen, bei dem es sich um Schwefelpuder zu handeln scheint. Eine Geheimtür in der Schlafzimmerwand ist aufgebrochen worden, um den Blick auf eine vom Speisesaal zu den Schlafzimmern führende Geheimtreppe freizugeben, über die sich Stuck vor unwillkommenen Gästen in Sicherheit zu bringen pflegte. In diesem kleinen, schwefelgelb ausgemalten Treppenhaus sieht man die Figur Stucks sowie einen Staubsauger – eine unerwartete und irritierende Ergänzung, die durch das Geräusch eines Staubsaugers noch verstärkt wird. Am 25. April 1944 wurde die Villa Stuck von Brandbomben getroffen. Das Dach und der gesamte zweite Stock der Villa wurden schwer beschädigt, im Schacht der Geheimtreppe brach Feuer aus. Die aufgebrochene Wand und der verlassen wirkende Treppenschacht erinnern nicht nur an die Bombardierung der Villa Stuck sondern auch an die psychischen Schäden infolge des

Dressing Room

The narrow, long room next to Mary von Stuck's bedroom, often described as her "dressing room," was used during her lifetime as a multi-purpose room for domestic activities such as ironing. It is here that Robert Wilson has created a tableau which juxtaposes a live, three-and-a-half-meter long tiger python snake with a late sculptural work by Franz von Stuck, *Monna Vanna*, 1920. The combination of a serpent and a naked female body immediately conjures

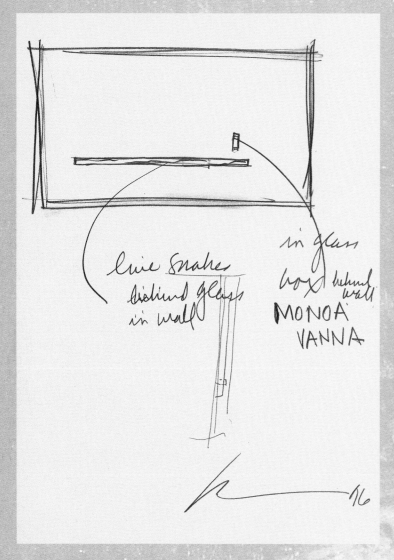

up associations of Stuck's early and highly controversial masterwork, *Die Sünde* (The Sin), from 1891/2.

A false wall runs the length of the room. A narrow glass window in the wall opens on to a box in which the Python lives. Next to the wall, on a narrow plinth, is Franz von Stuck's gilded sculpture of Monna Vanna, a fifteenth-century heroine of the City of Pisa. "When her native town was besieged by a Florentine army, she was prepared to give herself to the enemy *condottiere* in order to save the town and its citizens."[39] The Belgian Symbolist Maurice Maeterlinck, a contemporary of Franz von Stuck, first published his dramatic

Ankleidezimmer

Das schmale, langgezogene Zimmer neben Mary von Stucks Schlafzimmer, vielfach als ihr ›Ankleidezimmer‹ bezeichnet, wurde zu ihren Lebzeiten als Mehrzweckraum für häusliche Arbeiten wie Bügeln genutzt. In diesem Raum hat Robert Wilson ein Tableau gestaltet, das einen lebenden, drei Meter langen Tigerpython und eine späte Skulptur Franz von Stucks mit dem Titel *Monna Vanna* aus dem Jahr 1920 miteinander vereint. Das Nebeneinander einer Schlange und eines nackten weiblichen Körpers erweckt sogleich Assoziationen mit Stucks frühem, höchst umstrittenem Meisterwerk *Die Sünde* von 1891/92.

Eine Zwischenwand verläuft der Länge nach durch das Zimmer. Das schmale Glasfenster in dieser Wand gibt den Blick frei auf einen Kasten – die Behausung der Pythonschlange. Auf einer schmalen Plinthe neben der Wand steht Franz von Stucks vergoldete Skulptur der Monna Vanna, einer Pisaner Heldin aus dem 15. Jahrhundert. »Als ihre Vaterstadt von einem florentinischen Heer belagert wurde, war sie bereit, sich dem feindlichen Condottiere hinzugeben, um dadurch die Stadt und ihre Einwohner zu retten.«[39] Der belgische Symbolist Maurice Maeterlinck, ein Zeitgenosse Franz von Stucks, widmete diesem Sujet 1902 sein Schauspiel *Monna Vanna*. Henri Févriers Oper gleichen Titels, für die Maeterlinck das Libretto schrieb, wurde 1909 in Paris uraufgeführt. Giovanna (oder Vanna) erklärt sich bereit, Prinzivalle von Florenz lediglich mit einem Mantel bekleidet – wie Stucks Skulptur sie zeigt – aufzusuchen, auf daß die Stadt Pisa die Möglichkeit erhalte, sich mit Lebensmitteln und Waffen zu versorgen.

Ist Stucks und jetzt Robert Wilsons Monna Vanna eine bescheidene Maid mit gesenktem Blick, die zweifellos nur notgedrungen bereit ist, sich sexuell hinzugeben, um die Mitbewohner ihrer Stadt zu retten, so verkörpert Franz von Stucks *Sünde*, deren Körper verführerisch mit dem der Schlange verschränkt ist, das genaue Gegenteil: eine Frau, die sich ihrer sexuellen Macht voll und ganz bewußt ist und die den fleischlichen Lüsten frönt. Ungewöhnlich eindringlich beschrieb der zeitgenössische Kunstkritiker Otto Julius Bierbaum *Die Sünde*:

»Die glatte Kälte der schmeidigen Schlangenkraft schläft auf der weichen Wärme des weißen Leibes, der voller Verheißungen lockt und leuchtet. Die schlimme Huldin wartet mit ihren Augen, hinter denen die Hölle brennt. Ganz stille wartet sie, und sicher. Ihre Blicke gehen weit, weit, – bis tief in die Herzen der Menschen. Aber die Schlange mit dem hornigen platten Kopf ist ungeduldig. ... Hüte dich vor der Schlange und der Drohung ihres Blickes. Aber er sieht nur die höllentiefen, schönen Augen der Frau und die blühende Fülle ihres weißen Leibes.«[40]

Sexualität und die Betrachterrolle in der Kunst, insbesondere in der Kunst des 19. Jahrhunderts, sind Themen, mit denen sich die feministische Theorie eingehend auseinandergesetzt hat.[41] Im Mittelpunkt dieser Analysen steht der weibliche Blick und die Frage, ob und wie er den männlichen (und weiblichen) Betrachter fesselt. Begegnete dem männlichen Betrachter in *Die Sünde* ein ausgesprochen sexueller weiblicher Blick, der ihn hilflos machte, so sind in *Monna Vanna* Blick und Körper demütig. Dem Betrachter (der Betrachterin) steht es frei, ihren Körper ungehemmt und ohne Angst oder Scheu zu erforschen.

In Maeterlincks Libretto wird Vannas Keuschheit von Prinzivalle respektiert, er gesteht ihr seine Liebe. Wegen dieser Liebe gibt er ihrem Flehen nach, mit

work *Monna Vanna* in 1902. An opera of the same name, composed by Henri Février and based on Maeterlinck's libretto, premiered in Paris in 1909. Giovanna (or Vanna) agrees to visit Prinzivalle of Florence dressed only in a mantle — as shown in Stuck's sculpture — in order that Pisa may receive food and arms.

If Stuck's, and now Wilson's, Monna Vanna is a modest maid with lowered eyes who is willing to perform sexual favors — certainly out of necessity and without pleasure — to rescue her fellow citizens, Franz von Stuck's *Die Sünde*, her body seductively intertwined with that of the serpent, is her antithesis: a woman who is fully aware of her sexual prowess, in pursuit of its pleasures. In extraordinarily purple prose, the nineteenth-century critic Otto Julius Bierbaum described *Die Sünde* as follows:

"The smooth coldness of the snake's supple power sleeps on the soft warmth of her white body which glows and beckons with all manner of promised delights. The wicked temptress waits with eyes which burn with the fires of Hell. She waits quietly and confidently. Her gaze travels far and further — piercing deep into the hearts of her fellow creatures. But the snake, with its flat horny head, is impatient.... Beware of the serpent and the menace of its gaze. But he sees only the beautiful hell-deep eyes of the woman and the burgeoning fullness of her white body."[40]

Issues of sexuality and spectatorship in art, especially in the nineteenth century, have been analyzed in depth by feminist theorists.[41] Central to this discussion is the female gaze, and whether and how it engages the male (and female) viewer. If in *Die Sünde* a blatantly sexual female gaze confronted the male, rendering him helpless, the female gaze and the female body in *Monna Vanna* is suppliant. The male spectator — and the female — can search her body without restraint, without fear.

In Maeterlinck's libretto Vanna's chastity is respected by Prinzivalle, who professes his love for her. Because of this love, he succumbs to her pleas to go to Pisa with her, whereupon Vanna's husband imprisons him (his passion has resulted in his ruin). Nevertheless, his love is redeemed when Vanna rescues him, thereby placing her own chastity in question. This complicated tale of lust and temptation, chastity and betrayal, is underscored in Wilson's tableau by the sound of a man laughing hysterically.

ihr nach Pisa zu kommen, wo er von Vannas Ehegatten gefangengesetzt wird. Seine Leidenschaft gerät ihm also zum Verderben. Gleichwohl bleibt seine Liebe nicht völlig unerhört, da Vanna ihn rettet und so ihre eigene Keuschheit in Frage stellt. Diese vertrackte Erzählung von sinnlicher Begierde und Verführung, Keuschheit und Verrat wird untermalt durch Robert Wilsons und Peter Cerones Klangenvironment eines »hysterisch lachenden Mannes«.

80
Monna Vanna, 1920
Bronze, grün patiniert, Kopf, Hände und Körper feuervergoldet
Höhe: 54 cm
Privatbesitz

Mary's Room

The final tableau in the Villa Stuck was the first Idea developed by Robert Wilson for this project. We see the eleven-year-old Mary as "Torero," in one of the many costumes in which she was portrayed by Franz von Stuck. The occasion is a children's Fasching party in the Villa Stuck in 1907. In other photographs, apparently taken on the same day, we see her playing with her friend Hedda Kaulbach,[42] who is also dressed in a Spanish costume. Another of Mary's friends, Marcella Wolff, recalled many years later the "fairytale" atmosphere in the Villa:

"From the age of five onwards, I was invited there on countless occasions, and each time it was like a little party.... The door was answered by old Johann, the epitome of the dignified manservant, with grey, carefully parted hair and side whiskers, who helped me out of my little coat. I shall never forget the smell, a faint studio smell of paint and turpentine, mingled with many other ingredients.... I was allowed to play with Stuck's daughter Mary, a strikingly pretty girl. She was a few years older than me, and I admired her greatly.... Usually I was led straight into Mary's room where we would play until teatime. As far as I recall, we were always allowed to take tea with the 'grown-ups.'"[43]

As if to emphasize the fairytale quality of Mary's childhood, but also to quote his own early furniture sculptural works such as *Hanging Chair (Freud)*, Wilson suspends a simulacrum of Mary who floats above Stuck's "Spanish Chair." She sits as if she were perched on the chair, her right hand resting on the seat. She stares straight ahead, at an imaginary, non-existent camera, while the family dog, Pips, waits patiently for his mistress' attention.

In three of the Villa Stuck tableaux Wilson has included Stuck's original furniture (in the reception and music rooms, in the boudoir and here). The Spanish Chair, which was not designed by Stuck, was already in his possession before 1893, as photographs of his atelier in the Theresienstrasse show. Christian Burchard has suggested that the triangle design of the inlaid ivory decoration on the Spanish Chair may have inspired Stuck's design for his furniture in the music salon.

The sound score for this tableau is a "whispered text Ophelia" from Act IV, Scene V of *Hamlet*, where Ophelia, like Mary, is crazed with grief over the death of her father. On December 21, 1929, sixteen months after the death of Franz von Stuck, and eight weeks after the death of her adoptive mother, Mary Stuck is described in a letter to the Estates Court as having suffered a "'severe nervous breakdown,' with 'attacks of manic agitation,' whose duration could not be predicted at this stage."[44] In this, the last tableau, we are once again confronted with a magical, fantastic world and with premonitions of death and tragedy. The words of Ophelia echo as we leave the Villa Stuck:

> "White his shroud as the mountain snow,
> Larded all with sweet flowers,
> Which bewept to the grave did go
> With true-love showers."

Marys Zimmer

Das letzte Tableau in der Villa Stuck war die erste ›Idee‹, die Robert Wilson für dieses Projekt entwickelte. Wir sehen die elfjährige Mary als ›Torero‹ in einem der zahlreichen Kostüme, in denen Franz von Stuck sie porträtiert hat. Anlaß ist ein Kinderfasching 1907 in der Villa Stuck. Auf anderen Photos, die offenbar am selben Tag aufgenommen wurden, sehen wir sie beim Spielen mit ihrer Freundin Hedda Kaulbach[42], die ebenfalls ein spanisches Kostüm trägt. Eine andere Freundin Marys, Marcella Wolff, erinnerte sich viele Jahre später an die ›märchenhafte‹ Atmosphäre in der Villa:

»Von meinem fünften Jahr ab bin ich unzählige Male dort eingeladen gewesen und jedes mal war es ein kleines Fest … An der Stuckschen Türe empfing einen der alte Johann, der Inbegriff eines würdigen Dieners mit grauem Scheitel und Backenbart, und half mir aus dem Mäntelchen. Unvergeßlich der Geruch, ein leiser Atelierhauch von Farben und Terpentin, der aber noch viele andere Ingredienzien enthielt … Ich durfte mit Stucks Tochter Mary spielen, die ein auffallend hübsches Mädchen war. Sie war ein paar Jahre älter als ich und ich bewunderte sie sehr. Meistens wurde ich gleich in Marys Zimmer geführt, wo wir bis zum Tee spielten. So viel ich mich erinnere, durften wir fast immer mit den 'Großen' Tee trinken.«[43]

Als wollte er den märchenhaften Charakter von Marys Kindheit unterstreichen, zugleich aber auch seine eigenen frühen Möbelskulpturen wie *Hängender Stuhl (Freud)* zitieren, läßt Wilson über Stucks sogenanntem Spanischen Stuhl eine Figur von Mary schweben. Sie ist sitzend dargestellt, als ob sie auf dem Stuhl thronen würde, die rechte Hand auf die Sitzfläche gestützt. Ihr Blick ist geradeaus auf eine imaginäre, nicht vorhandene Kamera gerichtet, während der Hund des Hauses, Pips, geduldig darauf wartet, daß sich sein Frauchen ihm zuwendet.

In drei der Tableaus des Environments *Villa Stuck* hat Wilson Originalmöbel von Stuck einbezogen (im Empfangsraum und Musiksalon, im Boudoir und hier). Der Spanische Stuhl, den Stuck nicht selbst entworfen hat, befand sich bereits vor 1893 in seinem Besitz, wie Aufnahmen von seinem Atelier in der Theresienstraße belegen. Nach Auffassung von Christian Burchard könnte das Dreiecksmotiv der Elfenbeineinlegearbeit am Spanischen Stuhl Stucks Entwurf für die Möblierung des Musiksalons inspiriert haben.

Die Partitur für dieses Tableau ist ein »geflüsterter Text Ophelia« aus *Hamlet*, vierter Akt, 5. Szene, wo Ophelia – ähnlich wie Mary – von Gram über den Tod ihres Vaters erfüllt ist und wirr spricht. Am 21. Dezember 1929, sechzehn Monate nach dem Tod ihres Vaters Franz von Stuck und acht Wochen nach dem Tod ihrer Adoptivmutter heißt es in einem Brief an das Nachlaßgericht, Mary habe einen »›schweren Nervenzusammenbruch‹ erlitten und [kranke] an ›manischen Erregungszuständen‹, deren Dauer sich zu diesem Zeitpunkt nicht absehen ließ.«[44] In diesem letzten Tableau werden wir aufs neue konfrontiert mit einer magischen Phantasiewelt und mit Vorahnungen von Tod und Unglück. Ophelias Worte hallen nach, wenn wir die Villa verlassen:

> »Sein Grabtuch weiß, wie Schnee auf Höhn,
> Besprengt mit Blumenschauer;
> Die Blümlein naß zum Grabe gehn,
> Von Liebestrauer.«

Mary oder Franz von Stuck
(zugeschrieben)
MARY ALS TORERO
1907 (Kat. 195)

DER PIPS

List of Works/Exponate

Concept/Konzept: Robert Wilson
Artistic Collaboration/Künstlerische Mitarbeit: Stefan Hageneier and/und Hans Thiemann, Design; Heinrich Brunke, Light/Licht; Peter Cerone, Sound/Ton

Vestibule/Vestibül

Two paper figures, paint, fluorescent tubes, shirting, ceramic vase, three beetles, sound (based on a photograph by Friedrich Witzel, *Franz von Stuck in front of his painting "Sisyphos,"* c. 1927/1928, Franz von Stuck Estate, Inv. Nr. M 36 b l; on a vase by Haagsche Porselein-en Kunst-Aardewerk Fabriek ›Rozenburg,‹ Den Haag, 1903, designed by J. Jurrian Kok and R. Sterkenaus, Museum Villa Stuck, Inv. Nr. K 91 4–3 and on a letter by Franz von Stuck to Friedrich August von Kaulbach, 1919, Monacensia, Archive, Municipal Library, Munich, Inv. Nr. 1646/94)
Zwei Plastiken aus Papier, Farbe, Leuchtstoffröhren, Baumwolle, Vase aus Keramik, drei Käfer, Ton (nach der Photographie *Franz von Stuck vor seinem Gemälde ›Sisyphos‹,* um 1927/1928, Nachlaß Franz von Stuck, Inv. Nr. M 36 b l; nach einer Vase der Haagsche Porselein-en Kunst-Aardewerk Fabriek ›Rozenburg‹, Den Haag, 1903, Design: J. Jurrian Kok, Bemalung: R. Sterkenaus, Museum Villa Stuck, Inv. Nr. K 91 4–3 und nach einem Brief von Franz von Stuck an Friedrich August von Kaulbach, 1919, Monacensia Handschriften-Sammlung der Stadtbibliothek München, Inv. Nr. 1646/94)
Tableau: 500 x 400 cm; Figures/Plastiken: H: 172 cm; Vase: H: 38 cm

Reception Room and Music Salon/Empfangszimmer und Musiksalon

Styrofoam figures, paint, sheepskin, iron, wood, furniture, vitrine with text fragments from the opera *Der Freischütz,* Tiffany goblet, mask, sound (based on a painting *Phantastische Jagd,* Franz von Stuck, 1890, Museum Villa Stuck, Inv. Nr. G 96 1–2; furniture designed by Franz von Stuck, built by Ludwig Hießmannseder 1897/98; Goblet, Louis Comfort Tiffany, 1902, Museum Villa Stuck, Inv. Nr. GL-91-16-3, and mask of Cléo de Mérode with floral diadem, c. 1900 designed by Despret, Museum Villa Stuck, Inv. Nr. GL-91-7-1; excerpts from Agathe's arias, *Der Freischütz,* 1821, Carl Maria von Weber)
Bemalte Plastiken aus Styropor, Schafsfell, Eisen, Holz, Möbel, Vitrine mit Textstücken aus der Oper *Der Freischütz,* Tiffany-Stengelglas, Mädchenmaske, Ton (nach dem Gemälde *Phantastische Jagd,* Franz von Stuck, 1890, Museum Villa Stuck, Inv. Nr. G 96 1–2; mit Möbeln nach Entwürfen von Franz von Stuck, Ausführung Ludwig Hießmannseder 1897/98, Stengelglas, Louis Comfort Tiffany, 1902, Museum Villa Stuck, Inv. Nr. GL-91-16-3, Mädchenmaske mit Blütendiadem, Cléo de Mérode, um 1900, Design: Despret, Museum Villa Stuck, Inv. Nr. GL-91-7-1; Ausschnitte aus der Arie der Agathe, *Der Freischütz,* 1821, Carl Maria von Weber)
Tableau: 1500 x 640 cm; Figures/Plastiken: 280 x 167 cm (Hunter/Jäger), 176 x 160 cm (Hunted/Gejagter)

Dining Room/Speisesaal

Paper figures, paint, fabric, wood, styrofoam columns, painted insulating material, painted tin arrows, sound: winding up of a carillon (based on a photograph by Adolf Baumann, *Mary and Franz Stuck on the occasion of the artist's ball "In Arkadien,"* 1898, Franz von Stuck Estate, Inv. M 11)
Plastiken aus Papier, Farbe, Stoff, Holz, Säulen aus Styropor, bemalter Boden aus Dämmplatten, bemalte Pfeile aus Blech, Ton: Aufziehmechanismus eines Carillons (nach der Photographie von Adolf Baumann *Mary und Franz Stuck anläßlich des Künstlerfestes ›In Arkadien‹,* 1898, Nachlaß Franz von Stuck, Inv. M 11)
Tableau: 810 x 990 cm; Backdrop/Prospekt: 810 x 480 cm; Columns/Säulen: 47–417 cm; Figures/Plastik: H. 169 (Mary), H. 172 (Franz); Arrows/Pfeile: 85 cm

Boudoir

Paper figure, paper dog, paint, chair, leaves, mask, sound: dog barking (based on a photograph by Atelier Friedrich Müller/Theodor Hilsdorf, *Franz von Stuck with his dog,* 1914, Franz von Stuck Estate, Inv. Nr. M 34 a; Franz von Stuck death mask, Museum Villa Stuck, Inv. Ach-obj 91 1–2)
Plastik aus Papier, Hund aus Papier, Farbe, Stuhl, Laub, Maske, Ton: Hundegebell (nach der Photographie des Atelier Friedrich Müller/Theodor Hilsdorf *Franz von Stuck mit seinem Hund,* 1914, Nachlaß Franz von Stuck, Inv. Nr. M 34a, Abformung der Totenmaske Franz von Stucks, Museum Villa Stuck, Inv. Ach-obj 91 1–2)
Tableau: 800 x 415 cm; Figure/Plastik: H: 136 cm; Dog/Hund: 78 cm; Chair/Stuhl: H: 85 cm, Seat/Sitzfläche 65 x 68 cm

Smoking Salon/Rauchzimmer

Wooden backdrop, paint, live tree with fabric leaves, electric fan (based on a photograph attributed to Franz Stuck, *Landscape in the vicinity of Osternberg* (?), 1890 (?), Franz von Stuck Estate, Inv. Nr. Ph-bio-1890–4)
Prospekt aus Holz, Farbe, echter Baum aus Holz mit Textil-Blättern, Ventilator (nach der Photographie *Landschaft bei Osternberg* (?), 1890 (?), zugeschrieben Franz von Stuck, Nachlaß Franz von Stuck, Inv. Ph-bio-1890–4)
Tableau: 445 x 410 cm; Backdrop/Prospekt: 440 x 410 cm; Tree/Baum: H: 350 cm; Treetop/Baumkrone: Ø 180 cm

Atelier

Wooden box, stuffed rabbit, pencil and ink drawings, styrofoam figure, paint, paper and wood objects, sound (based on two drawings of *Serpentintänzerinnen,* 1895, Franz von Stuck Estate and on the painting *Trunkene Kentaurin,* c. 1889, Collection Katharina Büttiker, courtesy Gallery Wühre 9 – Art Deco, Zurich, all works by Franz von Stuck; Rabbit: Jagd- und Fischerei Museum München; sound: water and *Ave Maria* by Franz Schubert)
Box aus Holz, ausgestopfter Hase, Bleistift- und Tuschezeichnung, Figur aus Styropor, Objekte aus Papier und Holz, Prospekt aus Holz, Farbe, Ton (nach den beiden Zeichnungen *Serpentintänzerinnen,* 1895, Nachlaß Franz von Stuck, und dem Gemälde *Trunkene Kentaurin,* ca. 1895, Sammlung Katharina Büttiker, courtesy Galerie Wühre 9 – Art Deco, Zürich, alle Arbeiten von Franz von Stuck; Hase: Jagd- und Fischerei Museum München; Ton: Wassergeräusche und *Ave Maria* von Franz Schubert)
Tableau: 475 x 275 cm; Rabbit/Hase: H. 55 cm; Centaur/Kentaur: 275 cm; Objects/Objekte: H. 45 cm (Vessels/Gefäße), 80 cm (Stone/Fels)

Room/Zimmer

Paper figure, wood, feathers, cord paint, sound (based on a photographic reproduction *Cupid at a Masked Ball,* c. 1889, Museum Villa Stuck, Inv. Nr. 11 and on three letters by Franz von Stuck to his daughter Mary, 1926, Estate Franz von Stuck, to Friedrich August von Kaulbach, 1919, Monacensia, Archive, Municipal Library, Munich, Inv. Nr. 1646/94 and to Franz Gerlach, 1882, Museum Villa Stuck, Inv. Nr. Arch.-dok 97 l–l, sound: excerpts from *Mikrokosmos* by Béla Bartók, 1926–1937)
Plastik aus Papier, Holz, Federn, Kordel, Farbe, Ton (nach der photographischen Reproduktion *Amor auf dem Maskenball,* ca. 1889, Museum Villa Stuck, Inv. Nr. 11, und drei Briefen Franz von Stucks an seine Tochter Mary, 1926, Nachlaß Franz von Stuck, an Friedrich August von Kaulbach, 1919, Monacensia Handschriftensammlung der Stadtbibliothek München, Inv. Dr. 1646/94 und an Franz Gerlach, 1882, Museum Villa Stuck, Inv. Nr. Arch-dok 97 H, Ton: Auszüge aus dem *Mikrokosmos* von Béla Bartók, 1926-1937)
Tableau: 590 x 225 cm; Figure/Plastik: H: 148 cm

Franz von Stuck's Bedroom/Franz von Stucks Schlafzimmer

Two paintings, booklet, sound: roaring lion (based on a photograph attributed to Mary or Franz Stuck, *Ernst von Possart as Napoleon,* c. 1905, Museum Villa Stuck, Inv. Nr. Ph-P-94/797-84)
Zwei Gemälde, Buch, Ton: Löwengebrüll (nach der Photographie *Ernst von Possart als Napoleon,* ca. 1905, Mary oder Franz Stuck zugeschrieben, Museum Villa Stuck, Inv. Nr. Ph-P-94/979-84)
Tableau: 700 x 635 cm; Paintings/Gemälde: 300 x 200 cm

Bathroom/Badezimmer

Styrofoam figure, paint, iron, sound (based on the painting by Franz von Stuck, *Frühling,* c. 1920, Franz von Stuck Estate; sound: Untitled, 1997, composed and played by Stefano Scavani)
Plastik aus Papier, Farbe, Eisen, Ton (nach dem Gemälde *Frühling* von Franz von Stuck, um 1920, Nachlaß Franz von Stuck; Ton: ohne Titel, 1997, komponiert und gespielt von Stefano Scavani)
Tableau: 410 x 605 x cm; Figure/Plastik: H: 115 x 160 cm

Mary von Stuck's Bedroom/Mary von Stucks Schlafzimmer

Photographic reproduction on silk, styrofoam pyramid, sand, pigment, cork granules, bricks, electric fan, paper figure, paint, wood, vacuum cleaner, sound: noise of a vacuum cleaner (based on a photograph attributed to Franz Stuck, *Mary Stuck,* c. 1900, Museum Villa Stuck, Inv. Nr. Ph-P-94/797-83 and on a photograph by Friedrich Witzel, *Franz von Stuck in front of his painting "Sisyphos,"* c. 1927/1928, Franz von Stuck Estate, Inv. Nr. M 36 b l)
Photographische Reproduktion auf Seide, Kegel aus Styropor, Sand, Pigment, Korkgranulat, Ziegelsteine, Ventilator, Plastik auf Papier, Farbe, Holz, Staubsauger, Ton: Staubsaugergeräusche (nach der Photographie *Frau Mary Stuck,* um 1900, Museum Villa Stuck, Inv. Nr. Ph-P-94/797-83 und nach der Photographie *Franz von Stuck vor seinem Gemälde ›Sisyphos‹,* um 1927/1928, Nachlaß Franz von Stuck, Inv. Nr. M 36 b l;)
Tableau: 640 x 750 cm; Voile: 347 x 206,5 cm; Pyramid/Kegel: H: 85 cm; Figure/Plastik: H: 172 cm

Dressing Room/Ankleideraum

Sculpture, tiger python, wooden box, glass, sound: laughing man (*Monna Vanna,* gilded bronze, 1920, Franz von Stuck, Estate Franz von Stuck, Snake: courtesy Thomas Lücke, Reptilienhaus Oberammergau)
Skulptur, Tigerpython, Box aus Holz, Glas, Ton: Lachen eines Mannes (*Monna Vanna,* feuervergoldete Bronze, 1920, Franz von Stuck, Nachlaß Franz von Stuck, Schlange: Leihgabe Thomas Lücke, Reptilienhaus Oberammergau)
Tableau: 360 x 680 cm; Sculpture/Skulptur: H: 54 cm; Snake/Schlange: 250 cm; Box: 555 x 80 cm

Mary's Room/Marys Zimmer

Paper figure, paint, costume jewelery, paper dog, wooden chair with ivory decoration, sound (based on a photograph attributed to Mary or Franz von Stuck, *Mary als Torero,* 1907, and on a photographic reproduction of the painting *Der Pips,* 1902, by Franz von Stuck – presently in a private collection – distributed by the art publishers Franz Hanfstaengl in 1902. Original Spanish chair with ivory decoration, wood, Estate Franz von Stuck; excerpts from William Shakespeares *Hamlet,* Act 4, Scene 5)
Figur aus Papier, Farbe, Hund aus Papier, Stuhl, Holz mit Elfenbein-Intarsien, Ton (nach der Photographie *Mary als Torero,* 1907, Mary oder Franz von Stuck zugeschrieben und der photographischen Reproduktion des Gemäldes *Der Pips,* Franz von Stuck – heute in Privatbesitz –, vom Kunstverlag Franz Hanfstaengl 1902 vertrieben, originaler spanischer Stuhl mit Elfenbein-Intarsien, Holz, Nachlaß Franz von Stuck; Auszüge aus William Shakespeares *Hamlet,* Akt 4, Szene 5)
Tableau: 410 x 600 cm; Figure/Plastik: H:120 cm; Chair/Stuhl: H: 125 cm, Seat/Sitzfläche: 49,5 x 33 cm

Interview with Robert Wilson

Interview mit Robert Wilson

Excerpts from an interview with Robert Wilson by Anne Erfle conducted on November, 21, 1997, for the *Süddeutsche Zeitung*.

Mr Wilson, what fascinates you about the person of Franz von Stuck?

His personal vision. I think at this time it's fresh.

In his time he delved into another world, a mythic world, which he constructed himself. I assume, you are not transposing his pictures 1:1 in your tableaux. What relationship do you see this project having to our time?

I am building a center on Long Island, the Watermill Center. It is not exactly the same as what Stuck did, but it's a little bit the same. I am constructing a series of buildings, workshops, ateliers, a place where I live, and space for pieces I have designed. I am working in my own house, in my own environment with the chairs, the furniture, the ceramics which I collected — and glass, I love glass. Stuck lived surrounded by artbooks and art objects as I do. And I think that fascinates me, being in his house, seeing his vision, the furniture he had designed. I identify with it a little bit. It is not exactly my aesthetics but I like the fact, that it is not exactly my aesthetics. I find it so personal that this man had his vision, it was his. And in so many areas.

Do you regard your installations as sculpture or more as objects associated with your work in the theater?

It's all part of one. I have just been reading through notes, correspondences, and catalogues about Donald Judd. He said about his table that he was not sure whether the table was just a table (furniture) or sculpture. No, he said, a chair is a chair and is not sculpture. A table is a table and is not sculpture. I don't see so much separation between my work in theater or in the installation for the Venice Biennale. For me it is all the same. Marcel Breuer said: "In this chair that I have designed are all my aesthetics." The same aesthetics go into designing a building or designing a city.

But here you enter the aesthetics of another person. I would like to know whether you see any parallels in your work and Stuck's?

Yes I do. I think that sometimes we are parallel and sometimes we meet. But often we don't meet in terms of our aesthetics. We are parallel but different.

Do you counter his aesthetics in your tableaux?

I don't know if I am successful. If you are asked to do something as a celebration of a man on the one hand you have to be faithful and pay homage and respect to him but on the other hand you have to be careful not to become his slave. You have to keep your own identity. It's the fascination of this project to me — to counter, to make displacements and to find a balance. In some ways I make it even more kitsch. Sometimes it's very severe. I was asked how I would do this. I answered, I will make it "Steel Velvet". That we should have chosen as the title of the exhibition, *Steel Velvet*.

Auszug aus einem Interview vom 21. November 1997 mit Robert Wilson für die Süddeutsche Zeitung. Das Gespräch führte Anne Erfle.

Was fasziniert Sie an der Person Franz von Stucks?

Seine individuellen Visionen, sie wirken frisch, besonders in dieser Zeit.

In seiner Zeit taucht er ab in eine individuelle mythische Welt, die er sich selbst konstruiert hat. Da ich annehme, daß Sie seine Bilder in Ihre Tableaus nicht 1:1 übertragen, welchen Bezug stellen Sie mit diesem Projekt zur heutigen Zeit her?

Ich baue für mich ein Zentrum in der Nähe von New York, das Watermill Center. Es ist nicht genau dasselbe, was Stuck gemacht hat, aber ein wenig doch. Es entsteht ein Gebäudekomplex mit Ateliers, mit Räumlichkeiten für Workshops, für meine Skulpturen und mit meinen eigenen Wohnräumen. Ich arbeite in meinem eigenen Haus, meinem eigenen Ambiente mit all den Stühlen, Möbeln, Sammelobjekten, wie Keramik und Glas – ich liebe Glas. Stuck lebte wie ich, umgeben von Kunstbüchern und Kunstobjekten. Das ist es, was mich fasziniert, in seinem Haus zu sein, seine Visionen zu sehen und die Möbel, die er entworfen hat. Ein bißchen identifiziere ich mich mit ihm. Es ist nicht genau meine Ästhetik, das ist auch gut so. Ich finde es so persönlich, daß der Mann eine Vision hatte, es war seins. Und in vielfältigen Bereichen.

Würden Sie Ihre Installationen hier in der Villa als skulpturale Kunstwerke bezeichnen oder sie eher in Zusammenhang mit Ihrer Theaterarbeit sehen?

Es ist alles Teil eines Ganzen. Ich habe gerade Notizen, Briefwechsel und Kataloge über Donald Judd gelesen. Er war sich nicht sicher, ob sein Tisch eine Skulptur sei oder nur ein Tisch, ein Möbelstück. Er kam zu dem Fazit, ein Tisch ist ein Tisch und keine Skulptur, und ein Stuhl ist ein Stuhl. Ich sehe keine so großen Unterschiede, für mich ist alles eins, die Theaterarbeit oder die Installation auf der Biennale in Venedig. Marcel Breuer sagt: »In dem Stuhl, den ich entwerfe, ist all meine Ästhetik enthalten«. Das gleiche gilt für ein Gebäude oder für eine Stadt.

Hier sind Sie aber in die Ästhetik eines anderen eingestiegen. Wie verhält es sich dann? Gibt es Parallelen zu Stucks Ästhetik?

Parallelen ja, manchmal treffen wir uns, meist jedoch nicht. Jeder hat seine eigene Ästhetik, parallel, aber verschieden.

Und brechen Sie seine in den Tableaus?

Ich weiß nicht, ob es mir gelingt. Wir werden es sehen, wenn alles fertig ist. Wenn man aufgefordert wird, etwas zur Ehrung eines Menschen zu tun, wird man auf der einen Seite respektvoll mit ihm umgehen. Andererseits muß man sehr aufpassen, nicht sein Sklave zu sein. Man muß seine eigene Identität bewahren. Das ist die Faszination dieses Projektes – zu kontern, zu verschieben und die Balance zu finden. Kitsch wird noch kitschiger, anderes dagegen sehr hart. Man hat mich gefragt, wie ich es machen würde. Ich antwortete, wie stählerner Samt. So hätten wir die Ausstellung nennen sollen: »Steel Velvet«.

The Watermill "Ideas"

Watermill Center, Long Island, New York

Watermill Center, Interior, Long Island, New York

Illustrations: Concept drawings by Robert Wilson

Idea 1 (Mary's Room/Zimmer)

entire room dark green
white dog as sculpture on floor
Torero as sculpture with chair up on the left wall

Idea 2

Idea 2 (Mary von Stuck's Bedroom/Schlafzimmer)

back and sidewalls light brown
floor dark reddish-brown dirt
pile of yellow sulfur/with lightbulb hanging above it
(alternative: buckets with moving water and light tubes)
photo of Mary enlarged, reproduced on sepia-colored silk
fan slightly blowing the silk
sound: rain and thunder

Idea 3 (Franz von Stuck's Bedroom/Schlafzimmer)

entire room dark gray
reproduced photographs of Ernst Possart as Napoleon next to each other on two walls
Franz von Stuck in white coat as sculpture
vase of Franz von Stuck's collection on floor
sound: whispered text

Idea 4 (Dining Room/Speisezimmer)

dark green walls
orange clay floor
wax sculpture of Mary and Stuck in Roman costume (photo)
enlarged photo of Roman temple as backwall
golden arrows
broken or fallen columns on the floor
(plaster copies of orginals)

Idea 5 (Smoking Salon/Rauchsalon)

image of *Landschaft bei Osternberg*
landscape as backwall
cut out of tree in front
nature and road as floor

Idea 6 (Room/Zimmer)

entire room is wallpapered with Stuck's handwritten text
sculpture of *Amor* like Stuck's painting

Idea 7 (not realized/nicht realisiert)

wall divided into a gray section and enlarged drawing of *Lydia Feez*
white swan with pearl necklace

Idea 8 (Atelier – Trunkene Kentaurin)

dark brown room with a "stage" cut-out
3-dimensional copy of Stuck's painting *Trunkene Kentaurin* seen through the cut out

Idea 9

Idea 9 (not realized/nicht realisiert)

Stuck's drawing of Olga Lindpaintner in silver baroque frame on floor with real small turtles
one of Stuck's chairs hanging above this

Idea 10

Idea 10 (not realized/nicht realisiert)

3-dimensional copy of Stuck's painting *Meerweibchen* in an entire room, so people have to walk through it

Idea 11 (not realized/nicht realisiert)

Stuck's former studio in the Theresienstrasse rebuilt

Idea 12 (Bathroom/Badezimmer)

landscape of Stuck's painting *Frühling* on 3 walls of room
sculpture of centaur going up the wall

Idea 13

Idea 13 (not realized/nicht realisiert)

sculptures of men in black suits [members of the Munich Secession] with white sculptures (restaged photo)
sound: Bach, organ, church music

Idea 14

Idea 14 (not realized/nicht realisiert)

Stuck's painting *Der Nibelungen Not* seen through a partially opened doorway
painting in different levels

Idea 15

Idea 15 (not realized/nicht realisiert)

one leg of Stuck's chair stands on a lightbulb on the floor
walls are painted in golden/yellow like the seatcover of the chair

Idea 16 (Atelier)

all walls of the room wallpapered like Stuck's sketch *Serpentintänzerinnen* (repeated drawing)
Stuck in white coat as sculpture

Idea 17 (Atelier)

all walls of the room wallpapered like Stuck's sketch *Serpentintänzerinnen* (repeated drawing)
rabbit

Idea 18 (Vestibule/Vestibül)

3 sculptures of Stuck (photo) in white coat and white hair, like a ghost sound: man clearing his throat

Idea 19 (Boudoir)

Franz von Stuck as sculpture with dog (photo), in historical room of the building

Idea 20 (not realized/nicht realisiert)

2 historical rooms lit decadently

Idea 21 (Dressing Room/Ankleidezimmer)

Stuck's sculpture *Monna Vanna* on base
glass cage with real snake

Exhibitions/Ausstellungen/Environments

Compiled by/Zusammengestellt von Geoffrey Wexler, Byrd Hoffman Foundation

Poles, Grailville, Loveland, Ohio 1968

Solo Exhibitions/Einzelausstellungen

1967

Poles, Grail Retreat, Loveland, Ohio

1971

Willard Gallery, New York City

1974

Robert Wilson. Dessins et Sculptures Musée Galliera, Paris. 10.9.–26.9.1974

1975

Galerie Wünsche, Bonn

1976

Robert Wilson, Sculpture & Drawings, Iolas Gallery-Brooks Jackson, Inc., New York City. March/März 1976

1977

Robert Wilson, Furniture/Multiples. Marian Goodman Gallery, New York City. 22.11.–31.12.1977

1978

Robert Wilson, Skulpturen (in conjunction with the/in Zusammenarbeit mit der Berliner Festspiele GmbH). Galerie Folker Skulima, Berlin. 25.5.–27.6.1978

1979

Marian Goodman Gallery, New York City

Galerie Folker Skulima, Berlin

Galerie Zwirner, Köln

Paula Cooper Gallery, New York City

1980

Robert Wilson. From a Theater of Images. The Contemporary Arts Center, Cincinnati. 16.5.–29.6.1980

Neuberger Museum, State University of New York, Purchase. 13.7.–21.9.1980

1982

Franz Morat Institut, Freiburg

Robert Wilson. Die Goldenen Fenster/ Zeichnungen. Städtische Galerie im Lenbachhaus, München. 18.5.–13.6.1982

Galerie Annemarie Verna, Zürich. 31.8.–2.10.1982

Marian Goodman Gallery, New York City [*Drawings for The Golden Windows*]. 7.12.–29.12.1982

Robert Wilson. Dessins pour "Medea"/ "Great Day in the Morning". Galerie le Dessin, Paris. 30.9.–11.11.1982

1983

Works by Robert Wilson. Museum of Art, Rhode Island School of Design, Providence. 14.1.–13.2 1983

Drawings from "the CIVIL warS". Leo Castelli, Richard L. Feigen, James Corcoran, New York City. 3.5.–11.6.1983

Sogetsu School, Tokyo. May/Mai 1983

Robert Wilson. Drawings. Gallery Ueda, Warehouse, Tokyo. 10.5.–30.5.1983

Festival Mondial du Théâtre, Nancy. 20.5.–5.6.1983

Raum für Kunst, Produzentengalerie, Hamburg. 9.6.–30.6.1983

Museum Boijmans Van Beuningen, Rotterdam. 13.8.–11.9.1983

Robert Wilson. "the CIVIL warS". Galerie Brinkman, Amsterdam. 3.9.–30.9.1983

Robert Wilson. Dessins pour "the CIVIL warS". Pavillon des Arts, Paris. 15.11.–11.12.1983

Musée Galliera, Paris 1974, Stalin Chairs

1984

Robert Wilson. Zeichnungen und Skulpturen. Kölnischer Kunstverein, Köln. 13.1.–22.1.1984

Robert Wilson. Dessins pour trois Opéras: "Medea", "Great Day in the Morning", "the CIVIL warS"

ARCA (Centre d'Art Contemporain), Marseille. 19.3.–31.3.1984

Museo de Folklore, Roma. 20.3.–29.4.1984

Walker Art Center, Minneapolis. 25.4.–25.5.1984

Robert Wilson. Drawings for "the CIVIL warS: a tree is best measured when it is down" and selected videos. Jones Troyer Gallery, Washington, D.C. 29.5.–16.6.1984

Robert Wilson's "the CIVIL warS: a tree is best measured when it is down". Drawings, Models, and World Wide Documentation. Exhibition Center, Otis Art Institute, Los Angeles 11.6.–15.8.1984

Robert Wilson. Drawings. Paula Cooper Gallery, New York City. 4.12.–22.12.1984

1985

Lithographien für "Parsifal". Werkraum der Münchner Kammerspiele, München. June/Juni 1985

Institute of Contemporary Art, Boston [*Parsifal Lithographs*]. 15.1.–15.3.1985

Robert Wilson. "Medea" e "Parsifal": Disegni, Incisioni, Video. (Rossini Opera Festival). Galeria Franca Mancini, Pesaro. 19.8.–19.9.1985

1986

Robert Wilson. Drawings for "the CIVIL warS". Rhona Hoffman Gallery, Chicago. 10.1.–1.2.1986

Robert Wilson. Drawings: "Alcestis". The Harcus Gallery, Boston. February/Februar 1986

Robert Wilson. The Complete "Parsifal" Portfolio. Drawings for Theatre Pieces. The Alpha Gallery, Boston. 8.3.–2.4.1986

Robert Wilson. Transmutation of Archetypes: "Medea" & "Parsifal". Lehman College Art Gallery, City University of New York, New York City.

Hewlett Gallery, Carnegie-Mellon University, Pittsburgh. 30.3.–20.4.1986

Kuhlenschmidt Gallery, Los Angeles. 18.3.–16.4.1986

Drawings: "the CIVIL warS": Robert Wilson. Hewlett Gallery, Carnegie-Mellon University, Pittsburgh 1.4.–26.4.1986

"Hamletmachine": Drawings. Grey Art Gallery, New York University, New York City. May/Mai–June/Juni 1986

Musée Galliera, Paris 1974, Hanging Chair (Freud)

Theater in der Kunsthalle, Hamburg. 4.10.–15.11.1986

Robert Wilson. Drawings for the Stage. Laguna Gloria Museum, Austin. 10.7.–7.9.1986

"The Knee Plays": Drawings. KiMo Gallery, Albuquerque. 28.10.–30.11.1986

Robert Wilson. Drawings. University of Iowa, Iowa City. 1.11.–15.12.1986

1987

Robert Wilson. Drawings, Furniture and Props for "Alceste", "Alcestis", "the CIVIL warS", "Death, Destruction and Detroit II", "Hamletmachine", "Salome". Paula Cooper Gallery, New York City. 21.1.–14.2.1987

Aldrich Museum of Contemporary Art, Ridgefield, Connecticut. 23.9.1987–3.1.1988

Robert Wilson. Erinnerung an eine Revolution. Galerie der Stadt Stuttgart. 3.7.–16.8.1987

Robert Wilson. "Parzival". Galerie Harald Behm, Hamburg. 8.9.–31.10.1987

Zeichnungen. Galerie Biedermann, München. September 1987

Robert Wilson. Die lithographischen Zyklen 1984–1986: "Medea", "Parsifal", "Alceste". Galerie im Theater der Stadt Gütersloh. 30.10.–30.11.1987

Galerie Fred Jahn, München. 7.7.–30.7.1988

Museum Morsbroich, Leverkusen. 17.1.–5.3.1989

1988

Cosmopolitan Greetings. Galerie Harald Behm, Hamburg. June/Juni 1988

Drawings. Marlene Eleini Gallery, London. November 1988

Dreams and Images. The Theatre of Robert Wilson. (Selections from Robert Wilson's papers/eine Auswahl der Zeichnungen von Robert Wilson). Rare Book and Manuscript Library, Butler Library, Columbia University, New York City. 8.12.–17.2.1988

1989

Robert Wilson. Zeichnungen und Druckgrafik. Galerie Lüpke, Frankfurt. 21.4.–27.5.1989

Robert Wilson. Drawings for the Opera "De Materie" by Louis Andriessen. Stedelijk Museum, Amsterdam. 2.6.–16.6.1989

Erinnerung an eine Revolution. (Organized by/veranstaltet von Galerie Fabian Walter.) Kunst-Buffet Basel Badischer Bahnhof, Basel. 14.6.–14.7.1989

Robert Wilson. "La Nuit d'avant le jour": Dessins. Yvon Lambert, Paris. 9.9.–14.10.1989

Robert Wilson. "Orlando": 22 Drawings and Furniture. Annemarie Verna Galerie, Zürich. 28.10.1989–27.1.1990

"Swan Song". Galerie Fred Jahn, München. 20.12.1989–January/Januar 1990

From a Theater of Images, The Contemporary Arts Center, Cincinnati 1980

1990

Robert Wilson: Choreographie des Designs. Ambiente, Interior Design And... (AIDA), Hamburg. March/März 1990

King Lear. Schirn Kunsthalle, Frankfurt. 17.5.–17.6.1990

Robert Wilson. Drawings, Sculpture and Furniture, "the CIVIL warS". Virginia Lynch Gallery, Tiverton, Rhode Island. 29.7.–23.8.1990

Robert Wilson. "Alceste": Drawings and Furniture/Sculpture. Feigen Incorporated, Chicago. 7.9.–6.10.1990

1991

Robert Wilson. Sculpture, Furniture, Paintings and Drawings. Paula Cooper Gallery, New York City. 26.1.–23.2.1991

Robert Wilson's Vision. (Retrospective exhibition/Retrospektive) Museum of Fine Arts, Boston. 6.2.–21.4.1991

Contemporary Arts Museum, Houston. 14.6.–18.8.1991

San Francisco Museum of Modern Art, San Francisco. 12.9.–1.12.1991

Robert Wilson. Drawing and Sculpture. (Drawings from/Zeichnungen zu *When We Dead Awaken* and/und *Lohengrin*.) Barbara Krakow Gallery, Boston. 2.3.–13.4.1991

Robert Wilson. Drawing and Sculpture. (Drawings from/Zeichnungen zu *When We Dead Awaken*.) Thomas Segal Gallery, Boston. 2.3.–13.4.1991

Robert Wilson. Die lithografischen Zyklen und Zeichnungen. Städtische Galerie, Erlangen. 2.3.–31.3.1991

Die wundersame Welt des Robert Wilson. (*Video 50, Deafman Glance, Stations*.) (Organized by/veranstaltet von Freunde der Deutschen Kinemathek e.V.) Kino Arsenal, Berlin. 1.5.–4.5.1991

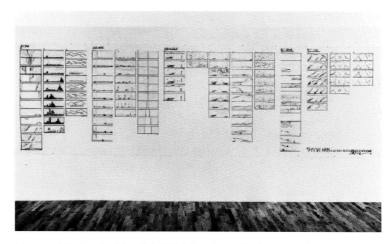

Museum of Modern Art, New York, 1984, Drawing to/Zeichnung zu 'the CIVIL warS'

Robert Wilson. Chairs for Marie and Pierre Curie, Sigmund Freud, Albert Einstein, A Table for Nijinski and "Parzival" Drawings. Busche Galerie, Köln. 6.9.–9.10.1991

Robert Wilson. Monuments. Kestner-Gesellschaft, Hannover. 7.9.–6.10.1991

Bayerische Akademie der Schönen Künste, München. 6.12.1991–19.1.1992

Robert Wilson. "Lohengrin" Drawings and Other Works. Annemarie Verna Galerie, Zürich. 20.9.–16.11.1991

Robert Wilson. Mr. Bojangles' Memory: og son of fire. Centre Georges Pompidou, Paris. 6.11.1991–27.1.1992

Robert Wilson. Zeichnungen – Zyklen. "A Letter for Queen Victoria"/"Golden Windows"/"the Civil WarS"/"Swan Song". Galerie Fred Jahn, München. 28.11.–21.12.1991

1992

Robert Wilson. White Raven Drawings. Paul Cooper Gallery, New York City. January/Januar

Robert Wilson. Drawings. Hiram Butler Gallery, Houston. 1.2.–31.3.1992

Robert Wilson. Drawings for "Alice in Wonderland". Laura Carpenter Fine Art, Santa Fe. 18.7.–5.8.1992

Robert Wilson. (In conjunction with the performance of/in Verbindung mit der Performance *Don Juan Último*.) Instituto Valenciano de Arte Moderno (IVAM), Valencia. 16.9.–22.11.1992

Robert Wilson. Galeria Gamarra y Garrigues, Madrid. 25.9. – November 1992

Einstein on the Beach. Kamakura Gallery, Tokyo. 12.10.–31.10.1992

Memory of a Revolution/Erinnerung an eine Revolution, Stuttgart 1987

Robert Wilson. *Convidados de piedra*
(Festival de OtoonviSala Goya, Círculo
de Bellas Artes) Madrid.
13.10.–5.11.1992

"La Flute Enchantée". Dessins. Galerie
Thaddaeus Ropac, Paris.
12.12.1992–14.1.1993

Robert Wilson. *Works, 1972–1992.*
Raum für Kunst e.V., Hamburg.
19.12.1992–20.2.1993

Objects. Produzentengalerie, Hamburg.
December/Dezember 1992–February/
Februar 1993

Binnenalster-Tür. (In conjunction with/
in Verbindung mit *Mediale '93,*
5.2.–28.3.1993.) Hamburg

1993

Robert Wilson. *Furniture and Other Works.*
Waco Creative Art Center, Waco.
18.2.–11.4.1993

Robert Wilson. Nathalie Beeckman Fine
Arts, Bruxelles. 29.3.–31.4.1993

Draft Notes for a Conversation on Dante.
(Presentation of a lithograph book/
Präsentation eines lithografischen
Buches.) Galerie van Rijsbergen,
Rotterdam. 15.5.–27.6.1993

Galerie Thaddaeus Ropac, Paris.
6.11.–30.11.1993

Portrait, Still Life, Landscape. Museum
Boijmans Van Beuningen, Rotterdam.
15.5.–9.9.1993

Memory/Loss. (Objects/Objekte: Robert
Wilson and/und Tadeusz Kantor; Sound
score/Ton: Hans Peter Kuhn; Text: Heiner
Müller.)

Biennale de Venezia, Granai delle Zitelle,
Venezia. 13.6.–10.10.1993

Monsters of Grace. Galerie Franck+Schulte,
Berlin. 16.9.–23.10.1993

Robert Wilson. *Memorie della Terra
Desolata.* (Exhibition in conjunction with
the performance of/Ausstellungen in
Verbindung mit der Performance *T.S.E.*)
Baglio delle Case di Stefano, Gibellina
Nuova. 24.9.–7.11.1993

*Fotografien der Produktionen Robert
Wilsons für deutsche Bühnen/
Photographs of Robert Wilson
Productions in Germany.* Goethe-Institut,
New York City. 2.11.–3.12.1993

Robert Wilson. *Deafman Glance. A Video
Installation.* 2.12.–23.12.1993

1994

Disegni de Gibellina. Paula Cooper
Gallery, New York City.
13.1.–27.1.1994

Three Rooms. Akira Ikeda Gallery,
New York City. 22.1.–26.2.1994

"Alice". Galeria Luís Serpa, Lisboa.
26.2.–9.4.1994

Zeichnungen zu "Der Mond im Gras".
Gallery Biedermann, München.
10.04.1994

Paula Cooper Gallery, New York 1987

1995

"Die Zauberflöte". Galerie Thaddaeus
Ropac, Salzburg. 20.1.–15.3.1993

Dragons and Silk from the Forbidden City.
Joyce Ma Gallery, Paris.
10.5.–20.7.1995

Robert Wilson. Hiram Butler Gallery,
Houston. May/Mai 1995

Robert Wilson. *The Rooms of Seven
Women und Zeichnungen zu den Neu-
inszenierungen "Blaubart"/"Erwartung".*
(Sponsored by/unterstützt durch
Direktorium der Salzburger Festspiele
and/und Galerie Thaddaeus Ropac)
Salzburg. Karl-Böhm-Saal des Kleinen
Festspielhauses, Salzburg.
24.07.–01.09.1995

H. G.. Clink Street Vaults, London.
12.09.–15.10.1995

"Erwartung". Oeuvres sur papier. Galerie
Thaddaeus Ropac, Paris.
5.12.1995–13.01.1996

1996

Robert Wilson. *Salle Multi* (*Obscure*
Festival), Québec City.
5.02.–12.02.1996

Robert Wilson. Paula Cooper Gallery,
New York City. 30.03.–27.04.1996

Robert Wilson. Galerie Lehmann,
Lausanne. 18.04.–18.05.1996

Robert Wilson. *Survey of Drawings,
1973–1993.* Modernism, San Francisco
20.06.–17.08.1996

Robert Wilson. Fotouhi Cramer Gallery,
East Hampton. 13.07.–4.8.1996

Le Festival de la Mode par Robert Wilson.
(Centennial installation/Installation zum
100jährigen Jubiläum) Galeries
Lafayette, Paris. 7.10.–31.10.1996

Robert Wilson. *"Oedipus Rex". Nouveaux
dessins.* Galerie Thaddaeus Ropac,
Paris. October/Oktober–21.12.1996

Water Jug Boy. Art Cologne, Köln.
10.11.–17.11.1996

1997

Robert Wilson. *"Pelléas et Mélisande".
Zeichnungen und Skulpturen.* (Organized
by/veranstaltet von Galerie Thaddaeus
Ropac.) Schüttkasten Salzburg.
19.07.–31.08.1997

Robert Wilson/*Villa Stuck.* Museum Villa
Stuck, München.
25.11.1997–08.02.1998

Paula Cooper Gallery, New York 1987

Selected Group Exhibitions/ Gruppenausstellungen (Auswahl)

1974

Galleria Salvatore Ala, Milano

1975

Paula Cooper Gallery, New York City

1980

Drawings. The Pluralist Decade. Institute of Contemporary Art, University of Pennsylvania, Philadelphia. 4.10.–9.11.1980

Museum of Contemporary Art, Chicago. 29.5.–26.6.1981

Further Furniture. Marian Goodman Gallery, New York City. 9.12.–31.12.1980

1981

1981 Biennial Exhibition. Whitney Museum of American Art, New York City. 20.1.–12.4.1981

Other Realities. Installations for Performance. Contemporary Arts Museum, Houston. 1.8.–27.9.1981

Artifacts at the End of a Decade. (Artist book, including *"The Golden Windows"* set designs/Künstlerbuch, u.a. mit den Bühnenbildern zu *"The Golden Windows".*) (Traveling exhibition sponsored by/ Wanderausstellung, unterstützt von The Gallery Association of New York)

Frankfurter Kunstverein, Frankfurt (*Kunstwerke am Ende eines Jahrzehnts*). 12.2.–14.3.1982

1982

Amerikanische Zeichnungen der Siebziger Jahre. Louisiana Museum of Modern Art, Humlebaek

Kunsthalle Basel

Städtische Galerie im Lenbachhaus, München

Wilhelm-Hack Museum, Ludwigshafen

The Next Wave. (Brooklyn Academy of Music.) Paula Cooper Gallery, New York City. 5.11.–27.11.1982

1983

Der Hang zum Gesamtkunstwerk. Kunsthaus Zürich

Städtische Kunsthalle, Düsseldorf

Museum Moderner Kunst, Wien

Große Orangerie, Schloß Charlottenburg, Berlin. March/März–April 1984

Designing for Opera. Grolier Club, New York City. 6.9.–8.10.1983

The Permanent Collection. Highlights and Recent Acquisitions. The Grey Art Gallery, New York University, New York City. 8.11.–10.12.1983

Art & Dance. Images from the Modern Dialogue, 1890–1980. Neuberger Museum, State University of New York, Purchase

Energiëën, Amsterdam 1990, Room for Salomé/Raum für Salomé

1984

Survey of Contemporary Painting & Sculpture. Museum of Modern Art, New York City. 17.5.–7.8.1984

Festival Nacional de Video. (*Video 50* and/ und *Stations*). Círculo de Bellas Artes de Madrid. 11.6.–16.6.1984

Familiar Forms/Unfamiliar Furniture. First Street Forum, St. Louis. 19.9.–10.11.1984

Highlights. Selections from the BankAmerica Corporation Art Collection. A.P. Giannini Gallery, San Francisco. 11.10.–27.11.1984

1985

Large Drawings.

Bass Museum of Art, Miami Beach. 15.1.–17.2.1985

Madison Art Center, Madison. 11.8.–22.9.1985

Norman MacKenzie Art Gallery, University of Regina, Saskatchewan. 8.11.–15.12.1985

Anchorage Museum of History and Art, Anchorage. 15.1.–1.3.1986

Santa Barbara Museum of Art, Santa Barbara. 11.4.–8.5.1986

Cinquante ans de dessins américains, 1930–1980. (Drawings for/ Zeichnungen zu *"Great Day in the Morning".*) École des Beaux-Arts, Paris. 3.5.–13.7.1985

Städtische Galerie im Städelschen Kunstinstitut, Frankfurt (*Amerikanische Zeichnungen*). 28.11.1985–26.1.1986

Ed Grazda and Douglas Sandhage. Photographs of Robert Wilson's "Deafman Glance" at the Brooklyn Academy of Music, 1971. Dance Theater Workshop, New York City. 14.5.–30.6.1985

New Works on Paper 3. Museum of Modern Art, New York City. 25.6.–3.9.1985

Spatial Relationships in Video. Museum of Modern Art, New York City. 4.7.–3.9.1985

High Style. (Sculpture/Skulptur *Stalin chairs*). Whitney Museum of American Art, New York City. 18.9.1985–16.2.1986

Contemporary American Prints. Recent Acquisitions. The Brooklyn Museum, New York City. 27.9.–30.12.1985

The New Figure. Birmingham Museum of Art, Birmingham. 4.10.–17.11.1985

Works on Paper. Joe Fawbush Editions, New York City. 16.11.–14.12 1985

Quatorzième Festival International du nouveau cinéma et de la vidéo Montréal. Montréal.

1986

Public and Private. American Prints Today. The 24th National Print Exhibition. (*"Parsifal".*) The Brooklyn Museum, New York City. 7.2.–5.5.1986

Flint Institute of Arts, Flint. 28.7.–7.9.1986

Rhode Island School of Design, Providence. 29.9.–9.11.1986

Museum of Art, Carnegie Institute, Pittsburgh. 1.12.1986–22.3.1987

Mr. Bojangles' Memory: og son of fire, Paris 1992

Walker Art Center, Minneapolis.
1.2.1987–22.3.1987

*Die Maler und das Theater im 20. Jahr-
hundert.* Schirn Kunsthalle, Frankfurt.
1.3.–19.5.1986

Mill Valley Film Festival. (Video *Deafman
Glance*). Sequoia Theatre, Mill Valley.
25.9.–2.10.1986

Works from the Paula Cooper Gallery.
John Berggruen Gallery, San Francisco.
14.10.–20.11.1986

1987

Sculpture. Procter Art Center, Bard
College, Annandale-on-Hudson.
1.3.–18.3.1987

Resolution. A Critique of Video Art.
Los Angeles Contemporary Exhibitions,
Los Angeles. 10.4.–16.5.1987

L'époque, la mode, le moral, la passion.
(Video *Deafman Glance*)

Centre National d'Art et de Culture
Georges-Pompidou, Paris.
21.5.–17.8.1987

Art Against AIDS. A Benefit Exhibition.
(Drawing/Zeichnung *"the CIVIL warS"*)

Paula Cooper Gallery, New York City.
4.6.–4.7.1987

Paula Cooper Gallery, New York City.
Summer/Sommer 1987

The Arts for Television (Video *Deafman
Glance*). (Co-organized by/Mitver-
anstalter Stedelijk Museum, Amsterdam
and/und Museum of Contemporary Art,
Los Angeles.) Stedelijk Museum,
Amsterdam. September 1987

Institute of Contemporary Art, Boston.
17.9.–1.11.1987

Museum of Contemporary Art, Los Angeles.
6.10.–15.11.1987

Contemporary Arts Museum, Houston.
10.6.–16.7.1989

Aarhus Videofestival '87. (Video *Deafman
Glance*). Aarhus. 5.9.–13.9.1987

*Ross Bleckner/Michael Byron/Roy Lerner/
Barry Le Va/Will Mentor/Deborah
Remington/Gary Stephan/Keung Szeto/
Gilbert & George. Pictures/Robert
Wilson. Drawings.* Aldrich Museum
of Contemporary Art, Ridgefield,
Connecticut. 27.9.1987–3.1.1988

Lead. Hirschl & Adler Modern, New York
City. 3.12.1987–16.1.1988

Sculptors on Paper. New Work. Madison
Art Center, Madison.
5.12.1987–31.1.1988

Kalamazoo Institute of Arts, Kalamazoo.
6.9.–16.10.1988

Pittsburgh Center for the Arts, Pittsburgh.
28.5.–19.6.1988

Sheldon Memorial Art Gallery, University
of Nebraska, Lincoln. 14.3.–30.4.1989

Robert Wilson, Deichtorhallen, Hamburg 1993

1988

*Focus on the Collection. Painting and
Sculpture from the 1970s and 1980s.*
Neuberger Museum, Purchase.
31.1.–27.3.1988

*Zeichenkunst der Gegenwart. Sammlung
Prinz Franz von Bayern.* Staatliche
Graphische Sammlung, München.
21.9.–18.12.1988

1989

Artist/Designer. Opening Exhibition.
Artist/Designer, New York City.
11.5.–30.6.1989

Parachute Magazine Benefit. Galerie René
Blouin, Montréal. August 1989

25 Jahre Video-Skulptur. Kongresshalle,
Berlin. 27.8.–24.9.1989

Guest Artist in Printmaking. College of Fine
Arts, University of Texas, Austin.
1.9.–29.9.1989

Festivalkrant. World Wide Video Festival.
(Video *La Femme à la Cafetière*).
Kijkhuis, Den Haag. 9.9.–16.9.1989

Festival des Programmes Audiovisuels.
(Video *La Femme à la Cafetière*).
Cannes. 7.10.–8.10.1989

La Rose des Vents. Soirée Bob Wilson.
(Video.) Café du Théâtre, Centre
d'Action culturelle, Villeneuve d'Ascq.
14.10.1989

Bienal Internacional de São Paulo.
São Paulo. 14.10.–10.12.1989

Biennale Festival of Cinema Art. (Video
La Femme à la Cafetière). Barcelona.
November 1989

Festival de Video Art Plastique. (Video
La Femme à la Cafetière). Herouville
St. Clair. 30.11.–3.12.1989

Artists' Furniture. The Harcus Gallery,
Boston. 9.12.1989–18.1.1990

1990

"Black Rider". Robert Wilson/William
S. Burroughs. XPO Galerie, Hamburg.
3.3.–28.4.1990

International Video Festival. (Video
La Femme à la Cafetière). Saint-Herbin.
22.3.–25.3.1990

Monsters of Grace, Berlin 1993

Akira Ikeda Gallery, New York 1994

Video Art. (Video *Deafman Glance*). University of Rhode Island, Kingston. 27.3.–13.4.1990

Video and Dream. (Video *Deafman Glance*). Museum of Modern Art, New York City. March/März 1990

Festival International du Film sur l'Art. (Video *La Femme à la Cafetière*.) Montréal. March/März 1990

Energiëën. (Tableau *Salomé's Room.*) Stedelijk Museum, Amsterdam. 7.4.–29.7.1990

Modèles Déposés–1. C.A.U.E., Limoges. 20.4.–26.5.1990

Art Against AIDS. (Drawing for/Zeichnung zu *"Parzival".*) 406 Seventh Street, N.W., Washington, D.C. 3.5.–26.5.1990

Second Harvest. Artists' Tribute to Paul Baker. The Art Center, Waco. 10.7.–19.8.1990

Festival du Film d'Art. (Video *La Femme à la Cafetière*). Paris. November 1990

Bienal de la imagen en Movimiento '90. (Video *La Femme à la Cafetière*.) Centro de Arte Reina Sofia, Madrid. 12.12.–24.12.1990

1991

Danses Tracées. Dessins et Notation des Chorégraphes. Centre de la Vieille Charité, Musées de Marseille. 19.4.–9.6.1997

Big Motion in Video. (Internationales Videotheater). Medienwerkstatt, Wien. 7.5.–8.5.1991

Interactions. Institute of Contemporary Art, Philadelphia. 23.5.–7.7.1991

The Artist's Hand. Drawings from the BankAmerica Corporation Art Collection. San Diego Museum of Contemporary Art, La Jolla. 8.6.–4.8.1991

Sélection. Œuvres de la collection. FAE Musée d'Art Contemporain, Pully-Lausanne. 10.6.–13.10.1991

Mara Eggert. Magische Augenblicke. Inszenierungen von Ruth Berghaus und Robert Wilson. Deutsches Theatermuseum, München. 24.7.–29.9.1991

1992

Drawings for the Stage. Stephen Solovy Fine Art, Chicago. 11.1.–February/Februar 1992

The Exploding Valentine. A Weekend of Video Romance and Revolt. (Video *La Femme à la Cafetière*). The Kitchen, New York City. 14.2.1992

10th World Wide Video Festival. (Video *Mr. Bojangles' Memory*). Kijkhuis, Den Haag. 7.4.–12.4.1992

Contemporary Masterworks. Feigen Incorporated, Chicago. 15.5.–20.6.1992

Six Operas. Six Artists. (Drawings from/ Zeichnungen zu *"Alceste".*) Marion Koogler McNay Art Museum, San Antonio. 17.5.–6.9.1992

Summer Drawing Show. Galerie Fred Jahn, Stuttgart. 1.7.–22.7.1992

1993

I Am the Enunciator. Thread Waxing Space, New York City. 9.1.–20.2.1993

Exploring Art in Contemporary Scale. Laguna Gloria Museum, Austin. 24.1.–February/Februar 1993

Mediale '93. Deichtorhallen und Hafen, Hamburg. 5.2.–28.3.1993

Magazin im Magazin. eine Ausstellung des Vorarlberger Kunstvereins–Magazin 4. Vorarlberger Kunstverein, Bregenz. 29.5.–26.6.1993

Architektur Zentrum, Vienna/Wien 23.11.–13.12.1993

Seeing the Forest Through the Trees. Contemporary Arts Museum, Houston. 14.8.–10.10.1993

1994

Outside the Frame. Performance and the Object. A Survey History of Performance Art in the USA since 1950. Cleveland Center for Contemporary Art, Cleveland. 11.2.–1.5.1994

Snug Harbor Cultural Center, Staten Island. 26.2.–18.6.1995

Dessiner. Une Collection d'Art Contemporain. Musée du Luxembourg, Paris. 6.5.–3.7.1994

Festival International des Jardins (Garden design by/Landschaftsdesign von Robert Wilson). Chaumont-sur-Loire. 1.7.–16.10.1994

1995

The Art Show. Art Dealers Association of America. (Paula Cooper Gallery.) Seventh Regiment Armory, New York City. 23.2.–27.2.1995

Die Muse? Transforming the Image of Woman in Contemporary Art. (Sponsored by/unterstützt durch Universität Salzburg and/und Galerie Thaddaeus Ropac.) Max Gandolph Bibliothek, Salzburg. 22.7.–2.9.1995

Galerie Thaddaeus Ropac, Paris [*Muses? Transformation de l'image féminine dans l'art contemporain*]. 26.9.–18.11.1995

Féminin/Masculin (le sexe de l'art). (Video 50.) Centre National d'Art et de Culture Georges-Pompidou, Paris. 26.10.1995–12.2.1996

Un Cuore Per Amico. Triennale de Milano, Milano. 30.10.1995

Prints To Benefit the Foundation for Contemporary Performance Arts. Brooke Alexander Gallery, New York City. 5.12–29.12.1995

Creative Arts Workshops for Kids (Mural, with contribution by/Wandgemälde mit einem Beitrag von Robert Wilson.) 124th Street, between 2nd & 3rd Ave, New York City. 1995

The Pleasures of Merely Circulating (Publication/Publikation). Zürich, 1995, p./S. 31

Waterjug Boy, Cologne/Köln 1996

1996

Black, Grey & White. Galerie Bugdahn
und Kaimer, Düsseldorf.
29.5.–23.8.1996

*Puppets and Performing Objects in the
20th Century*. (Puppet from/Puppe aus
"the CIVIL warS—Knee Plays"). New
York Public Library for the Performing Arts,
New York City. 11.6.–28.9.1996

The Chair Event. (Auction to benefit/
Auktion zugunsten von *Friends in Deed*).
The Metropolitan Pavillon, New York
City. December/Dezember 1996

1997

1997 Biennial Exhibition. (Video *Death of
Molière*). Whitney Museum of American
Art, New York City. 20.3.–15.6.1997

Love Hotel. (Traveling exhibition of the/
Wanderausstellung der National Gallery
of Australia.) Plimsoll Gallery, University
of Tasmania, Hobart. 30.8.–28.9.97

Australian Centre for Contemporary Art,
Melbourne. 18.10.–30.11.97

Brisbane City Gallery, Brisbane.
26.3.–10.5.98

Auckland Art Gallery, Auckland.
30.5.–2.8.98

The John Curtain Gallery, Curtin University
of Technology, Perth. 4.9.– 4.10.98

Robert Wilson/Villa Stuck, Munich/München 1997

**Works by Robert Wilson in Public
Collections/Arbeiten von Robert Wilson
in öffentlichen Sammlungen**

The Art Institute of Chicago

National Gallery of Australia, Canberra

Bank of America, San Francisco

Centre National d'Art et de Culture
Georges-Pompidou, Paris

The Contemporary Arts Center, Cincinnati

Cooper-Hewitt National Design Museum,
New York City

Fonds d'Art Contemporain, Paris

Galerie der Stadt, Stuttgart

Hamburger Bahnhof – Museum für
Gegenwart, Berlin

Huntington Art Museum, University
of Texas, Austin

Kunstmuseum Bern

Lannan Foundation, Los Angeles

The Menil Collection, Houston

The Metropolitan Museum of Art,
New York City

Musée d'Art Contemporain,
Pully/Lausanne

Museum of Art, Rhode Island School
of Design, Providence

Museum Boijmans Van Beuningen,
Rotterdam

The Museum of Contemporary Art,
Los Angeles

Museum of Fine Arts, Boston

The Museum of Fine Arts, Houston

The Museum of Modern Art,
New York City

Philadelphia Museum of Art

Stedelijk Museum, Amsterdam

The Toledo Museum of Art, Ohio

Virginia Museum of Fine Arts, Richmond

Walker Art Center, Minneapolis

Robert Wilson/Villa Stuck, Munich/München 1997

Notes

"Freedom Machines" (pp. 9–31)

1. Louis Aragon, "Lettre ouverte à André Breton sur *Le Regard du Sourd*, l'art, la science, et la liberté." *Les Lettres Francaises* (June 2, 1971) cited and translated by Trevor Fairbrother in: *Robert Wilson's Vision* (Museum of Fine Arts, Boston, 1991): 114.
2. *Deafman Glance* had been inspired by the drawings of Raymond Andrews, whom Robert Wilson adopted after seeing the deaf-mute eleven-year-old black child being harassed by a policeman on the street. Ibid: 111.
3. John Perreault, "Art: Trying Harder," *Village Voice*, January 1, 1970: 16.
4. Richard Foreman, "The Life and Times of Sigmund Freud," *Village Voice*, May 21, 1970.
5. Trevor Fairbrother, 1991 (see note 1): 110.
6. Richard Foreman, 1970 (see note 4). Foreman also applied the term "impenetrable (holy) objects" to Wilson's performers.
7. The Getty Information Institute's ULAN (Union List of Artist Names) consists of "some 200,000 names representing approximately 100,000 individual artists (or 'creators,' including performance artists, decorative artists, etc.) and architects, cumulated from nine participating Getty documentation projects": http://www.ahip.getty.edu/ulan_browser/intro.html
8. Marie-Claude Dane, "Exposition Robert Wilson," in: *Robert Wilson: Dessins et Sculptures* (Musée Galliera, Paris, 1974): "cette exposition devrait le démontrer, que ce jeune auteur, acteur, cinéaste, metteur en scène, Président de la Byrd Hoffman Foundation, etc, etc, dessine et peint bien plutôt qu'il n'écrit et se considère lui-même comme un artiste plastique."
9. These include the Galerie Wünsche in Bonn, Galerie Folker Skulima in Berlin; Galerie Zwirner in Cologne; Galerie Annemarie Verna in Zurich; Galerie le Dessin, Paris; Produzentengalerie in Hamburg; Galerie Brinkman, Amsterdam; Galleria Franca Mancini in Pesaro; Galerie Fred Jahn and Galerie Biedermann in Munich; Galerie Harald Behm, Hamburg; Marlene Eleini Gallery, London; Galerie Lüpke, Frankfurt; Galerie Fabian Walter, Basel; Yvon Lambert, Paris; Busche Galerie, Cologne; Galerie Gamarra y Garrigues, Madrid; Galerie Thaddaeus Ropac, Paris and Salzburg; Nathalie Beeckman Fine Arts, Brussels; Galerie Franck + Schulte, Berlin; and Galeria Luís Serpa, Lisbon.
10. Both Jacqueline Brody in 1985 and Robert Enright in 1994 noted that Robert Wilson constantly made points during an interview by drawing on a piece of paper in front of him. Enright commented: "It was a telling example of what he means when he advises us to listen to the pictures," in: "A Clean, Well-Lighted Grace," *Border Crossings*, 1994: 16.
11. Interview with Gynter Quill, *Waco Tribune Herald*, July 25, 1965, cited by Trevor Fairbrother, 1991 (see note 1): 110.
12. Interview with Rüdiger Schaper, "Überall ist Texas," *Süddeutsche Zeitung*, March 23, 1996.
13. Robert Stearns, *Robert Wilson: From a Theater of Images* (The Contemporary Arts Center, Cincinnati, 1980): 50.
14. Jacqueline Brody, "Robert Wilson: Performance on Paper," in: *The Print Collector's Newsletter*, Vol. XVI, No. 4, September-October 1985: 124.
15. Dorine Mignot, "Room for Salomé: An Interview with Robert Wilson," in: *Energieën* (Stedelijk Museum, Amsterdam, 1990): 112–113.
16. Roland H. Wiegenstein, "Die Skulpturen von Robert Wilson" in: *Robert Wilson: Skulpturen* (Galerie Folker Skulima, Berlin, 1978).
17. Richard Foreman 1970 (see note 4). For further information on the history of tableaux vivants and the so-called Attitudes see Birgit Joos, "Tanz der Statuen — die Attitüden des 18. Jahrhunderts" in: *Loie Fuller: Getanzter Jugendstil* (Museum Villa Stuck, Munich, 1995): 81–84.
18. Craig Owens, "Robert Wilson: Tableaux," *Art in America*, No. 68, November 1980: 114.
19. Ibid.
20. Brigitte Reinhardt, "Zum Environment von Robert Wilson" in: *Robert Wilson: Erinnerung an eine Revolution* (Galerie der Stadt, Stuttgart, 1987): 17.
21. Johann-Karl Schmidt, "Robert Wilson *still life is real life*," in: *Robert Wilson: Erinnerung an eine Revolution* (see note 20): 6. The environment was exhibited again in the Kunst-Buffet Badischer Bahnhof, Basel, Switzerland in 1989, with an actor, and in the retrospective exhibition *Robert Wilson's Vision*, organized by the Museum of Fine Arts, Boston, USA in 1991, with a costumed, animated mannequin.
22. It was also presented in the exhibition *Monuments*, organized by the Kestner-Gesellschaft in Hanover in 1991.
23. Robert Enright, 1994 (see note 10): 20. Wilson commented: "So [a chair is] a piece of sculpture and it's like an actor."
24. Dorine Mignot, 1990 (see note 15): 113.
25. Ibid.
26. Ibid.
27. Sanssouci was the favorite castle of Frederick the Great (1712–1786). Constructed in the eighteenth century in a large park, it is situated in Potsdam, near Berlin. The photographs *Forest Portraits, East Berlin* were taken by Robert Wilson as research for *The Forest*, 1988, a collaboration with Heiner Müller and David Byrne.
28. Rebecca Nemser, "Night and day: 'Vision' isn't an exhibit, it's an experience," *The Boston Phoenix*, February 8, 1991.
29. Golem means, in Hebrew, shapeless mass. "According to the Kabbala, a wise man who knows the secret name of God, composed of 72 letters, can temporarily create an artificial human by breathing life into a golem of clay.": dtv-Lexikon.
30. The papier mache is made from Asian newspapers: Trevor Fairbrother, 1991, "Room I" (see note 1).
31. According to Trevor Fairbrother, 1991 "Room II" (see note 1), the restored Bourbon Monarchy employed an old Bonapartist to reside in one of the elephant legs and act as caretaker of the plaster monument after Napoleon's demise.
32. Ibid, Room III.
33. Ibid.
34. *The Christian Science Monitor*, February 21, 1991.
35. Thierry Grillet, "Conversation: An interview of Robert Wilson," in: *Visitor's Guidebook: Robert Wilson: Mr. Bojangles' Memory: og son of fire* (Centre Georges Pompidou, Paris, 1991): n.p.
36. Wilson originally planned to also include the work of the following artists: Alexander Calder, Charles Simonds, Joseph Cornell, René Magritte, and Claes Oldenburg.
37. Robert Hewison, *Sunday Times*, November 16, 1991.
38. Joseph Hantmann, "Strandpartie mit Rudolf Heß: Geschichtspanorama für Stadtbewohner: Robert Wilsons Möbel im Centre Pompidou," in: *Frankfurter Allgemeine Zeitung*, November 21, 1991.
39. The *Binnenalster Door* is an enlarged version of the door created by Wilson for *Orlando*, a theater work based on Virginia Woolf's novel of the same name from 1928, which was performed at the Schaubühne in Berlin in 1989. A smaller version of the work was exhibited in *Mediale* in February of 1993.
40. The installation, which was later purchased by the National Gallery in Berlin, consisted of three rooms: Room 1 — white wax figure of an arm and hand grabbing a second hand, dagger, and recorded sound; Room 2 — fragment of a face mask made from the skin of a pig's bladder tinted gray, lead helicopter, square barred windows, names in graffiti in Arabic and other languages; Room 3 — wood bench of oak or ash (like a church pew), white wax figure of a giant nude male, wax figure of a youth covered with a gray felt blanket, wax figure of a middle-aged woman dressed in a black and gray tailored suit, vertical window which emits cold white daylight and recorded sound. (Description provided by the Byrd Hoffman Foundation.) "Monsters of Grace is an environment containing elements of light, sound and sculpture. Wilson created the work at the Galerie Franck + Schulte in 1993, using plaster casts from the collection of the State Museum." Wulf Herzogenrath, *'Es ist gehauen nicht und nicht gestochen ...': Erwerbungen von Werken mit neuen Medien für die Nationalgalerie 1992–1994*, Nationalgalerie, Berlin.
41. This exhibition, organized by Carmen Albroch, the director of IVAM, was presented on the occasion of the premiere of the opera *Don Juan 'Ultimo* by Vicente Molina Foix and Robert Wilson in the Teatro María Guerrero in Madrid in conjunction with the Festival de Otono in Madrid.
42. The letter from Heiner Müller was written to Wilson in response to the environment *Memory of a Revolution* in Stuttgart in 1987.
43. *Robert Wilson: Memory/Loss* (Biennale di Venezia, Venice, 1993): n.p. Objects by Robert Wilson and Tadeusz Kantor, sound score by Hans Peter Kuhn, text by Heiner Müller, lighting by Heinrich Brunke and Robert Wilson. Curated by Achille Bonito Oliva.
44. Diodorus Siculus called the Ramesseum (of Rameses II) at Thebes "the tomb of Ozymandias." This name was adopted by Shelley (1792–1822) for his poem *Ozymandias* : The Oxford Companion to English Literature.
45. Thomas Hutchinson (ed.), *The Complete Poetical Works of Percy Bysshe Shelley* (London, 1905 reprinted 1965): 550.
46. Antje Weber, "Das Sehen ist so wichtig wie das Hören," *Süddeutsche Zeitung*, Munich, July 10, 1997.
47. The chief works of the American-born poet Thomas Stearns Eliot (1888–1965) were *The Waste Land* (1922), *Ash Wednesday* (1930), and *Murder in the Cathedral* (1935).
48. Antje Weber, 1997 (see note 46).
49. Hans Peter Kuhn has worked with Robert Wilson since the production of *Death Destruction & Detroit* at the Schaubühne am Halleschen Ufer in Berlin in 1979. Compact disc recordings of Kuhn's sound environments were published on the occasion of both the Boston and the Paris exhibitions.
50. Roberto Andò, "For Robert Wilson," in: *Robert Wilson: Disegni di Gibellina — Memorie della Terra Desolata* (Gibellina Nuova, Sicily, 1993). Wilson produced a stage work titled *T.S.E.* in a former granary in Gibellina, an extension of his project for the Venice Biennale: "Ich dachte dabei an eine Art Porträt von Eliot," Antje Weber, 1997 (see note 46).
51. Hans Peter Kuhn in: *Robert Wilson: Disegni di Gibellina* (see note 50).
52. Wim Crouwel, Foreword, *Robert Wilson: Portrait, Still Life, Landscape* (Museum Boijmans Van Beuningen, Rotterdam, 1993).
53. Wilson noted in an interview with Piet de Jonge in Robert Wilson: *Portrait, Still Life, Landscape*, (see note 52) that "This idea of three separate spaces could be very much related to *The Life and Times of Sigmund Freud*. The first act on the beach, the beach in bright daylight. The second act in a Victorian drawing room, gray. And the third act in a cave, darker and with animals. And in some ways these three spaces (in the museum) are part of this continuum. "
54. Unless otherwise indicated all quotations are taken from the catalogue to the exhibition and from a letter to the author from Piet de Jonge dated October 15, 1997.
55. Robert Wilson: "The walls are painted white. You have light from exposed light-bulbs that's rather harsh and aggressive, there's aluminium shelving. It looks like a warehouse. You can walk through this labyrinth and see things up close," in: Robert Enright, 1994 (see note 10): 21.
56. Ibid: 22.
57. "In the case of the Boston exhibition, he [Wilson] examined the 15-foot-square coffered units that make up the ceiling of the Gund Gallery, and diagrammed the grid these squares defined. It was three units wide and nine units long, making the proportions of the floor plan one to three. Wilson plotted walls to divide the space into three square rooms (each comprising nine ceiling units)," Trevor Fairbrother, 1991 (see note 1): 36. Wilson also used the same principle in his installation titled "Three Rooms" in the Akira Ikeda Gallery in New York in 1994.
58. Michael Ratcliffe, "The Magus of Clink Street," *The Observer Review*, September 3, 1995.
59. Ibid.
60. Lyn Gardner, "Where angels peer," *The Guardian*, London, September 22, 1995.
61. Tom Lubbock, "Beyond, caverns beckon, the darkness lit in pools," *The Independent*, September 19, 1995.
62. Lyn Gardner, 1995 (see note 60).
63. Ibid.
64. Tom Lubbock, 1995 (see note 61).
65. Ibid.
66. See Jo-Anne Birnie Danzker, "Max Beckmann und die Wissenschaft der Sklaven," in: *Max Beckmann: Welt-Theater* (Museum Villa Stuck, Munich, 1993): 11–14.
67. Rüdiger Schaper, 1996 (see note 12).
68. Dorine Mignot, 1990 (see note 15).

"Robert Wilson/Villa Stuck" (pp. 32–37)

1. Michael Petzet and Gerhard Hojer, *The Castle of Neuschwanstein* (Munich, 1975):4.
2. Ibid:10 and p.12.
3. See Barbara Hardtwig, "Die Sünde" in: *Franz von Stuck: Die Sammlung des Museums Villa Stuck* (Museum Villa Stuck, Munich, 1997): 64–71.
4. In 1905.
5. *Der Mond im Gras: einmal keinmal immer* by Robert Wilson, based on stories by the Brothers Grimm and Georg Büchner, music by Robyn Schulkowsky. An exhibition of drawings for this project was also shown at the Gallery Biedermann in Munich.
6. Wilson had worked with the Kammerspiele before, having premiered his stage work *The Golden Windows* there in 1982 and having directed Chekhov's *Swan Song* in 1989. His drawings for *The Golden Windows* were exhibited in Munich at the Lenbachhaus and in the Gallery Fred Jahn in 1982. *Monuments*, an exhibition of his sculptural furniture works, was shown at the Bavarian Academy of Fine Arts in Munich in 1991.
7. A revival of *La Maladie de la Mort* by Marguerite Duras, music by Hans Peter Kuhn, performed by Lucinda Childs and Michel Piccoli, Ruhr Festspielhaus, Recklinghausen, Germany.
8. Trevor Fairbrother also notes in Robert Wilson's *Vision* (Museum of Fine Arts, Boston, 1991) that "after three years of general discussion in Boston and elsewhere, the moment was suddenly right": 36. The time span for the preparation of this project was almost identical to that of the Villa Stuck.

9. Watermill is situated in a 9,000 square-meter brick building constructed in the 1920s. Robert Wilson: "Watermill ist eine Art Think-Tank, ein Ort, wo neue Arbeiten entwickelt, Projekte auf den Weg gebracht werden, ob es sich um Film, Architektur, Skulptur, Oper, Tanz oder Theater handelt... Die Finanzierung läuft über den Verkauf meiner Kunstwerke und über meine Theaterarbeit" in: "Überall ist Texas," Süddeutsche Zeitung, March 3, 1996.

10. "I've been working on it for years. It took me a long time to figure it [Parsifal] out — two or three years.... You see, I spend so long working on something that the furniture or whatever is usually very carefully made." Interview with Robert Wilson by Jacqueline Brody in: The Print Collector's Newsletter, Vol. XVI, No.4. September–October 1985: 119 and 121.

11. In the 1960s an additional floor was added to Stuck's atelier in order to create more exhibition space.

12. Eleven Ideas (1–5, 7, 9, 11, 13, 18 and 19).

13. The two hand-painted photographs are also designed to look like "identical" mechanical reproductions.

14. Two other especially ambitious projects (a reconstruction of Stuck's former atelier in the Theresienstraße and a group photo of Stuck with other members of the Munich Secession) were also technically and financially impossible to realize.

15. Another traced photograph which interested Robert Wilson, that of Stuck's stepdaughter Olga Lindpaintner, was originally planned for the "dome room," Stuck's atelier after 1914. If, as originally planned, both the historic villa and the later addition from 1914 had been included in the project Villa Stuck, then both of Stuck's ateliers — the place where his work was produced — would have been used for tableaux based on tracings and drawings on the reverse of Stuck's photographs.

16. Cited by Trevor Fairbrother (see note 8): 109.

17. Robert Enright, "A Clean, Well-Lighted Grace," Border-Crossings, 1994: 17.

18. Jacqueline Brody, 1985 (see note 10): 124.

19. Christine Dössel, "Ich will die Welt nicht verändern!", Die Woche, November 7, 1997: 54.

"Tableaux"
(pp. 38–87)

1. The sound was originally to have been that of a man clearing his throat. Later this was changed to "some text, letter, old recording."

2. Friedrich August von Kaulbach (1850–1920) was the director of the Academy in Munich. His daughter, Hedda, was a close friend of Stuck's daughter, Mary.

3. For a detailed account of the hostage taking see Franz von Stuck: Die Sammlung des Museums Villa Stuck (Museum Villa Stuck, Munich, 1997): 222–224.

4. Interview with Rüdiger Schaper, "Überall ist Texas," Süddeutsche Zeitung, March 23, 1996.

5. "Der Musiksalon" in: Villa Stuck (Museum Villa Stuck, Munich, 1992): 18.

6. Ibid: 19.

7. For a detailed analysis of this painting see Barbara Hardtwig, "Phantastische Jagd" in: Franz von Stuck (see note 3): 50–53. "However, the fantasy figure of the Deer-Man-Centaur is clearly a product of Stuck's own imagination. A further original idea was to take the hunting motif, revived by Gustave Courbet in the mid-nineteenth century, and transpose it into a mythological setting."

8. A centaur is a fabulous creature with the head, arms, and torso of a man, and the lower body and legs of a horse.

9. "Dying Lioness": a gypsum carving from c. 645 BC. Nineveh (ancient Ninua) was the capital of the Assyrian empire on the left bank of the Tigris from 704 BC until its destruction in 612 BC. The palaces of Sennacherib and Ashurbanipal were excavated from 1842 onwards by, among others, P.E. Bottas and Sir A.H. Layard. The original reliefs are presently in the collection of the British Museum.

10. Alexander Rauch, "Symbolismus zwischen 'Paradies' und 'Sünde': Das Werk des Künstlers und seine Villa" in: Die Villa Stuck in München (Bayerische Vereinsbank, Munich, 1992): 48.

11. One of the tableaux in the environment H.G. in London in 1995 also had a heaven filled with golden arrows.

12. Fasching is a pre-Lenten celebration in Germany. For a description of this photograph and for information on the photographer, see pages 31, 142–143, and 187 of Franz von Stuck und die Photographie: Inszenierung und Dokumentation (Museum Villa Stuck, Munich, 1996).

13. See Ulrich Pohlmann, "'Als hätte er sich selbst entworfen'" in: Franz von Stuck und die Photographie (see note 12): 31.

14. "I think the idea is that it is something different [from a Stuck painting] — like he was having a party and there was a decorator who did something": letter from Robert Wilson to the author and Stefan Hageneier, August 11, 1997.

15. Willi Geiger, "The age of the Great War begins, a time of frenzied political and intellectual upheaval. Futurism, Cubism, Expressionism and other artistic movements generated in this tumultuous period sweep through Europe.... How strange Stuck's enchanted garden remains, populated as it is with nymphs, fauns, centaurs and Amazons, how quaint it seems in comparison with these explosions of the new!" in: Franz von Stuck (Villa Stuck, Munich, 1968), n.p.

16. This room was also used for intimate dinners.

17. Franz von Stuck spent the summer of 1890 with Ludwig von Herterich, K.J. Becker-Gundahl, Wilhelm Dürr, Julius Exter, and other artists on the property of the painter Hugo von Preen in the Osternberger Artists' Colony. See Franz von Stuck und die Photographie (see note 12): 153.

18. Alexander Rauch (see note 10): 54.

19. Illustrierte Zeitung, 99/2580: 684 cited in: Jo-Anne Birnie Danzker, Loïe Fuller: Getanzter Jugendstil (Museum Villa Stuck, Munich, 1995): 12.

20. See Franz von Stuck und die Photographie (see note 12): 104 and 168.

21. Robert Enright, "A Clean, Well-Lighted Grace" in: Border Crossings, 1994: 16.

22. For a discussion of this painting see Edwin Becker, Franz von Stuck: Eros & Pathos (Van Gogh Museum, Amsterdam, 1995): 36.

23. Letter from Piet de Jonge to the author, dated October 15, 1997.

24. Otto Julius Bierbaum, Franz Stuck, Munich, 1893: 58.

25. "Still Life: Room II" in: Robert Wilson: Portrait, Still Life, Landscape (Museum Boijmans Van Beuningen, Rotterdam, 1995).

26. Hans Ottomeyer, Weg in die Moderne (Kassel, 1996): 103.

27. See Helmut Hess, "Stuck und Hanfstaengl — Künstler und Verleger" in: Franz von Stuck und die Photographie (see note 12): 116 ff and 128.

28. See Barbara Hardtwig, "Amor Imperator" in: Franz von Stuck (see note 3): 39.

29. For further information on Ernst von Possart (1848–1921) see Birgit Jooss in: Franz von Stuck und die Photographie (see note 12): 97 and 161 and Norbert Götz in: Die Prinzregentenzeit (Münchner Stadtmuseum, Munich, 1988): 360.

30. See Helmut Hess in: Franz von Stuck und die Photographie (see note 12): 128.

31. Jill Johnston, "Family Spectacles," in: Art in America, December, 1986.

32. Dorine Mignot, "Room for Salomé: An Interview with Robert Wilson" in: Energiëen (Stedelijk Museum, Amsterdam, 1990): 113. See also Robert Enright (see note 21): 16.

33. "His wife also paid frequent visits to the studio.... But then the calm was shattered. In a high, shrill voice, she would cry, 'Wonderful, wonderful, you're a genius!' Stuck generally failed to respond." Richard Knecht cited by Barbara Hardtwig in: Franz von Stuck (see note 3): 98.

34. Stuck did not allow his stepchildren to live in the Villa: see Jo-Anne Birnie Danzker: 11–17.

35. See Jo-Anne Birnie Danzker, "The Franz von Stuck Estate," ibid: 14.

36. Cited by Barbara Hardtwig, "Mary von Stuck," ibid: 98.

37. Marcella Wolff (1900–1996), "Das Haus Stuck," ibid: 221–222.

38. Mary von Stuck died shortly afterwards, and Stuck's daughter suffered an emotional breakdown, ibid: 14–16 and 62–63.

39. Eva Heilmann, "Das Plastische Werk" in: Franz von Stuck: Gemälde.Zeichnung.Plastik aus Privatbesitz (Museum Moderner Kunst, Passau, 1993): 127.

40. Otto Julius Bierbaum, Franz Stuck (see note 24): 71, cited by Barbara Hardtwig in: Franz von Stuck (see note 3): 64.

41. See for example Griselda Pollock, Vision & Difference: Feminity, Feminism and the Histories of Art (Routledge, London, 1988).

42. Hedda Kaulbach (1900–1992) was Friedrich August von Kaulbach's second daughter; her sister Mathilde, or Quappi, was married to Max Beckmann.

43. Marcella Wolff, Estate Marcella Wolff cited in: Franz von Stuck (see note 3): 221.

44. Cited by Barbara Hardtwig, ibid: 62.

Anmerkungen
»Freedom Machines« (S. 9-31)

1. Louis Aragon, ›Lettre ouverte à André Breton sur *Le Regard du sourd*, l'art, la science et la liberté‹, in: *Les Lettres Françaises*, 2. Juni 1971, zit. nach der englischen Übersetzung von Trevor Fairbrother in: ders., *Robert Wilson's Vision*, Museum of Fine Arts, Boston 1991, S. 114.
2. *Deafman Glance* war durch die Zeichnungen von Raymond Andrews angeregt worden, einem elfjährigen schwarzen Jungen, den Wilson adoptiert hatte, nachdem er Zeuge geworden war, wie der Junge von einem Polizisten auf der Straße schikaniert wurde. Ebenda, S. 111.
3. John Perreault, ›Art: Trying Harder‹, in: *Village Voice*, 1. Januar 1970, S. 16.
4. Richard Foreman, ›The Life and Times of Sigmund Freud‹, in: *Village Voice*, 21. Mai 1970.
5. Trevor Fairbrother 1991 (wie Anm. 1), S. 110.
6. Foreman (wie Anm. 4). Foreman verwendete auch den Begriff »impenetrable (holy) objects« (undurchdringliche [heilige] Objekte) für Wilsons Darsteller.
7. Die vom Getty Information Institute zusammengestellte ›Union List of Artist Names‹ (ULAN) umfaßt »rund 200 000 Namen, darunter ca. 100 000 einzelne Künstler (beziehungsweise ›Kulturschaffende‹ einschließlich darstellende Künstler, Gebrauchskünstler usw.) und Architekten. Sie faßt die Ergebnisse von neun verschiedenen Dokumentationsprojekten der Getty-Stiftung zusammen« (die Internet-Adresse lautet: http://www.ahip.getty.edu/ulan_browser/-intro.html).
8. Marie-Claude Dane, ›Exposition Robert Wilson‹, in: *Robert Wilson: Dessins et sculptures*, Musée Galliera, Paris 1974.
9. Darunter die Galerie Wünsche, Bonn, Galerie Folker Skulima, Berlin, Galerie Zwirner, Köln, Galerie Annemaria Verna, Zürich, Galerie le Dessin, Paris, Produzentengalerie, Hamburg, Galerie Brinkman, Amsterdam, Galleria Franca Mancini, Pesaro, Galerie Fred Jahn und Galerie Biedermann, München, Galerie Harald Behm, Hamburg, Marlene Eleini Gallery, London, Galerie Lüpke, Frankfurt am Main, Galerie Fabian Walter, Basel, Yvon Lambert, Paris, Busche Galerie, Köln, Galerie Gamarra y Garrigues, Madrid, Galerie Thaddaeus Ropac, Paris und Salzburg, Nathalie Beeckman Fine Arts, Brüssel, Galerie Franck + Schulte, Berlin, und Galeria Luís Serpa, Lissabon.
10. Sowohl Jacqueline Brody 1985 wie auch Robert Enright 1994 erwähnen, daß Robert Wilson während der Interviews immer wieder Dinge deutlich zu machen versuchte, indem er auf ein Stück Papier zeichnete. Enright meinte dazu: »Es ist ein treffliches Beispiel dafür, was er meint, wenn er uns rät, den Bildern zu lauschen.« Zit. nach Enright, ›A Clean, Well-Lighted Grace‹, in: *Border Crossings*, 1994, S. 16.
11. Interview mit Gynter Quill, in: *Waco Tribune Herald*, 25. Juli 1965, zit. bei Fairbrother (wie Anm. 1), S. 110.
12. Interview mit Rüdiger Schaper, ›Überall ist Texas‹, in: *Süddeutsche Zeitung*, 23. März 1996.
13. Robert Stearns, *Robert Wilson: From a Theater of Images*, Ausst.Kat., The Contemporary Arts Center, Cincinnati 1980, S. 50.
14. Jacqueline Brody, ›Robert Wilson: Performance on Paper‹, in: *The Print Collector's Newsletter*, XVI/4 (September/Oktober 1985), S. 124.
15. Dorine Mignot, ›Room for Salomé: An Interview with Robert Wilson‹, in: *Energieën*, Ausst.Kat., Stedelijk Museum, Amsterdam 1990, S. 112 f.
16. Roland H. Wiegenstein, ›Die Skulpturen von Robert Wilson‹, in: *Robert Wilson: Skulpturen*, Ausst.Kat., Galerie Folker Skulima, Berlin 1978.
17. Foreman (wie Anm. 4). Näheres über die Geschichte der ›tableaux vivants‹ und der sogenannten Attitüden bei Birgit Jooss, ›Tanz der Statuen – die Attitüden des 18. Jahrhunderts‹, in: *Loïe Fuller: Getanzter Jugendstil*, Ausst.Kat., Museum Villa Stuck, München 1995, S. 81–84.
18. Craig Owens, ›Robert Wilson: Tableaux‹, in: *Art in America*, 68 (November 1980), S. 114.
19. Ebenda.
20. Brigitte Reinhardt, ›Zum Environment von Robert Wilson‹, in: *Robert Wilson: Erinnerung an eine Revolution*, Ausst.Kat., Galerie der Stadt, Stuttgart 1987, S. 17.
21. Johann-Karl Schmidt, ›Robert Wilson – *still life is real life*‹, in: *Robert Wilson: Erinnerung an eine Revolution* (wie Anm. 20), S. 6. Das Environment wurde 1989 ein weiteres Mal, wieder mit einem Schauspieler, im Kunst-Büfett Badischer Bahnhof in Basel ausgestellt und 1991, diesmal mit einer beweglichen Puppe in Kostüm, in die vom Bostoner Museum of Fine Arts organisierte Retrospektive *Robert Wilson's Vision* einbezogen.
22. Das Tableau wurde außerdem in der 1991 von der Kestner-Gesellschaft, Hannover, veranstalteten Ausstellung *Monuments* gezeigt.
23. Enright (wie Anm. 10), S. 20. Der Stuhl, so Wilson, ist »also eine Skulptur und hat etwas von einem Schauspieler«.
24. Mignot (wie Anm. 15), S. 113.
25. Ebenda.
26. Ebenda.
27. Das im 18. Jahrhundert errichtete Schloß Sanssouci in Potsdam war das Lieblingsschloß Friedrichs des Großen (1712–1786). Es ist umgeben von einem großen Schloßpark. Wilson hatte die *Forest Portraits, East Berlin* genannten Photos als Vorarbeit für die 1988 uraufgeführte Inszenierung *The Forest*, eine Gemeinschaftsarbeit mit Heiner Müller und David Byrne, gemacht.
28. Rebecca Nemser, ›Night and day: 'Vision' isn't an exhibit, it's an experience‹, in: *The Boston Phoenix*, 8. Februar 1991.
29. »Das Wort ›Golem‹ bedeutet auf Hebräisch ›ungestaltete Masse‹. Nach der Kabbala hat ein Mensch, der den geheimnisvollen Namen Gottes von 72 Buchstaben kennt, die Macht, einen Golem aus Lehm auf Zeit zu beleben und so einen künstlichen Menschen zu schaffen« (dtv-Lexikon).
30. Das Pappmaché war aus asiatischen Zeitungen hergestellt; Fairbrother (wie Anm. 1), ›Room I‹.
31. Nach Angaben von Fairbrother (wie Anm. 1), ›Room II‹, ließ die nach Napoleons Sturz wiedereingesetzte Bourbonen-Monarchie einen alten Bonapartisten in einem der Elefantenbeine wohnen, um auf das Gipsdenkmal aufzupassen.
32. Ebenda, ›Room III‹
33. Ebenda.
34. *The Christian Science Monitor*, 21. Februar 1991.
35. Thierry Grillet, ›Conversation: An Interview of Robert Wilson‹, in: *Visitor's Guidebook: Robert Wilson: Mr. Bojangles' Memory: og son of fire*, Centre Georges Pompidou, Paris 1991.
36. Wilson hatte ursprünglich vorgehabt, auch Werke folgender Künstler einzubeziehen: Alexander Calder, Charles Simonds, Joseph Cornell, René Magritte und Claes Oldenburg.
37. Robert Hewison, *Sunday Times*, 16. November 1991.
38. Joseph Hantmann, ›Strandpartie mit Rudolf Heß. Geschichtspanorama für Stadtbewohner: Robert Wilsons Möbel im Centre Pompidou‹, in: *Frankfurter Allgemeine Zeitung*, 21. November 1991.
39. Die Binnenalster-Tür ist eine vergrößerte Version der Türe, die Wilson für eine Bühnenbearbeitung von Virginia Woolfs Roman *Orlando* (1928) gestaltet hatte, ein Stück, das 1989 an der Berliner Schaubühne aufgeführt wurde. Eine kleinere Version wurde im Februar 1993 auf der *Mediale* gezeigt.
40. Diese Installation, die später von der Berliner Nationalgalerie erworben wurde, bestand aus drei Räumen – Raum 1: ein weißer Wachsabguß eines Arms mit einer Hand, die eine andere Hand ergreift, ein Dolch und eine Tonaufnahme; Raum 2: das Fragment einer Gesichtsmaske aus der grau gefärbten Membrane einer Schweinsblase, ein Hubschrauber aus Blei, Fenster mit quadratischem Fenstergitter, als Graffiti angebrachte Namen in Arabisch und anderen Sprachen; Raum 3: eine Holzbank aus Eiche oder Esche (einer Kirchenbank ähnlich), eine weiße Wachsfigur eines riesigen nackten Mannes, eine Wachsfigur eines in eine graue Filzdecke gehüllten Jünglings, eine Wachsfigur einer Frau mittleren Alters in einem schwarzgrauen Maßkostüm, ein hochformatiges Fenster, das kaltes weißes Tageslicht ausstrahlt und eine Tonaufnahme (Beschreibung: Byrd Hoffman Foundation). »Das Licht-Ton-Skulptur-Environment *Monsters of Grace* realisierte Wilson mit Abgüssen aus der Abgußsammlung der Staatlichen Museen in der Galerie Franck + Schulte 1993 als dreiteilige Arbeit«, Wulf Herzogenrath, *»Es ist gehauen nicht und nicht gestochen ...«: Erwerbungen von Werken mit neuen Medien für die Nationalgalerie 1992–1994*, Nationalgalerie, Berlin.
41. Diese von der Direktorin des IVAM, Carmen Alborch, organisierte Ausstellung wurde präsentiert anläßlich der Uraufführung der Oper *Don Juan 'Ultimo* von Vicente Molina Foix und Robert Wilson im Teatro María Guerrero in Madrid in Verbindung mit dem Festival de Otono, Madrid.
42. Heiner Müller hatte diesen Brief an Wilson in Reaktion auf das Environment *Erinnerung an eine Revolution* 1987 in Stuttgart geschrieben. Der Brief geht weiter: »Ein früher Entwurf zur totalen Verwertung der Arbeitskraft, bis zur Verwandlung in Rohstoff, in den Konzentrationslagern. Ich konnte den Vorgang, den Zerfall von Denken, das Verlöschen von Erinnerung, nicht darstellen, nur beschreiben, und die Beschreibung verstummt, wie schon unser Versuch mit Kafka-Texten, vor der Fliehkraft Deiner Bilder: Literatur ist geronnene Erfahrung. Die Toten schreiben mit auf dem Papier der Zukunft, nach dem von allen Seiten schon die Flammen greifen.«
43. *Robert Wilson: Memory/Loss*, Biennale di Venezia, Venedig 1993, o.S. Objekte: Robert Wilson und Tadeusz Kantor, Klangpartitur: Hans Peter Kuhn, Text: Heiner Müller, Beleuchtung: Heinrich Brunke und Robert Wilson. Kurator der Ausstellung: Achille Bonito Oliva.
44. Diodorus Siculus bezeichnete das – Ramses II. geweihte – Ramesseum in Theben als »die Grabstätte des Osymandias«. Shelley (1792–1822) griff diesen Namen auf für sein Gedicht *Ozymandias*.
45. Percy Bysshe Shelley, *Gedichte*, Heidelberg 1958, S. 33.
46. Antje Weber, ›Das Sehen ist so wichtig wie das Hören‹, in: *Süddeutsche Zeitung*, 10. Juli 1997.
47. Zu den Hauptwerken des 1888 in Amerika geborenen und 1965 gestorbenen Dichters Thomas Stearns Eliot zählen *The Waste Land* (1922), *Ash Wednesday* (1930) und *Murder in the Cathedral* (1935).
48. Weber (wie Anm. 46).
49. Hans Peter Kuhn arbeitet seit der Inszenierung von *Death Destruction & Detroit* an der Schaubühne am Halleschen Ufer in Berlin 1979 mit Robert Wilson zusammen. Sowohl anläßlich der Retrospektive in Boston wie auch anläßlich der Pariser Ausstellung wurden CD-Aufnahmen von Kuhns Klangenvironments herausgebracht.
50. Roberto Andò, ›For Robert Wilson‹, in: *Robert Wilson: Disegni di Gibellina – Memorie della Terra Desolata*, Gibellina Nuova, Sizilien, 1993. Wilson inszenierte in einem ehemaligen Getreidespeicher in Gibellina ein Bühnenwerk mit dem Titel *T.S.E.*, ein Ableger seines Projektes für die Biennale von Venedig: »Ich dachte dabei an eine Art Porträt von Eliot«; Weber (wie Anm. 46).
51. Hans Peter Kuhn, in: *Robert Wilson: Disegni di Gibellina* (wie Anm. 50).
52. Wim Crouwel, ›Vorwort‹, in: *Robert Wilson: Portrait, Still Life, Landscape*, Ausst.Kat., Museum Boijmans Van Beuningen, Rotterdam 1993.
53. Wilson sagte in einem Interview mit Piet de Jonge im Rotterdamer Ausstellungskatalog: »Diese Idee mit den drei getrennten Räumen hat möglicherweise eine ganze Menge mit *The Life and Times of Sigmund Freud* zu tun. Der erste Akt auf dem Strand, der Strand am hellichten Tag. Der zweite Akt in einem viktorianischen Salon, grau. Und der dritte Akt in einer Höhle, dunkler und mit Tieren. Und in mancherlei Hinsicht sind diese drei Räume [im Museum] Teil dieses Kontinuums.«
54. Sämtliche im folgenden angeführten Zitate wurden, sofern nicht anders angegeben, dem Ausstellungskatalog und einem Brief Piet de Jonges vom 15. Oktober 1997 an die Autorin entnommen.
55. Wilson: »Die Wände sind weiß gestrichen. Das Licht kommt von nackten Glühbirnen und ist grell und aggressiv. Es gibt Regale aus Aluminium. Das Ganze wirkt wie ein Speicher. Man kann dieses Labyrinth begehen und sich die Sachen aus der Nähe ansehen.« Zit. bei Enright (wie Anm. 10), S. 21.
56. Ebenda, S. 22.
57. »Im Falle der Bostoner Ausstellung unterzog er [Wilson] die 5 x 5 großen Felder, aus denen sich die Kassettendecke der Gund Gallery zusammensetzt, einer näheren Betrachtung und machte eine schematische Skizze der orthogonalen Struktur, die die Quadrate ergaben. Es handelte sich um drei Felder in der Breite und neun in der Länge, also ein Grundrißverhältnis von eins zu drei. Wilson plante Trennwände, die den Saal in drei quadratische Räume (mit jeweils neun Deckenfeldern) aufteilten«; Fairbrother (wie Anm. 1), S. 35. Bei seiner Installation ›Drei Räume‹ in der Akira Ikeda Gallery in New York ging Wilson nach dem gleichen Prinzip vor.
58. Michael Ratcliffe, ›The magus of Clink Street‹, in: *The Observer Review*, 3. September 1995.
59. Ebenda.
60. Lyn Gardner, ›Where angels peer‹, in: *The Guardian*, London, 22. September 1995.
61. Tom Lubbock, ›Beyond, caverns beckon, the darkness lit in pools‹, in: *The Independent*, 19. September 1995.
62. Gardner (wie Anm. 60).
63. Ebenda.
64. Lubbock (wie Anm. 61).
65. Ebenda.
66. Siehe zu diesem Punkt auch Jo-Anne Birnie Danzker, ›Max Beckmann und die Wissenschaft der Sklaven‹, in: *Max Beckmann: Welt-Theater*, Ausst.Kat., Museum Villa Stuck, München 1993, S. 11–14.
67. Schaper (wie Anm. 12).
68. Mignot (wie Anm. 15).

»Robert Wilson/Villa Stuck« (S. 32-37)

1. Michael Petzet und Gerhard Hojer, *Schloß Neuschwanstein*, München 1975, S. 4.
2. Ebenda, S. 19.
3. Siehe Barbara Hardtwig, ›Die Sünde‹, in: *Franz von Stuck: Die Sammlung des Museums Villa Stuck*, München 1997, S. 64–71.
4. Im Jahr 1905.
5. *Der Mond im Gras: einmal keinmal immer* von Robert Wilson, nach Erzählungen der Brüder

Grimm und Georg Büchners, Musik Robyn Schulkowsky. Die Münchner Galerie Biedermann zeigte die Zeichnungen für dieses Projekt im Rahmen einer Ausstellung.

6. Wilson hatte bereits zuvor mit den Kammerspielen zusammengearbeitet: 1982 war dort sein Bühnenwerk *Die Goldenen Fenster/The Golden Windows* uraufgeführt worden und 1989 hatte er bei Tschechows *Schwanengesang* Regie geführt. Seine Zeichnungen zu *The Golden Windows* wurden 1982 in München in der Städtischen Galerie im Lenbachhaus und in der Galerie Fred Jahn ausgestellt. *Monuments*, eine Ausstellung seiner Möbelskulpturen, wurde 1991 in der Bayerischen Akademie der Schönen Künste in München gezeigt.

7. Eine Wiederaufnahme von *La Maladie de la Mort* von Marguerite Duras, Musik Hans Peter Kuhn, Darsteller Lucinda Childs und Michel Piccoli, Ruhr-Festspiele, Recklinghausen.

8. Auch Trevor Fairbrother erwähnt in *Robert Wilson's Vision*, Museum of Fine Arts Boston, 1991, S. 36, »daß nach drei Jahren eher allgemeiner Erörterungen in Boston und anderswo plötzlich der richtige Augenblick da war«. Die Vorbereitungszeit für das Ausstellungsprojekt in Boston war fast genauso lang wie für das Projekt *Villa Stuck*.

9. Watermill ist in einem 9 000 m² großen Gebäude aus den zwanziger Jahren untergebracht. »Watermill ist eine Art Think-Tank, ein Ort, wo neue Arbeiten entwickelt, Projekte auf den Weg gebracht werden, ob es sich um Film, Architektur, Skulptur, Oper, Tanz oder Theater handelt ... Die Finanzierung läuft über den Verkauf meiner Kunstwerke und über meine Theaterarbeit«, Robert Wilson, zit. in ›Überall ist Texas‹, in: *Süddeutsche Zeitung*, 23.3.1996.

10. »Ich habe jahrelang daran gearbeitet. Ich brauchte lange, um die Sache [Parsifal] auszuknobeln ... Sehen Sie, ich brauche so viel Zeit für die Arbeit an einer Sache, daß die Möbel oder etwaige andere Sachen mit sehr großer Sorgfalt gemacht worden sind.« Robert Wilson im Gespräch mit Jacqueline Brody, in: *The Print Collector's Newsletter*, Nr. XVI/4 (September/Oktober 1985), S. 119 und 121.

11. In den sechziger Jahren erhielt Stucks Atelier einen zusätzlichen, dritten Stock zwecks Vergrößerung der Ausstellungsfläche.

12. Insgesamt elf Ideen (Nr. 1–5, 7, 9, 11, 13, 18 und 19).

13. Die beiden von Hand gemalten ›Photographien‹ sollen außerdem wie ›identische‹ mechanische Reproduktionen wirken.

14. Zwei andere, besonders aufwendige Projekte (eine Rekonstruktion von Stucks ehemaligem Atelier in der Theresienstraße und die Nachbildung eines Gruppenphotos von Stuck mit anderen Mitgliedern der Münchner Secession) konnten ebenfalls aus technischen und finanziellen Gründen nicht realisiert werden.

15. Eine andere abgepauste Photographie, die Robert Wilson interessierte, eine Aufnahme von Stucks Stieftochter Olga Lindpaintner, war ursprünglich für den ›Kuppelsaal‹, Stucks Atelier nach 1914, geplant. Wären, wie ursprünglich vorgesehen, sowohl die historischen Räume der Villa wie der Anbau von 1914 in das Projekt *Villa Stuck* einbezogen worden, so wären beide Ateliers des Künstlers – der Ort der Entstehung seines Werks – für Tableaus verwendet worden, denen Pausen oder Zeichnungen auf den Rückseiten von Stucks Photographien zugrunde gelegen hätten.

16. Zitiert bei Fairbrother (wie Anm. 8), S. 109.

17. Robert Enright, ›A Clean, Well-Lighted Grace‹, in: *Border Crossings*, 1994, S. 17.

18. Brody (wie Anm. 10), S. 124.

19. Christine Dössel, ›Ich will die Welt nicht verändern!‹, in: *Die Woche*, 7. November 1997, S. 54.

»Tableaus«
(S. 38-87)

1. Nach dem ersten Entwurf für dieses Projekt sollte ursprünglich das Räuspern eines Mannes zu hören sein. Später wurde daraus »irgendein Text, Brief, alte Aufnahme«.

2. Friedrich August von Kaulbach (1850–1920) war Direktor der Akademie der bildenden Künste in München. Seine Tochter Hedda war eng befreundet mit Stucks Tochter Mary.

3. *Franz von Stuck: Die Sammlung des Museums Villa Stuck*, Ausst.Kat., Museum Villa Stuck, München 1997, S. 224. Näheres über die Geiselnahme auf S. 222 ff.

4. Interview mit Rüdiger Schaper, ›Überall ist Texas‹, in: *Süddeutsche Zeitung*, 23. März 1996.

5. ›Der Musiksalon‹, in: *Villa Stuck*, Museum Villa Stuck, München 1992, S. 18.

6. Ebenda, S. 19.

7. Eine ausführliche Erörterung dieses Gemäldes findet sich bei Barbara Hardtwig, ›Phantastische Jagd‹, in: *Franz von Stuck* (wie Anm. 3), S. 50–53. »Jedoch ist die Phantasiegestalt des Hirschmensch-Kentauren offenbar eine originäre Stucksche Erfindung. Ebenfalls seine ureigene Idee ist die Umsetzung des Jagdmotivs, das der französische Maler Gustave Courbet um die Jahrhundertmitte neu belebt hatte, in ein mythologisches Ambiente.«

8. Ein Kentaur ist ein Fabelwesen mit menschlichem Oberkörper und Pferdeleib.

9. *Sterbende Löwin*, ein um 645 v.Chr. entstandenes Gipsrelief. Ninive oder Ninua war die Hauptstadt des Assyrerreiches am linken Ufer des Tigris von 704 bis zur Zerstörung 612 v.Chr. Die reliefgeschmückten Paläste Sanheribs und Assurbanipals wurden seit 1842 u.a. durch P.E. Bottas und Sir A.H. Layard ausgegraben. Die Originalreliefs befinden sich heute im British Museum, London.

10. Alexander Rauch, ›Symbolismus zwischen 'Paradies' und 'Sünde': Das Werk des Künstlers und seine Villa«, in: *Die Villa Stuck in München*, Bayerische Vereinsbank, München 1992, S. 48.

11. Zu einem der Tableaus des Environments *H.G.* 1995 in London gehörte ebenfalls ein Himmel voller goldener Pfeile.

12. Näheres über dieses Photo und über den Photographen in dem Ausst.Kat. *Franz von Stuck und die Photographie: Inszenierung und Dokumentation*, Museum Villa Stuck, München 1996, S. 31, 142 f. und 187.

13. Siehe Ulrich Pohlmann, ›Als hätte er sich selbst entworfen‹, in: *Franz von Stuck und die Photographie* (wie Anm. 12), S. 31.

14. »Ich glaube, worum es geht, ist, daß es etwas anderes ist [als ein Gemälde Stucks] – so, als ginge es um eine Party, und jemand hätte den Raum für die Party dekoriert«; Robert Wilson in einem Brief an die Autorin vom 11. August 1997.

15. »Die Zeit des großen Krieges, die Periode schwerster politischer und geistiger Umwälzungen bricht herauf; Futurismus, Kubismus, Expressionismus, Folgeerscheinungen dieser bewegten Jahre, erfassen ganz Europa ... Wie seltsam erscheinen neben diesen Explosionen all die Nymphen, Faune, Zentauren und Amazonen, die weiterhin Stucks Zaubergarten bevölkern«; Willi Geiger in: *Franz von Stuck*, Ausst.Kat., Villa Stuck, München 1968, o.S.

16. Dieses Zimmer wurde auch für intime Abendessen genutzt.

17. Franz von Stuck verbrachte den Sommer 1890 zusammen mit Ludwig von Herterich, K.J. Becker-Gundahl, Wilhelm Dürr, Julius Exter und anderen Künstlern auf dem Gut des Malers Hugo von Preen in der Künstlerkolonie Osternberg; *Franz von Stuck und die Photographie* (wie Anm. 12), S. 153.

18. Rauch (wie Anm. 10), S. 54.

19. *Illustrierte Zeitung*, 99/2580, S. 685, zit. bei Jo-Anne Birnie Danzker (Hrsg.), *Loïe Fuller:*

Getanzter Jugendstil, Ausst.Kat., Museum Villa Stuck, München 1995, S. 12.

20. Siehe *Franz von Stuck und die Photographie* (wie Anm. 12), S. 104 und 168.

21. Robert Wilson, befragt von Robert Enright in ›A Clean, Well-Lighted Grace«, in: ders, *Border Crossings*, 1994, S. 16.

22. Näheres über dieses Gemälde bei Edwin Becker, *Franz von Stuck: Eros & Pathos*, Ausst.Kat., Van Gogh Museum, Amsterdam 1995, S. 36.

23. Brief von Piet de Jonge an die Autorin vom 15. Oktober 1997.

24. Otto Julius Bierbaum, *Franz Stuck*, München 1893, S. 58.

25. ›Still Life: Room II‹, in: *Robert Wilson: Portrait, Still Life, Landscape*, Ausst.Kat., Museum Boijmans Van Beuningen, Rotterdam 1995.

26. Hans Ottomeyer, *Weg in die Moderne*, Kassel 1996, S. 103.

27. Siehe Helmut Hess, ›Stuck und Hanfstaengl – Künstler und Verleger‹, in: *Franz von Stuck und die Photographie* (wie Anm. 12), S. 128.

28. Siehe Barbara Hardtwig, ›Amor Imperator‹, in: *Franz von Stuck* (wie Anm. 3), S. 39.

29. Näheres über Ernst von Possart (1848–1921) bei Birgit Jooss, in: *Franz von Stuck und die Photographie* (wie Anm. 12), S. 97 und 161, sowie Norbert Götz, in: *Die Prinzregentenzeit*, Ausst.Kat., Münchner Stadtmuseum, München 1988, S. 360.

30. Siehe Helmut Hess, in: *Franz von Stuck und die Photographie* (wie Anm. 12), S. 128.

31. Jill Johnston, ›Family Spectacles‹, in: *Art in America* (Dezember 1986).

32. Dorine Mignot, ›Room for Salomé: An Interview with Robert Wilson‹, in: *Energieën*, Ausst.Kat., Stedelijk Museum, Amsterdam 1990, S. 113. Siehe auch Enright (wie Anm. 21), S. 16.

33. »Auch seine Frau kam öfters ins Atelier ... Dann war es allerdings mit der Ruhe vorbei. Sie hatte eine hohe, schrille Stimme, wenn sie rief: 'Wunderbar, wunderbar, du bist ein Genie!' Stuck gab meistens gar keine Antwort«; Richard Knecht, zit. bei Barbara Hardtwig, in: *Franz von Stuck* (wie Anm. 3), S. 98.

34. Stuck ließ nicht zu, daß seine Stiefkinder in der Villa wohnten; siehe Jo-Anne Birnie Danzker, ›Die Geschichte des Museums Villa Stuck: der Nachlaß Franz von Stucks«, ebenda, S. 14.

35. Siehe Jo-Anne Birnie Danzker, ebenda, S. 14.

36. Zit. bei Barbara Hardtwig, ›Mary von Stuck‹, ebenda, S. 98.

37. Marcella Wolff (1900–1996), ›Das Haus Stuck‹, ebenda, S. 221 f.

38. Abgesehen davon, daß Mary von Stuck wenig später starb, erlitt Stucks Tochter einen Nervenzusammenbruch; ebenda, S. 14–16 und 62 f.

39. Eva Heilmann, ›Das plastische Werk‹, in: *Franz von Stuck: Gemälde, Zeichnung, Plastik aus Privatbesitz*, Ausst.Kat., Museum Moderner Kunst, Passau 1993, S. 127.

40. Bierbaum (wie Anm. 24), S. 71, zit. nach Barbara Hardtwig, in: *Franz von Stuck* (wie Anm. 3), S. 64.

41. Siehe z.B. Griselda Pollock, *Vision & Difference: Femininity, Feminism and the Histories of Art*, London 1988.

42. Hedda Kaulbach (1900–1992) war Kaulbachs zweite Tochter; ihre Schwester Mathilde, genannt Quappi, war mit Max Beckmann verheiratet.

43. Marcella Wolff (aus den 1950er Jahren), Nachlaß Marcella Wolff, zit. in: *Franz von Stuck* (wie Anm. 3), S. 221.

44. Zit. bei Barbara Hardtwig, ebenda, S. 62.

Photo Credits/Photonachweis

Shigeo Anzai: 96
John Berens: 98
Dirk Bleicker: 21, 97
Byrd Hoffman Foundation, New York: 9, 90, 92
Centre National d'Art et de Culture Georges-Pompidou, Paris, Photo: Jean-Claude Planchet: 18, 96
James Dee : 95 (2)
Lutz Deppe : 97
Wolf Dieter Gericke: 15, 94
Philippe Gras: 10, 92, 93
Ron Forth: 12, 93
Jorge Hernandez: 13
The Independent, London, Photo: Peter Macdiarmid: 31
Köln Messe: 98
Jannes Linders: 26, 27, 28, 29
Armin Linke: 22, 23, 25
Monacensia, München: 72/73
Münchner Stadtmuseum: 38/39, 46/47, 50/51, 85
Museum of Fine Arts, Boston: 16, 17
Museum of Modern Art, New York: 94
Museum Villa Stuck, München: 42/43, 67, 68/69, 77; Photo: Brigitte Maria Mayer: Cover, endpapers, frontispiece/Umschlag, Vorsatz, Frontispiz, 40/41, 44/45, 48/49, 52/53, 56/57, 57, 60/61, 64/65, 70/71, 74/75, 78/79, 82/83, 86/87, 99 (2); Wolfgang Pulver: 43; Alexander Rauch: 80/81
Nachlaß Franz von Stuck: 54/55, Photo: Adolf Baumann: 46
Stefan Neuenhausen: 19
Privatbesitz, Baldham: 58/59, 62/63
Christian Wassmann: 90